TO

MY THREE CHILDREN

Contents

List of Illustrations

TEXT FIGURES

List of Illustrations

PLATES

ge 129). For Italian Mannerism I have largely taken
d permission of Messrs Routledge, what I had
e first volume of *The Mint*. The ̶ ̶ ̶ ̶ que
it was, except for ̶ ̶ ̶ ̶

Acknowledgements

The author wishes to express his thanks to the following for permission to reproduce photographs and drawings: Messrs B. T. Batsford Ltd (plate 27, figs. 36, 37, 39 and 75); Professor K. C. Conant (plate 11b); Country Life Ltd. (plates 59b and 60b); Mr H. Felton (plate 30a); The Sir John Soane Museum (plate 61b).

Foreword

THIS third edition differs from the second chiefly by another increase in the number of plates. There are now 64 instead of 48, that is twice as many as in the first edition. This increase has enabled me to enlarge the text in several ways as well. Most of the additions were made two years ago for a library edition brought out by Messrs John Murray. The following are the chief differences between the editions of 1945 and 1948. A few new lines appear on pages 21 and 22 on Roman architecture, and a few on pages 25 to 27 on the origin of the Christian basilica and on Constantinian basilicas. On pages 29 and 30 a little more is said on Anglo-Saxon and Merovingian churches, and on pages 31 to 34 a little more on Carolingian architecture, especially Centula. The treatment of the Romanesque style has scarcely been altered. Minor additions will be found regarding two-tower façades (page 47), the characteristics of French pilgrimage churches (page 49), the school of Cologne (page 51), and relations forward and backward between Rhineland and Lombardy (page 52).

In the chapter on Early and High Gothic the wonderfully logical development from St Denis to Chartres, Rheims, and Amiens via Sens, Noyon, Laon, and Paris is described in words and drawings on pages 63 to 71.

Regarding the Italian Renaissance, pages 112 to 115 have a paragraph or two on late Brunelleschi and Michelozzo, followed by several pages on the evolution of central planning through the 15th century, with due stress on Filarete and Milan. Then apropos Alberti a little is put in on page 121 about the Palazzo Venezia and the Palace of Urbino and about such combinations of longitudinal with central conceptions as Faenza. Bramante's early work in Milan has also received a little more

e Italian Bar
some paragraphs with drawings
on oval and kindred plans (pages 162 and 163).

Coming now to France and England since the Renaissance, page 119 contains something on theoretical books of the 16th century, and pages 205 to 209 a good deal on Paris buildings between 1600 and 1660 – Levau and Antoine Lepautre for instance. On pages 221 and 222 some comment can be read on the coming and characteristics of the Rococo in France. After that there are only two more additions worth mentioning : a page or so on the historical revivals after 1830 in England and on the Continent (pages 251 to 255), and half a page on the two great contemporaries of Morris and Norman Shaw, on H. H. Richardson and Philip Webb (pages 257 to 259).

The present edition is almost identical with the library edition of 1948. The only alterations of any importance are those on page 56, where Gothic vaulting is explained in, I hope, a more satisfactory manner than before, and on pages 88 to 91 where more appears on the churches of the Friars, whose importance for an understanding of the Late Gothic style grows as one goes on studying them. On page 185 I have added yet a little more on staircases, which keep fascinating me. Of other changes I need mention only the following : page 27, a little more on Early Christian and Byzantine centrally planned churches; page 44, a little more on tunnel-vaults before 1060; pages 34 and 40, some notes on the recent excavations at Cologne and Hildesheim; pages 99–100, some necessary paragraphs on municipal buildings of the Middle Ages in Italy and the Netherlands; pages 118 and 119, a little on the relatively late appearance of Tuscan Renaissance forms in North Italy; page 119, a paragraph on Alberti's personality; page 121, something more on Urbino, Francesco di Giorgio, Laurana, and again Alberti; page 135, an insertion on the Villa Madama; page 151, an insertion on 16th-century town planning; and finally page 243, with a few new remarks on Ledoux.

LONDON, CHRISTMAS 1949

Introduction

A BICYCLE shed is a building; Lincoln Cathedral is a piece of architecture. Nearly everything that encloses space on a scale sufficient for a human being to move in is a building; the term architecture applies only to buildings designed with a view to aesthetic appeal. Now aesthetic sensations may be caused by a building in three different ways. First, they may be produced by the treatment of walls, proportions of windows, the relation of wall-space to window-space, of one storey to another, of ornamentation such as the tracery of a 14th-century window, or the leaf and fruit garlands of a Wren porch. Secondly, the treatment of the exterior of a building as a whole is aesthetically significant, its contrasts of block against block, the effect of a pitched or a flat roof or a dome, the rhythm of projections and recessions. Thirdly, there is the effect on our senses of the treatment of the interior, the sequence of rooms, the widening out of a nave at the crossing, the stately movement of a baroque staircase. The first of these three ways is two-dimensional; it is the painter's way. The second is three-dimensional, and as it treats the building as volume, as a plastic unit, it is the sculptor's way. The third is three-dimensional too, but it concerns space; it is the architect's own way more than the others. What distinguishes architecture from painting and sculpture is its spatial quality. In this, and only in this, no other artist can emulate the architect. Thus the history of architecture is primarily a history of man shaping space, and the historian must keep spatial problems always in the foreground. This is why no book on architecture, however popular its presentation may be, can be successful without ground plans.

But architecture, though primarily spatial, is not exclusively spatial. In every building, besides enclosing space, the architect models volume and plans surface, i.e. designs an exterior and sets out individual walls. That means that the good architect requires the sculptor's and the painter's modes of vision in addition to his own spatial imagination. Thus architecture is the most comprehensive of all visual arts and has a right to claim superiority over the others.

This aesthetic superiority is, moreover, supplemented by a social superiority. Neither sculpture nor painting, although both are rooted in elementary creative and imitative instincts, surround us to the same extent as architecture, act upon us so incessantly and so ubiquitously. We can avoid intercourse with what people call the Fine Arts, but we cannot escape buildings and the subtle but penetrating effects of their character, noble or mean, restrained or ostentatious, genuine or meretricious. An age without painting is conceivable, though no believer in the life-enhancing function of art would want it. An age without easel-pictures can be conceived without any difficulty, and, thinking of the predominance of easel-pictures in the 19th century, might be regarded as a consummation devoutly to be wished. An age without architecture is impossible as long as human beings populate this world.

CHAPTER ONE

Twilight and Dawn

THE Greek temple (pl. 1) is the most perfect example ever achieved of architecture finding its fulfilment in bodily beauty. Its interior mattered infinitely less than its exterior. The colonnade all round conceals where the entrance lies. The faithful did not enter it and spend hours of communication with the Divine in it, as they do in a church. Our Western conception of space would have been just as unintelligible to a man of Pericles's age as our religion. It is the plastic shape of the temple that tells, placed before us with a physical presence more intense, more alive than that of any later building. The isolation of the Parthenon or the temples of Paestum, clearly disconnected from the ground on which they stand, the columns with their resilient curves, strong enough to carry without too much visible effort the weight of the architraves, the sculptured friezes and sculptured pediments – there is something consummately human in all this, life in the brightest light of nature and mind: nothing harrowing, nothing problematic and obscure, nothing blurred.

Roman architecture also thinks of the building primarily as of a sculptural body, but not as one so superbly independent. There is a more conscious grouping of buildings, and parts are less isolated too. Hence the all-round, free-standing columns with their architrave lying on them are so often replaced by heavy square piers carrying arches. Hence also walls are emphasized in their thickness, for instance, by hollowing niches into them; and if columns are asked for, they are half-columns, attached to, and that is part of, the wall. Hence, finally, instead of flat ceilings – stressing a perfectly clear horizontal as against a perfectly clear vertical – the Romans used vast tunnel-vaults or cross-vaults to cover spaces. The arch and the vault on a large scale are engineering achievements, greater than any of the Greeks, and it is of them as they appear in the aqueducts, baths, basilicas (that is, public assembly halls), theatres, and palaces, and not of temples, that we think when we remember Roman architecture (pl. 1b).

However, with very few exceptions, these grandest creations of the Roman sense of power, mass, and plastic body belong to a period later than the Republic, and even the Early Empire. The Colosseum is of the late 1st century A.D., the Pantheon of the early 2nd, the Baths of Caracalla of the early 3rd, the Basilica of Maxentius (usually called of Constantine) of the early 4th.

By then a fundamental change of spirit and no longer only of forms had taken place. The relative stability of the Roman Empire was overthrown after the death of Marcus Aurelius (180); rulers followed one another at a rate such as had been known only during short periods of civil war. Between Marcus Aurelius and Constantine, in 125 years, there were forty-seven emperors; less than four years was the average duration of a reign. They were no longer elected by the Roman Senate, that enlightened body of politically experienced citizens, but proclaimed by some provincial army of barbarian troops, often barbarians themselves, rude soldiers of peasant stock, ignorant of and unsympathetic to the achievements of Roman civilization. There was constant internecine warfare, and constant attacks of barbarians from outside had to be repulsed. Cities declined and were in the end deserted, their market-halls and baths and blocks of flats collapsed. Soldiers of the Roman army sacked Roman towns. Goths, Alemans, Franks, Persians sacked whole provinces. Trade, seaborne and landborne, came to an end, estates and farms and villages became self-supporting once again, payments in money were replaced by payments in kind; taxes were often paid in kind. The educated bourgeoisie, decimated by wars, executions, murder, and a lower and lower birthrate, had no longer a share in public affairs. Men from Syria, Asia Minor, Egypt, from Spain, Gaul, and Germany, held all the important positions. The subtle political balance of the Early Empire could no longer be appreciated and was no longer maintained.

When a new stability was brought about by Diocletian and Constantine about 300, it was the stability of an oriental autocracy, with a rigid oriental court ceremonial, a merciless army, and far-reaching State control. Soon Rome was no longer the capital of the Empire; Constantinople took her place. Then the Empire fell into two: that of the East to prove mighty, that of the West to become the prey of Teutonic invaders, the Visigoths, the Vandals, the Ostrogoths, the Lombards, and then for a while to be part of the Eastern – the Byzantine – Empire.

Now during these centuries the massive walls, arches, vaults, niches, and apses of Roman palaces and public buildings with their grossly inflated decorations grew up all over the vast Empire. But while this new style left its mark on Trier as much as on Milan, its centre was the Eastern Mediterranean: Egypt, Syria, Asia Minor, Palmyra – that is the country in which the Hellenistic style had flourished in the last century B.C. And the Late Roman style is indeed the successor to the Late Greek or Hellenistic.

The Eastern Mediterranean led in matters of the spirit too. From the East came the new attitude towards religion. Men were tired of what human intellect could provide. The invisible, the mysterious, the irrational were the need of that orientalized, barbarized population. The various creeds of the Gnostics, Mithraism from Persia, Judaism, Manichaeism, found their followers. Christianity proved strongest, found lasting forms of organization, and survived the danger under Constantine of an alliance with the Empire. But it remained Eastern in essence. Tertullian's: 'I believe in it because it is absurd' would have been an impossible tenet for an enlightened Roman. Augustine's : 'Beauty cannot be beheld in any bodily matter' is equally anti-antique. Of the greatest of the late Pagan philosophers, Plotinus, his pupil and biographer said that he walked like one ashamed of being in the body. Plotinus came from Egypt, St Augustine from Libya. St Athanasius and Origen were Egyptians; Basil was born and lived in Asia Minor, Diocletian was a native of Dalmatia, Constantine and St Jerome came from the Hungarian plains. Judged by the standards of the age of Augustus, none of them was a Roman.

Their architecture represents them, their fanaticism, and their passionate search for the invisible, the magic, the immaterial. S. Apollinare Nuovo in Ravenna (pl. 3 and fig. 1) was built early in the 6th century by Theodoric, ruler of the Ostrogoths in Italy. Yet there is nothing specifically Teutonic in it; it belongs wholly to that universal but, in its essentials, Eastern style that goes under the name of Early Christian. The functional elements of a Christian church are here already so completely

1. *Ravenna: S. Apollinare Nuovo, early 6th century*

established that neither a Gothic nor a present-day church has gone beyond it. The church is taken as the visible symbol of the way of the faithful towards the mystery of the Real Presence. The altar under the apse and the miracle of the Real Presence are the goal. There may be a transept as a halt between nave and apse – a rare motif incidentally, confined mainly to some major churches of Rome built under Constantine and his immediate successors (Old St Peter's, S. Paolo fuori le mura, S. Giovanni in Laterano, S. Maria Maggiore). With or without transepts, the main axis of propelling movement is indicated by the nave with its uninterrupted sequence of columns dividing off the aisles. It is this that drives us irresistibly on towards the East. There is no articulation in that long colonnade to arrest our eyes, nor in the long row of window after window up in

the clerestory; and the solemn and silent mosaic figures of
martyrs and holy virgins, with their motionless faces and stiff
garments, march with us.
One monotonous mesmeriz-
ing rhythm fills the whole
of the church – no secondary
motifs weaken its fanatical
single-mindedness.   This
type of plan and spatial development is so fitting that
one feels tempted to regard
it as a Christian invention.
That is, however, not so.
Basilica is the name under
which such churches with
nave, clerestory, aisles, and
apse are known to this day.
We have met it before meaning a public hall in Rome or
the Roman Empire. The
word is Greek and means
royal. So it may have come
to Rome with Hellenistic
regal pomp. But Roman
basilicas are in no surviving
form the immediate prede-
cessors of the Early Christian church building. They
usually have colonnades
not only between 'nave'
and 'aisles', but also on
the narrow sides, that is a
complete ambulatory, like a
Greek temple turned inside
out – or rather outside in

2. *Pompeii: basilica, c.* 100 B.C.

(fig. 2). Apses were not uncommon; even two apses are
found; but they are as a rule cut off from the main body by
the colonnades. Thus as a general term for a large-aisled hall

the word basilica may have been transferred from Pagan to
Christian, but hardly the building type as such. Other guesses
have been made : the *scholae*, or the private halls in large houses
and palaces (for instance, that of the Flavian emperors on the

3. *Rome: palace of the Flavian emperors, late 1st century* A.D.

4. *Rome: 'Basilica' of Porta Maggiore, 1st century* A.D.

Palatine (fig. 3), smaller apsed rooms, which may indeed have
been used for private worship by Christians.

But since 1917 we know of a much more direct connection
between Christian and Pagan religious architecture. The so-
called Basilica of Porta Maggiore (fig. 4) is a little subterranean
building of only about forty feet length. With its nave and

aisles, its piers and apse, it looks exactly like a Christian chapel. Stucco reliefs reveal that it was the meeting-place of one of the many mystical sects which had come to Rome from the East, before and after the advent of the sect of the Christians. It is attributed to the 1st century A.D. Considering the close dependence of Early Christian thought on that of the other oriental religions believing in a saviour, in sacrifice and re-birth, the Basilica of Porta Maggiore is the most convincing single source of Early Christian architecture yet found.

During the 4th century Constantine and his successors built vast basilicas in East and West; by the 5th century Christian churches existed everywhere – even in England (Silchester). Most of them are varieties of the basilican plan. An exception were baptisteries and memorials or mausoleum chapels for which, on a Roman precedent, centrally planned buildings were preferred: circular with an ambulatory (S. Costanza, Rome) or octagonal with an ambulatory (Baptistery of S. Giovanni in Laterano, Rome), or octagonal without an ambulatory but with niches in the four corners (Baptisteries, Ravenna), or in the shape of a Greek cross, that is with the four arms all of the same length (Mausoleum of Galla Placidia, Ravenna). On a large scale central planning was developed chiefly in Byzantium itself. It culminated in Justinian's magnificent churches, Holy Apostles, a Greek cross with five domes, of which nothing survives, St Sophia, a complicated interpenetration of various central and longitudinal motifs, and SS Sergius and Bacchus, reflected on Italian soil with unparalleled splendour at S. Vitale in Ravenna. Ravenna had, after the fall of the Visigoths, become the capital of Byzantine Italy. Thus S. Vitale was built for Justinian himself. It was completed in 547, ten years after St Sophia and probably ten or twelve after SS Sergius and Bacchus. It is an octagon with a two-storied octagonal ambulatory, a chancel and apse added at the east end, and at the west end a narthex or anteroom for the congregation to collect in before entering the House of God. The spatial motif that determines the character of the room, a motif of purely aesthetic, i.e. no functional, purpose is the use of the niches into which the central octagon expands. As these niches are not enclosed by walls, but open out with arcades into the ambulatories on the ground floor and the first floor, no clear distinction exists between the two main parts of the building. The central space flows into the ambulatory, and the ambulatory becomes a senseless shape if looked at as an independent unit. The same sensation of uncertainty, of a dreamlike floating, is created,

5. *Ravenna: S. Vitale, completed* 547

where solid walls remain, by the mosaics covering them. These glowing surfaces, with austere, gaunt figures in sombre tints, seem just as immaterial, as magical and weightless as the surging and drooping curves of the octagon.

The Franks in Gaul, the Angles and Saxons in Britain, the Visigoths in Spain could not possibly appreciate the complexity and sophistication of such churches. Theirs was still the outlook of native tribes although Clovis had accepted in 496 what he understood as Christianity. With the same merciless cruelty in which the Anglo-Saxon warrior revelled in England, all but exterminating what had remained of civilization on the island, the princes of the Merovingians sought to exterminate whole families of rivals. The pages of Gregory of Tours, who wrote in the second half of the 6th century, are full of assassination, rape, and perjury. Yet this is how our own civilization began, and how all civilizations begin – in the darkness of tribal barbarism. The Church was the only tie between these shifting kingdoms and the spiritual achievements of the South. Thus Anglo-Saxon brutality was tamed by Irish monasticism (inspired in some obscure way by the Coptic Church of Egypt) in the north and by missionaries from Rome in the south, until, early in the 8th century, the Venerable Bede and the circle around him attained a height of education unparalleled anywhere else in Europe. What they built seems primitive to us, but descriptions seem to indicate that large churches reflected more faithfully early Italian magnificence. Eddius in his Life of Wilfrid calls Hexham a building 'columnis variis et porticibus multis suffultum, mirabili longitudine et altitudine', and Ripon also 'variis columnis et porticibus suffultam', and Alcuin speaks of York as possessing thirty altars, and again many columns and arches, beautiful ceilings, and many *porticus* – whether these mean outer colonnades, or galleries, or aisles, or indiscriminately all of them.

Yet what survives or has been excavated does not bear out such accounts. Churches appear small throughout the country, more Mediterranean in form in the south-east, more original in the north. At Canterbury and elsewhere in Kent apses were, it seems, usual; in Northumberland and the neighbouring counties there are long, narrow unaisled buildings, for instance at Monkwearmouth and Jarrow, founded in 674 and 685. Chancels are separate, and the effect of the interiors is of a tall, tight gangway leading towards a small chamber. Externally masonry is rude and primeval. Geographically between the two regions lies Brixworth in Northamptonshire, the only partly preserved aisled basilica, built with the use of Roman bricks, probably in the 7th century.

Among the Franks of present-day France and the west of Germany the position was very much the same. There are a

few odd Merovingian survivals, small in scale and of debased
Roman and Early Christian forms (St Jean Poitiers, Baptistery
Venasque, etc.), and there are plenty of descriptions of buildings seemingly much more ambitious and accomplished – for
instance, of the 6th century in Gregory of Tours' *History of the
Franks*. A change which we can follow from buildings still upright or which can be reconstructed in our minds with some
certainty came only with Charlemagne, heralded perhaps by a
few major enterprises of his father, Pepin the Short. Charlemagne had grown up illite-
rate; he never wrote with
ease. But he had a con-
scious programme of edu-
cating his people or peoples
to a conception of Roman
urbanity and Roman gran-
deur in a new Christian
guise. Hence he gathered
round his person the flower
of European scholarship
and poetry, men from
England, Spain, France,
and Italy – all ecclesiastics,
of course. Hence he built
for himself palaces with
hall, chapel, and large ranges of rooms, all as clearly organized
in their relative positions as the palaces of the Roman emperors
on the Palatine, and all connected by vast colonnades of
evidently Roman Eastern derivation (fig. 6). To visualize
these palaces we have to rely on excavations and description.
Only in one case a substantial piece of one of Charlemagne's
palaces still stands: the Chapel Palatine of Aachen (Aix-la-
Chapelle), one of the emperor's principal residences. It was
originally connected with the Great Hall (not now traceable
beyond parts of the foundation walls) by colonnades nearly
400 feet long (pl. 3b). An equestrian statue of Theodoric, believed to be Constantine, looted from Rome, was significantly
placed in this colonnaded forecourt, and columns of the chapel

6. *Ingelheim: Charlemagne's palace, early
9th century*

also came from Italy. So did undoubtedly its ground plan. There can be little doubt that the architect took his inspiration from S. Vitale. But he could see no sense in the curved-out niches, so he flattened them out, thus re-establishing the straightforward division between central octagon and ambulatory. He also eliminated the columns on the ground floor. Simple wide openings alternate with short, sturdy piers. The plainness and massiveness of this ground floor (and also of the giant niche of the façade) strike a note utterly different from the subtle spatial harmonies of S. Vitale. Yet the upper floors with their polished antique columns, superimposed in two orders, re-echo something of the transparency, and the floating of space from one unit into another, which make the beauty of Justinian's churches.

Aachen sums up the historic position of Carolingian architecture at the extreme end of Early Christian and at the beginning of Western developments. Roman-Christian intentions – it is eminently significant that on Christmas Day of the year 800 Charlemagne made the Pope crown him with the crown of a new Holy Roman Empire – are everywhere traceable, but appear marred or in other cases rejuvenated by the naïve vigour of an unskilled, but very determined, somewhat barbarous youth. Of the major churches of which we know some are in plan surprisingly pure Early Christian – St Denis and Fulda derive directly from St Peter's and the other Roman basilicas with transepts[1]. Fulda was begun in 802 (fig. 7), the other one, St Denis, even before Charlemagne came to the throne, about 760.

Centula (or St Riquier near Abbeville), on the other hand (fig. 8), is in most features unprecedented. The church which was built in 790–99 no longer stands, and is known to us only by an old engraving and a still older description. First of all it had in its exterior just as much accent on the west as on the east

[1]. The plan may have suggested itself to the Carolingian rulers on a Northumbrian precedent, if the published plans of excavations at Hexham (apparently badly handled and recorded) are at all reliable. They show a large church of the same type of plan, and there is no reason not to assume that it is Wilfrid's, that is a building of the 7th century.

parts. Both were strongly emphasized by towers over the cross-ings rising in several stages and by additional lower staircase towers – a group, varied and interesting, and very different from the simple detached campanile or clocktower which Early Christian churches occasionally possessed. Then there were two transepts, one in the east and one in the west. Also

7. *Fulda: abbey church, begun 802*

the east apse was separated from the transepts by a proper chan-cel. This became almost a matter of course in the coming centuries. The western part has a complicated spatial organiza-tion, with a low, probably vaulted entrance hall and a chapel above, open towards the nave. Such a Westwork, as it is called in Germany, was also a popular feature of later churches, es-pecially in Germany, as was the bold grouping of manifold blocks with manifold towers.

Some of the ideas of Centula appear again in an immensely interesting original plan on vellum which, about the year 835, had been sent by some bishop or abbot close to the emperor's

8. *Centula: abbey church, 790–99 (reconstruction)*

court to the Abbot of St Gall as an ideal scheme ('exemplar') for the rebuilding of his monastery and may, according to excavations carried out after the Second World War, have been based on the Carolingian Cathedral of Cologne. But all this premature flowering of architectural imagination, and of thought and civilization altogether, withered away under the grim frosts of the later 9th and the 10th centuries. Less than thirty years after Charlemagne's death in 814 the Empire was divided. France and Germany henceforth took separate courses. Internal struggles, earl against earl, duke against duke, shook both. And from outside, the Vikings ravaged the North-West – Normans they called them in France, Danes in England – the Hungarians menaced the East, the Saracens, i.e. Mohammedan Arabs, the South. No progress was possible in art and architecture. What we know is almost as primitive as Merovingian work, although forms taken up under Charlemagne and his immediate successors were still used. But the spirit in which they were used was blunt and crude. And since during the pre-Carolingian centuries intercourse with Roman architecture had not entirely ceased, the period between about 850 and 950 seems even more barbaric.

Not much of this dark age has stood the ravages of war and the zeal of later builders in France and Germany. To see greater numbers of 9th- and 10th-century buildings in anything like their original state one must go to the borderlands of Western civilization, to Spain and Britain.

In Spain the Visigoths, rulers from the 5th to the early 8th century, had built churches of an oddly mutilated basilican type. S. Juan de Baños, for example, dedicated in 661, consisted originally (fig. 9 shows the plan before the later alterations) of a short nave separated from the aisles by arcades with horseshoe arches, exaggeratedly projecting transepts, a square apse, two rectangular eastern chapels or vestries inorganically detached from the apse and, as another inorganic appendix, a rectangular west porch. There is no spatial flow nor even a unity of plan in this minute building. The exterior colonnades originally running along the north, south, and west walls are of Late Antique-Oriental origin, as incidentally is the horseshoe arch.

This motif, however, the Arabs, when they conquered the South of Spain in the 8th century, made so much their own that for several centuries to come it remained the hall-mark of Mohammedan and Mozarabic, i.e. Christian Spanish, architecture under Arab influence. The Arabs, as against the Vikings and Hungarians, were far from un-civilized. On the contrary, their religion, their science, and their cities, especially Cordova with her half-million inhabitants, were far ahead of those of 8th-century Franks in France or Asturians in Northern Spain. The Mosque at Cordova (786–990), a building of eleven aisles, each twelve bays long, with interlaced arches and complicated star-ribbed vaults, has a filigree elegance more in keeping with the spatial transparency of S. Vitale than of the sturdy uncouthness of the North.

9. *S. Juan de Baños, dedicated 661. The east parts have later been altered*

Owing to their proximity to Mohammedan sophistication, the Asturias show a certain airiness here and there which is absent in any other contemporary Christian buildings. At S. Maria de Naranco near León, for example (pl. 4 and 5a), the fluted buttresses outside – as a structural device and a decorative motif still remotely evocative of Rome – and the slender arcade inside which now separates nave from choir are in strange contrast to the heavy tunnel-vault, the odd shield-like or seal-like medallions from which spring the transverse arches of the vault and the clumsy spiral shafts with their crude block capitals along the walls.

The building incidentally is of very special interest, in so far as in all probability it was designed between 842 and 848 as a Royal Hall for Ramiro I of Asturias – the only surviving early medieval example of such a building. It has a low vaulted cellar or crypt, and above this the hall proper, now the nave of the church. This is reached by flights of outside steps leading to porches in the centres of both the long sides of the building. On the east and the west there were originally open loggias, communicating with the main room by arcades, of which one, as has been said before, survives. The present choir is in fact one of the loggias blocked up towards the outside.

In British 9th- and 10th-century architecture one would

look in vain for such subtleties. Where buildings are preserved complete or nearly complete, we can see that their ground plans were just as elementary. At Bradford-on-Avon (fig. 10), e.g., the nave has no aisles. The chancel is accessible from the nave only by a narrow door with crudely worked joints. The porches on the north and south sides are also separated from the main room.

10. *Bradford-on-Avon: an Anglo-Saxon church plan*

Compartment is added to compartment, very much as in the Visigothic churches of Spain. Anglo-Saxon decoration is just as elementary. The craftsmen who worked the Ruthwell Cross in Bede's time seem superior to those who, one or two generations before the Conquest, decorated the tower of Earl's Barton. The only structural part of its decoration is the emphasizing of the three stories by plain string courses (pl. 5b). All the rest, the wooden-looking strips arranged in rows vertically like beanstalks, or higher up in crude lozenge patterns, is structurally senseless. Yet they are in a similar relation to Carolingian architecture as Asturian decoration was to the Muslim style. But while the day-to-day proximity of Arab to Spanish civilization created the mixed idiom of Naranco and the Mozarabic style of the 10th century, the British builders reduced the Romanizing motifs of Carolingian decoration to ungainly rusticity. The so-called long-and-short work up the edges of Earl's Barton tower, and so many other contemporary English towers, is another indication of the rawness of the minds and the heaviness of the hands of these late Anglo-Saxon architects, if architects they can be called.

CHAPTER TWO

The Romanesque Style

c. 1000–*c*. 1200

YET during these dark and troubled years the foundations of medieval civilization were laid. The feudal system grew, one does not know from what roots, until it had become the framework round which all the social life of the Middle Ages was built, a system as characteristic and unique as medieval religion and medieval art, strictly binding lord and vassal, and yet so vague, so dependent on symbolical gestures that we to-day can hardly recognize it as a system at all. By the end of the 10th century it had received its final form. By then political stability too had been re-established in the Empire. Otto the Great was crowned in Rome in 962. At the same time the first of the reform movements of monasticism set out from Cluny in Burgundy. The great abbot Majeul was enthroned in 965. And again at the same time the Romanesque style was created.

To describe an architectural style it is necessary to describe its individual features. But the features alone do not make the style. There must be one central idea active in all of them. Thus several essential Early Romanesque motifs can be traced singly in Carolingian architecture. Their combination, however, is new and determines their meaning.

The most significant innovations of the late 10th century are those in the ground plan – three above all, and all three caused by a new will to articulate and clarify space. This is most characteristic. Western civilization was only just beginning to take shape, but already at that early stage its architectural expression was spatial, as against the sculptural spirit of Greek and Roman art – and spatial in an organizing, grouping, planning way, as against the magic floating of space in Early Christian and

Byzantine art. The two chief plans for the east ends of Roman-esque churches were conceived in France; the radiating plan somewhere near the future centre of the country (perhaps at St Martin's in Tours, begun after a fire in 997, dedications in

11. *Tours: St Martin's. The thick black lines are the walls of the church begun shortly after 997, dedications in 1014 and 1020*

1014 and 1020[1]), and the staggered plan at Cluny, apparently in Abbot Majeul's rebuilding dedicated in 981 (figs. 11 and 12). The functional reasons were the growing worship of saints on the one hand, and on the other the growing custom of every priest saying Mass every day. So more altars were needed, and to accommodate them more chapels in the eastern parts, i.e. the parts reserved for the clergy, were the obvious solution. One can imagine how crudely Anglo-Saxon or Asturian architects would have added them. The architect of the new age groups them into one coherent unified entity, either by laying an ambulatory round the apse and adding radiating chapels, or by running the aisles on past the transepts, finishing them in small apses parallel or nearly parallel with the main apse and, in addition, placing one, two, or even three apses along the east wall of each transept.

1. But some French archaeologists attribute the same plan to the re-building of Notre Dame at Clermont-Ferrand in 946. The case is un-certain and would require further investigations on the spot.

Almost exactly at the time when the French began to evolve these new schemes, in Saxony, the centre province of Otto's

12. *Cluny: abbey church, as begun c. 960 and dedicated in 981. (Black – existing foundations; shaded – hypothetical.)*

empire, just north of the Harz mountains, another and even more thorough 'metrical system' was found to articulate the whole of a church, the system followed by Central European

13. *Hildesheim: St Michael's, begun shortly after 1000*

architects for the next two centuries. St Michael's at Hildesheim (fig. 13) was begun immediately after the year 1000. It had (for now, alas, it is completely gutted) two transepts, two chancels, and two apses, a logical development of ideas first

tried out in a rudimentary form at Centula.[1] Thus the mono-
tony of the Early Christian arrangement was replaced by a
grouping less single-minded and rhythmically more interesting. And St Michael's went decisively beyond Centula in dividing the nave into exactly three squares, with aisles separated
from the nave by arcades that have an alternation of supports,
pillars to stress the corners of the squares, columns in between.
Each transept again consisted of a centre square flanked by a
rectangle. The centre squares were clearly singled out by means
of chancel arches not only to the east and west, but also to the
north and south. In later buildings each transept was to be
square too, and the aisles consisted of sequences of squares. On
the east side at Hildesheim a square chancel was inserted between crossing and apse. Chapels branched off the transepts
parallel to the main apses – a complex ground plan, yet fully
ordered by an active conquering power of reason.

Who conceived this 'metrical system' we do not know.
What we do know, however, and have no reason to question,
is the fact, recorded by his biographer, that St Bernward, the
bishop who was responsible for the building of St Michael's,
was 'foremost in writing, experienced in painting, excellent in
the science and art of bronze founding and in all architectural
work'. Similarly we know, e.g., of Aethelwold, the great
English bishop, that he was a 'theoreticus architectus', well
versed in the building and repairing of monasteries, of Benno,
Bishop of Osnabrück in the 11th century, that he was 'an outstanding architect, a skilful planner ("dispositor") of masonry
work'. We also possess the plan of about 835 for St Gall, which
has been mentioned before, and was obviously the sender's –
that is a bishop's or abbot's – conception. Such and many
similar contemporary references justify the view that, while
actual building operations were of course at all times the job of
the craftsman, the designing of churches and monasteries in the

1. The west end had an outer ambulatory around the apse as had been
designed for Carolingian St Gall, had existed at Carolingian Cologne,
and still exists at Brixworth. On the Hildesheim excavations after the
Second World War see *Kunstchronik*, vol. 1, 1948, No. 10, p. 10; on the
Cologne excavations, O. Doppelfeld in *Der Kölner Dom*. 1948.

early Middle Ages may often have been due to clerics – at least to the same extent to which Lord Burlington was responsible for the design of his Chiswick villa. After all, in those times nearly all the literati, the educated, the sensitive were clerics.

The same tendency towards an elementary articulation which the new ground plans reveal can be found in the elevations of the 11th-century churches. At St Michael's, Hildesheim, the system of alternating supports, the rhythm of *a b b a b b a* (*a* representing square piers and *b* columns), serves to divide up the long stretch of wall, and ultimately the space enclosed by the walls, into separate units. This system became the customary one in Central European Romanesque architecture. In the West, and especially in England, another equally effective method was developed for achieving the same aim. It had been created in Normandy early in the 11th century. The Normans by then had lived in the north-west of France for a hundred years and from being Viking adventurers had become clear-minded, determined, and progressive rulers of a large territory, adopting French achievements where they saw possibilities in them – this applies to the French language, suppler than their own, to feudalism, and to the reform of Cluny – and imbuing them with the energy of their native spirit. They conquered Sicily and parts of Southern Italy in the 11th and 12th centuries and created an eminently interesting civilization there, a blend of what was most advanced in the administration of Normandy and in the thought and habits of the Saracens. In the meantime they had also conquered England, to replace there by their own superior mode of life that of the Northern invaders who had come before them. The Norman style in architecture, the most consistent variety of the Romanesque style in the West, strongly influenced France during the 11th century: in England it did more than that: it made English medieval architecture. One cannot discuss the Romanesque style without taking into consideration English Norman cathedrals and abbey churches. French writers too often forget that – the fulfilment of what had been initiated at Jumièges about 1040 (pl. 9) and Caen about 1050 lies at Ely, at Winchester, at Durham, to mention only a few.

The new principle was the separation of bay from bay by tall shafts running through from the floor to the ceiling – a flat ceiling everywhere; for the art of vaulting the width of a nave was all but lost. Thus again an articulation was achieved that conveys to us at once a feeling of certainty and stability. There is no wavering here – as there was none in the ruthless policy of William the Conqueror in subduing and normanizing England. Blunt, massive, and overwhelmingly strong are the individual forms which architects used in these early buildings, sacred as well as secular. For the Norman keep (pl. 6), the other architectural type which the Normans brought from France, has got the same compactness, the same disdain of embellishment as the Norman church. There were, of course, reasons of defence for the bareness of the keep, but it was a matter of expression, i.e. of aesthetics, too, as a comparison with such a piece of building as the transept of Winchester Cathedral (c. 1080–90) proves. At Winchester (pl. 7) the solid wall, though opened up in arcades on the ground floor and the gallery floor and again in a passage-way in front of the clerestory window, remains the primary fact. We feel its mighty presence everywhere. The tall shafts are bound to it and are themselves massive, like enormous tree-trunks. The columns of the gallery openings are short and sturdy, their capitals rude blocks (cf. fig. 14), the simplest statement of the fact that here something of round section was to be linked up with something of square section. If the elementary block form of the capital is given up, it is replaced by fluting, the future favourite motif of the Anglo-Norman capital, in its most primitive form (fig. 17). This plainness is typical of the 11th century, a plainness of statement expressed in terms of the plainest of forms.

By the end of the century changes began to appear, all pointing towards a new differentiation. More complex, more varied, more lively forms can be found everywhere. There is perhaps less force in them, but more individual expression. Now comes the age of St Bernard of Clairvaux (died 1153), who called it his aim as a preacher (and he was one of the greatest of medieval preachers) to move hearts, not to expound scripture, the age of Abelard (died 1142), the first to write an autobiographical account of his personal problems of love and scholarship, and in England the age of Henry II and Thomas Becket (died 1170). They stand before us as human beings; William the Conqueror as a natural phenomenon, irresistible and relentless. Just before 1100 – when Western Christianity rallied round the banners of the first Crusade – the pioneer work was done in architecture;

Early Romanesque was transformed into High Romanesque. Durham is the crucial monument in England, begun in 1093, the east parts vaulted in 1104, the nave *c.* 1130 (pl. 8). The nave appears higher than it is because, instead of the flat ceiling usual until then and usual in England for some time to come, it is covered by a rib-vault. As our eyes follow the lines of the shafts upwards, this movement does not come to a standstill where the walls end, but is carried farther up

14. *Block capital from St Michael's, Hildesheim, early 11th century*

with the ribs. The vaults of Durham choir (now renewed) are the earliest rib-vaults of Europe. In this lies Durham's eminence in the history of building construction.

Engineering skill had developed considerably during the century between the earliest examples of the Romanesque style and 1100. To vault in stone naves of basilican churches was the ambition of the craftsmen, for reasons of safety against fires in church roofs as well as for reasons of appearance. The Romans had known how to vault on a large scale; but in the West there were before the late 11th century only vaulted apses, tunnel- or groin-vaulted aisles, or narrow tunnel-vaulted naves without aisles (for instance Naranco), and even smaller tunnel-vaulted naves with aisles (French oratories and crypts such as St Irénée at Lyons of the 5th century, Glanfeuil of the 6th century, St Germain at Auxerre of *c.* 850, and outside France the east parts of S. Maria della Valle at Cividale of the 8th or 9th century, St Wipert at Quedlinburg in Saxony of *c.* 930, and St Martin de Canigou in French Catalonia of 1009, a latecomer, not a pioneer, and vastly overrated in its historical importance by Puig y Cadafalch). Now the vaulting of the wider naves of major churches was mastered, and – as always happens when an innovation is the full expression of the spirit of an age – mastered independently by several ingenious architects in several centres of building activity at about the same time. Burgundy remained faithful to massive tunnel-vaults. The earliest that can be dated seem to belong to about 1060 (Conques); those at Cluny, when this mightiest monastery of Europe was rebuilt, about 1100, had the widest span anywhere. Speier, the imperial cathedral on the Rhine, received her first groin-vaults in the 'eighties. And then there is Durham. A good deal of controversy still remains about dates of early vaults (especially concerning S. Ambrogio in Milan, whose rib-vaults some count amongst the pioneer works, while others date them about the second and third quarters of the 12th century). The new powerful initiative of the late 11th century, however, is beyond doubt.

Now the most remarkable fact about the vaults of Durham is that rib-vaults as against ribless groin-vaults are accepted as one of the *leitmotivs* of the Gothic style. Their structural advantages, chiefly the possibility of erecting the ribs and other arches first and independently on a separate centering and then filling in the cells between the ribs in a lighter material, will be discussed later (p. 56). To some people these structural advantages are still the only reason why the Gothic style came about. Durham proves this materialistic theory to be wrong. The ribs here are not built up independently, the filling masonry is not

lighter. The motif is there, but its constructional potentialities
have not yet been discovered. The reason of the Durham
builders for introducing so telling a feature must have been the
very fact that it is so telling, that it represents the ultimate fulfilment of that tendency towards articulation which had driven
Romanesque architects forward for over a hundred years.
Now the bay has become a unity not only by the two-dimensional means of lines of demarcation along the walls, but by
the three-dimensional means of those diagonal arches set across.

Where the two arches meet, where later
architects inserted their bosses, there
each unified bay has its centre. We
move along through the cathedral, not
driven towards the altar without halt as
in Early Christian churches but stepping
from spatial compartment to spatial
compartment in a new measured
rhythm.

The rib-vault imparts indeed at Durham to the whole structure an alertness
opposed to the weight of inert wall so

15. *Decorated block capital
from the crypt of Canterbury
Cathedral, early 12th century*

oppressive in 11th-century interiors. This alertness is taken up
in the more animated expression of the arcades and their mouldings, and the introduction of a few sharp ornamental forms, the
zigzag above all. Still, in spite of this quickening of rhythm
Durham is far from playful or busy. The circular pillars of
the arcades are still of overpowering strength, their sheer bulk
being emphasized by the elementary decoration, lozenges, zig-
zags, flutes exquisitely carved into their surfaces. The fact, incidentally, that all ornament at Durham is abstract, is typical
only of Norman architecture in England and Normandy, not
of Romanesque architecture in general. In France and Italy
many types of foliated decoration, especially of capitals, exist.
The best-known instance in England is characteristically
enough in the crypt of Canterbury, the gateway through
which a Continental style had passed once before, about
600, and another one was going to pass in 1175. The capitals
here (fig. 15) have foliated decoration, and some even beasts.

But nature had no immediate influence on these. They derive from sample-books kept in the lodges of the masons and based on illuminated manuscripts, ivories, previous work of the lodge, etc. Originality was a conception unknown; so was observation of nature. Style as a restrictive force of discipline ruled as unchallenged as authority in religion. Still, Durham seems more humane than Winchester, and 12th-century capitals seem more humane than the block shapes of the 11th, just as the sermons of St Bernard seem more humane and more personal than those of the theologians before him.

The exterior of Durham Cathedral is one of the most magnificent sights of England. There it stands, flanked on one side by the Bishop's Castle, on the top of its steep wooded hill with its mighty tower over the crossing and the two slenderer western towers to balance its weight. They are not Norman in their present form, the western towers dating from the 13th, the central tower (originally with a spire) from the 15th century. But towers were planned from the beginning, and where they were carried out, they ended in spires of moderate pitch such as those at Southwell (pl. 11b). The outside appearance of Romanesque churches thus differed just as widely from that of Early Christian churches as their interiors. While at S. Apollinare Nuovo the exterior hardly mattered – even church towers, when they were introduced, stood separate from their churches – a few Carolingian and then most larger Romanesque churches were designed to display variety and magnificence outside as well as inside. St Michael's at Hildesheim, with its two choirs, towers over both crossings and staircase turrets on both ends of both transepts, is the earliest surviving example of a truly Romanesque exterior (fig. 16).

Altogether Germany was eminently important for the development of art and architecture in the early 11th century. These were the years of Ottonian and Salian power, the years before the Emperor Henry IV had to humiliate himself before a Cluniac pope. There is nothing in the arts of Italy or France to emulate the bronze doors of Hildesheim Cathedral. Similarly, in architecture the introduction of yet another key element of the Romanesque (and Gothic) style seems to be due to

Germany: the two-tower façade. Its first appearance has been traced to the cathedral of Strassburg in its form of 1015. Then, however, the motif was at once taken up by the most active

16. *Hildesheim: St Michael's, begun shortly after* 1000 *(axonometric reconstruction of the original state)*

province of France: by Normandy; and from Jumièges (1040–67), and the two abbeys of William the Conqueror at Caen (Holy Trinity and St Stephen's, *c.* 1065–80), it reached Britain.

Perhaps we should not speak at all of France concerning the 11th and 12th centuries. The country was still divided into separate territories fighting each other, and consequently there was no one universally valid school of architecture, as, thanks to the Norman kings, there already was in England. The most important schools in France are those of Normandy, Burgundy, Provence, Aquitaine (or rather, broadly speaking, the whole South-West), Auvergne, and Poitou. Their comparatively static customs were crossed by a strong current from the north and west of France right down to the far north-west of Spain, the current of the principal pilgrimage routes. Pilgrimages were one of the chief media of cultural communication in the Middle Ages, and their effects on church planning are evident. They can be seen from Chartres via Orléans, Tours, Poitiers, Saintes to Spain; from Vézelay via Le Puy, Conques, or via Périgueux to Moissac and on to Spain; and from Arles to St Gilles and Toulouse and then to Spain. The goal was Santiago de Compostela, a sanctuary as celebrated as Jerusalem and Rome. The Cluniac Order had much to do with the development of the pilgrimage routes, and characteristics of Cluny can be found in the chief monasteries all the way along. What these were, we can read from the many surviving Cluniac houses – the Order, according to Dr Joan Evans's calculations, possessed some 1,450 priories at the height of its power – and also from the excavations and reconstruction of Cluny itself, carried out for the Medieval Academy of America by Professor Conant.[1] Cluny, as rebuilt at the end of the 11th century (High Altar consecrated in 1095) and early in the 12th and destroyed by the French themselves in 1810, had two transepts (as later became the rule in English cathedrals), each with an octagonal tower over the crossing. The more important of these, the one farther west, had octagonal towers to the right and left of the crossing as well (one of these survives), and two eastern apses to each arm. The eastern transept had four apses too. Moreover, the chancel apse had an ambulatory with five radiating chapels. Thus one saw looking at the church

1. I am greatly indebted to Professor Conant for allowing me to illustrate his reconstruction.

from the east (pl. 11b) a graded development in many carefully proportioned steps from the low radiating chapels over the ambulatory, the main apse, the chancel roof, the tower over the eastern crossing, to the tallest tower farther west – a structure so complex, so polyphonous, as earlier centuries in the West could not have conceived, and the Greeks would have detested, but the ideal expression no doubt of that proudest moment in medieval Christianity, when the Reform had conquered the throne of the popes, asserted the superiority of the papal tiara over the imperial crown, and called up the knights of Europe to defend the Holy Land in the first Crusade (1095).

Of the architectural elements of the Cluniac Order, it was especially the tunnel-vaulted naves with galleries (pl. 11b) and the stepped-up east ends which appear in the great churches on the pilgrimage route: St Stephen's in Nevers (begun in 1063), St Martial in Limoges (near completion in 1095 and now destroyed), St Sernin in Toulouse (begun *c.* 1075, and the grandest of all in its exterior, pl. 11a), and Santiago itself (begun in 1077). The motif of the radiating chapels, it need hardly be added, had been used at Tours long before any of these churches took it over. Regional modifications of this pilgrimage style make the individual churches all the more fascinating.

Of the main regional characteristics only a few can here be mentioned. Of Normandy with its basilicas, flat-roofed or with plain cross-vaults or rib-vaults, and with galleries, we have already spoken (pl. 9). The school of Provence liked tunnel-vaulted churches without any aisles. In Poitou the same height for tall naves and tall narrow aisles was the rule. In Auvergne aisles are also as a rule as high as the nave, but they do not look it, because they have galleries. Burgundy (in accordance with her geographical position between Provence, the North Italian sphere of influence, and the Rhineland) kept to the basilican tradition and used for vaulting either tunnel-vaults or groined vaults. Cluny belonged to the first kind; Vézelay, begun in 1096 and completed, it seems, in 1132, is the supreme example of the second (pl. 13). The church was supposed to possess the relics of the Magdalen; they made it a favourite goal of pilgrimages. It stretches out at the top of a small town climbing up the hill towards it. The main entrance is through an aisled narthex or galilee of three bays (a Cluniac motif), and on through one of the wildest of Romanesque figure portals. The nave has nothing of that violence. With its later and lighter choir in the far distance, its length of about 200 feet between narthex and crossing, its unusually high nave vaults, its arches of alternating grey and pink courses, and its inexhaustible profusion of capitals with sacred stories, it possesses a noble proportion and a proud magnificence without being less robust than Durham.

One more school must be mentioned, with a system quite apart from all the others: the school of Aquitaine, with Angoulême and Périgueux as its centres. They preferred aisleless churches – only occasionally are there aisles of nave height – consisting of several domed bays, with or without transept. Their simplicity and grave majesty are unparalleled (pl. 15). The centralizing tendency which is apparent wherever domes are used culminates at St Front in Périgueux (pl. 16), where during the second quarter of the 12th century the decision was taken to create a purely central building – a great rarity in the High Middle Ages – by leaving without the western bay of its nave an Aquitanian aisleless church which had already its transepts. Thus a Greek cross resulted, with a square for the centre and four squares for the arms. Each square has in its turn short arms again and is covered by a vast dome. The interior (for the exterior is badly restored) is the classic expression of Romanesque clarity and determination.[1] There is no sculptural decoration anywhere except for some arcading along the walls. The system goes back to the age of Justinian. It was created for his church of the Holy Apostles, of which nothing now remains. From there it was taken over by the Venetians

1. The term *classic* is used throughout in this book with a meaning different from *classical*. *Classical* applies to anything inspired by, or copied from, the style of Antiquity, *classic* to the short moments of perfect balance achieved by many styles. When we say of a work of literature or art that it is *a classic*, we mean something similar, namely that it is perfect of its kind, and universally accepted as such.

when they began to rebuild St Mark's in 1063. Whether the
inspiration for Périgueux came from Byzantium or Venice cannot be said. The impression inside St Mark's is certainly utterly
different from that of Périgueux. Venice, the most oriental and
most romantic of European cities, and the most powerful
centre of trade with the East, had endowed her grandest church
with all the magic of the Orient, mosaics, luxuriant capitals,
arcades to separate centres from arms, and concealed spatial
relations in the sense which we have seen at Ravenna. At Périgueux it is stripped of all that suspicious glamour and appears
pure and sheer, great for its architectural nobility and none
other. St Mark's belongs to Eastern, Périgueux to Western
architecture. There is even something strikingly Roman in the
bareness of Périgueux. No wonder that the ground plan was
re-invented in almost identical form by the Italians of the Renaissance.

So much for France. Germany could not do better than
develop the theme set at Hildesheim, and the cathedrals and
monastery churches of the central Rhineland, notably Speier,
Mainz, Worms, and Laach, make a splendid display of towers
over their crossings and staircase towers, of double transepts
and double chancels in an unending variety of proportion and
detail (pl. 15b). The second main school of German Romanesque architecture is that of Cologne. Of the Saxon school
something has already been said – the others are more provincial. Cologne, before 1940, possessed an unrivalled number
of churches dating back to the 10th, 11th, 12th, and early 13th
centuries. Their loss is one of the most grievous casualties of the
war. Their hall-mark (since St Mary in Capitol, consecrated
in 1065) is a resolutely centralizing scheme for the east
ends, a scheme in which both transepts and the chancel end
in identical apses. Oriental influence has been presumed. The
exteriors were as glorious and varied as any higher up the
Rhine.

North Italy has one church of the same type: S. Fedele at
Como. Some have tried to construct a dependence of Cologne
on Como, but it is now certain that if there is any relation it
must have operated the other way. In other respects the

connections between Lombardy and the Rhine are still contro-
versial. Nobody can deny them; but priority in types and
motifs can never be established beyond doubt. The most likely
answer to the question is that along the routes of the Imperial
campaigns into Italy there was a continuous give and take of
ideas and workmen. Probably Saxony and the Rhine were
leading to the end of the 11th century, and North Italy in the
12th. At that time gangs of Lombard masons must have
travelled far and wide, just as they did again in the Baroque.
We find their traces in Alsace as well as in Sweden, and one
man from Como appears in Bavaria in 1133. The *leitmotiv* of
this Lombardo-Rhenish style is the dwarf-gallery, that is the
decoration of walls, and especially those of apses, high up under
the eaves with little arched colonnades.

In her ground plans North Italy was less enterprising. Some
of the most famous churches have not even a projecting transept, that is, keep close to Early Christian traditions. This
applies, for instance, to the cathedral of Modena and S. Ambrogio in Milan. S. Ambrogio is the most impressive of them
all (pl. 16), with its atrium and its austere front, its low squat
nave, its massive piers, its wide domed cross-vaults, and its
broad primitive ribs (on these see page 44). Generally speaking
the interior characteristics of these Lombard cathedrals are
cross-vaults or rib-vaults, galleries in the aisles, polygonal
domes over the crossings, their outside characteristics isolated
towers (*campanile* is their Italian name), and those miniature
arcadings already referred to. The extreme case of such decorative arcading is the front and the leaning tower of the cathedral of Pisa in Tuscany, both of the 13th century.

Pisa strikes one altogether as of rather an alien character –
Oriental more than Tuscan. Similarly alien is the style of Venice
with its Byzantine and of Sicily with its Arab connections. To
see the Italian Romanesque at its most Italian, that is at its most
purely Tuscan, one has to look to such buildings as S. Miniato
al Monte in Florence (pl. 17a), which, in spite of its early date
(its ground floor may even be contemporary with the transept
of Winchester, pl. 7), possesses a delicacy of treatment, a civilized restraint in sculptural decoration and a susceptibility to

the spirit of Antiquity unparalleled anywhere in the
North – a first synthesis of
Tuscan intellect and grace
with Roman simplicity
and poise.

Yet in those parts of
France in which classical
remains abound, and men,
climate, and scenery strike
one as so akin to Italy, a
new sympathy with the
heritage of Rome also
appeared with the 12th
century. The most im-
portant monuments of this
blend of the Romanesque
and the Roman stand in
Burgundy and Provence.
The Burgundian church
of St Lazare at Autun
(pl. 14) has fluted pilasters,
and Autun as well as Vézelay and others possess
capitals in which the de-
based 'Corinthian' of the
earlier Romanesque style
(fig. 18) is restored to
something like its original
meaning by a new live un-
derstanding of the vegetal
and decorative character
of the acanthus leaf (fig.
19). A similar understanding, not of Roman detail
but of Roman architecture
as a whole, distinguishes
the façade of St Gilles in

17. *Fluted capital from Winchester
Cathedral, late 11th century*

18. *Debased Corinthian capital from
St Stephen's, Nevers, late 11th century*

19. *Capital from Vézelay, c. 1120: revived interest in Antiquity*

20. *Crocket capital from Laon, c. 1190: early Gothic resilience*

Provence (pl. 15a). For while its three round-headed porches and the manifold mouldings to their arches are unmistakably Romanesque, the columns in front of the walls between the doorways have straight entablatures, a feature of antique, never of Western architecture, and luxuriant Corinthian capitals. Moreover, there are figures of saints standing upright in straight-headed recesses. Life-size sculpture had been the greatest achievement of Classical Antiquity. In the days of S. Apollinare Nuovo it had all but disappeared. There is no large-scale Carolingian figure sculpture either. Only during the 11th century, when the plastic sense returned to church architecture, it reappeared; only towards its end did it begin to produce work of an aesthetic standard equalling that of the buildings themselves, and only centuries later did it gain independence from architecture.

CHAPTER THREE

The Early and Classic Gothic Style

c. 1150–c. 1250

IN 1140 the foundation stone was laid for the new choir of St Denis Abbey near Paris (fig. 21). It was consecrated in 1144. Abbot Suger, the mighty counsellor of two kings of France, was the soul of the enterprise. There are few buildings in Europe so revolutionary in their conception and so rapid and unhesitating in their execution. Four years was an exceptionally short time in the 12th century for rebuilding the choir of a large abbey church. Whoever designed the choir of St Denis, one can safely say, invented the Gothic style, although Gothic features had existed before, scattered here and there, and, in the centre of France, the provinces around St Denis, even developed with a certain consistency.

21. *St Denis: abbey church, consecrated* 1144

The features which make up the Gothic style are well enough known, too well in fact, because most people forget that a style is not an aggregate of features, but an integral whole. Still, it may be just as well to recapitulate them and re-examine their meaning. They are the pointed arch, the flying buttress, and the rib-vault. Not one of them is a Gothic invention. Pointed arches appear occasionally in Romanesque churches, e.g., in Burgundy and Provence, and at Durham. Flying buttresses were common in several parts of France and also used at Durham. They are not usually realized as such, because they were kept underneath the roofs. Of the ribs of Durham and North Italy something has been said in the previous chapter. What the Gothic style brought to these motifs was their combination for a new aesthetic purpose. This purpose was to enliven inert masses of masonry, to quicken spatial motion, to reduce a building to a seeming system of innervated lines of action. These aesthetic advantages are infinitely more significant for an understanding of the Gothic style than whatever technical advantages the use of ribs, flying buttresses, and pointed arches may have meant. Such technical advantages were not absent, although they have been vastly overestimated by Viollet-le-Duc and his innumerable followers.

The technical advantages are threefold. First of all a tunnel-vault presses down on the whole of the two walls on which it rests. The groin-vaults of Romanesque Germany or Vézelay pressed down on only four points. But Romanesque groin-vaults require square bays to be constructed satisfactorily. If you try to build a Romanesque, that is an essentially round-arched groin-vault over an oblong bay, you will have to use arches of three distinct diameters, over the long and short side of the rectangle and across the diagonal. Only one of the three can be semicircular; the others must be stilted or depressed. If the transverse arch, that is the most visible one, is made semicircular, then the diagonal becomes depressed, and depressed arches are structurally dangerous, because obviously the safety of an arch increases the closer its thrust approaches the vertical, and decreases the nearer the horizontal its thrust. Complete verticality would result in complete safety, complete horizontality would burst the two walls apart at once.

The pointed arch enables the designer to get nearer the desired verticality than the semicircular, and in addition to construct vaults over bays other than square. Instead of stilting and depression there will now simply be three different degrees of pointing. The rectangular bay is useful for another reason as well. In a square bay the four points of support are far from each other, and as they are the points on to which the whole weight of the vault is conducted, they carry a disproportionately great responsibility in securing the stability of the building. With oblong bays you can double the number of the supports and thus halve the share of each of them in holding the building together.

Moreover, the oblong Gothic vault was constructed with ribs to strengthen the groins, and that also was technically advantageous. For a tunnel-vault or a Romanesque groin-vault needs a wooden centering underneath its whole length and width to build it up. In the case of rib-vaults a centering is erected only strong enough to support the transverse arches and diagonal ribs until their mortar has set. The cells between the transverse arches and ribs can then be filled in with the help of a light, movable, hanging centering device, a so-called *cerce*. The saving in timber is evident. Whether the ribs also kept the cells independent of one another, even after the vault had been completed, and actually reduced the cells to the nature of membranes, remains doubtful. There are cases where after shelling or bombing ribs have remained intact while cells have come down, but there are others also where quite clearly vaults have stood although parts of their ribs have fallen out. So it can be regarded as certain that the primary object of the Gothic vault was its appearance of immaterial lightness rather than any actual lightness, that is once again an aesthetic rather than a material consideration.

The various technical and visual innovations appeared for the first time combined into a Gothic system at St Denis. Rib-vaults cover the varying shapes of bays, buttresses replace the massive walls between the radiating chapels which now form a continuous wavy fringe to the ambulatory. Their side walls have disappeared entirely. If it were not for the five-ribbed vaults, one would feel like walking through a second, outer ambulatory, with exceedingly shallow chapels. The effect inside the church is one of lightness, of air circulating freely, of supple curves and energetic concentration. No longer is part demonstratively separated from part. The transept, recent excavations have shown, was not intended to project much beyond the nave and chancel walls as it had always done until then.[1] Articulation remains; but it is a far more sophisticated articulation. Who was the great genius to conceive this? Was it Abbot Suger himself, who so proudly wrote a little book about the building and consecration of his church? Hardly; for the Gothic, as against the Romanesque style, is so essentially based on a co-operation between artist and engineer, and a synthesis of aesthetic and technical qualities, that only a man of profound structural knowledge can have invented such a system. We are here at the beginning of a specialization that has gone on splitting up our activities into smaller and smaller competencies, until to-day the patron is not an architect, the architect not a builder, the builder not a mason, let alone such distinctions as those between the quantity surveyor, the heating engineer, the air-conditioning engineer, the electrical installation expert, and the sanitation expert.

The new type of architect to whom St Denis and the later French and English cathedrals must be ascribed is the master craftsman as a recognized artist. Creative master craftsmen had of course existed before, and probably always designed most of what was built. But their status now began to change. It was a very gradual development. Suger in his book does not say one word about the architect of St Denis, nor in fact about the designer of the church as such. It seems curious; surely he must have known very well what a daring work he had put up. To explain his silence one must remember the often-quoted and often-misunderstood anonymity of the Middle Ages. It does not mean of course that cathedrals grew like trees. They were all designed by someone. But in the earlier medieval centuries the names of these men, immortal as their work seemed, did not count. They were content to be workmen working for a cause greater than their own fame. However, during the 12th and, above all, the 13th centuries the self-confidence of the individual grew, and personality came to be appreciated. The

1. See *College Art Journal*, vol. 6, 1947, p. 236.

names of the architects of Rheims and Amiens cathedrals were recorded in a curious way on the pavement of the naves. A preacher complained that master-masons got higher wages than others by simply going about with their staffs in their hands and giving orders, and – he adds – 'nihil laborant'. A century after this the King of France was godfather to the son of one of these men and made him a considerable present in gold to enable him to study at a university. But two hundred years had to elapse after the time of Suger to make such intimacy possible.

One of the earliest cases in which we can form a live impression of the personality of one of the great master-masons of the early Gothic style is that of William of Sens, architect to the choir of Canterbury Cathedral – a work as revolutionary in England as St Denis was in France. A fire had destroyed the old choir in 1174, as we are told by Gervase, the chronicler of the cathedral, who had himself lived through the events he relates. There was great despair among the brethren, until after a while they began to consult 'by what method the ruined church might be repaired. Architects, both French and English, were assembled; but they disagreed. Some suggested repair, while others insisted that the whole church must be taken down, if the monks wished to dwell in safety. This overwhelmed them with grief. Among the architects there was one, William of Sens, a man of great abilities and a most ingenious workman in wood and stone. Dismissing the rest, they chose him for the undertaking. And he, residing many days with the monks and carefully surveying the burnt walls . . . did yet for some time conceal what he found necessary to do, lest the truth should kill us in our hopelessness. But he went on preparing all things that were necessary, either himself or by the agency of others. And when he found that the monks began to be somewhat comforted, he confessed that the damaged pillars and all that they supported, must be destroyed, if the monks wished to have a safe and excellent building. At length they agreed . . . to take down the ruined choir. Attention was given to procure stones from abroad. He made the most ingenious machines for loading and unloading ships, and for drawing the mortar and stones.

He delivered also to the masons models (cut-out wooden templates) for cutting the stones. . . .' Then the chronicler tells us exactly what during each of the following four years was done. At the beginning of the fifth year, however, William, while on the scaffolding, fell down to the ground from a height of fifty feet. He was badly hurt and had to 'entrust the completion of the work to a certain ingenious monk who was overseer of the rough masons. . . .' But though lying in bed, he gave orders 'what was first and what was last to be done. . . . At length, finding no benefit from the skill of his surgeons, he went to France to die at home', and an English successor was appointed.[1]

So here we have the craftsman, equally skilled in masonry and engineering work, diplomatic with his patrons and appreciated by them, but never while conducting work abroad forgetting the land of his youth. At Sens, wherefrom he came, a new cathedral had been begun about thirty years before he went over to Canterbury, a cathedral with certain features evidently imitated at Canterbury.

We are fortunate in possessing at least one even more complete record of the personality and work of a Gothic architect, a notebook, or rather textbook, prepared about 1235 by Villard de Honnecourt, an architect from the Cambrai region of Northern France. This textbook, preserved at the National Library in Paris, is an eminently personal document. Villard addresses his pupils. He promises them tuition in masonry and carpentry, drawing of architecture and figures, and geometry. Of all this the book contains examples, drawn and briefly described. It is invaluable as a source of information on the methods and attitude of the 13th century. Villard, although an architect, draws a Crucifixion, a Madonna, and figures of the sleeping disciples as they were represented in the scene on the Mount of Olives (fig. 22), all these evidently for stone carvers to work from. He also drew figures of Pride and Humility, the Church Triumphant and the Wheel of Fortune. But there are worldly scenes too, wrestlers (fig. 23), men on horseback, a

1. The quotations are from Mr Charles Cotton's edition (*Canterbury Papers* No. 3. Published by the Friends of Canterbury Cathedral, 1930).

king with his retinue. Then there are many animals, some surprisingly realistic, others quite fantastic. There are simple geometrical schemes for drawing human heads and animals. He
records parts of buildings, the ground plans of church choirs

22. *A Cistercian plan, and a disciple on the Mount of Olives. From
Villard de Honnecourt's textbook, c. 1235*

(fig. 23), a tower of Laon Cathedral (he says: 'I have been in
many countries, as you can see from this book, but I have never
seen such another tower'), windows from the choir of Rheims
(fig. 24; he says: 'I was on my way to Hungary, when I drew
this, because I liked it best'), and a rose window at Lausanne.

He traces a labyrinth, and draws foliage. He designs a foliated end for a choir stall and a lectern with three evangelists. He has diagrams of mouldings and of timber construction. He adds proudly a good many pieces of machinery, a sawmill, a device

23. *Pair of wrestlers, a Cistercian church plan, and the plan of the cathedral of Cambrai. From Villard de Honnecourt's textbook, c. 1235*

for lifting heavy weights, and also such automata as a lectern eagle that turns its head, or a heatable metal orb for a bishop to hold in his hand. He even notes a recipe for getting rid of super-fluous hair.

Such was the range of knowledge and experience of the men who built the great Gothic cathedrals. They were invited abroad as the bringers of the new Gothic style, the 'opus francigenum', as it is called in a German record of that time; they kept their eyes open while they travelled, and noted buildings, sculptures, and paintings with the same eagerness. They knew as much of the carving of figures and ornaments as of building construction, although their drawing technique was still elementary.

St Denis must owe its novelty to a master-mason of this calibre. And many a bishop and architect burned with ambition to emulate Suger and St Denis. Between 1140 and 1220 new cathedrals were begun on an ever-growing scale at Sens, Noyon, Senlis, and then Paris (Notre Dame, *c.* 1163 seqq.), Laon (*c.* 1170 seqq.), Chartres (*c.* 1195 seqq.), Rheims (1211 seqq.), Amiens (1220 seqq.), and Beauvais (1247 seqq.). These are by no means all; there are many more all over France. We must, however, here confine ourselves to a brief analysis of the main development in the Ile de France and the surrounding regions, which just then became the centre of a national French kingdom. It is a development as consistent and as concise as that of the Greek temple.

24. *One of the radiating east chapels of Rheims Cathedral. From Villard de Honnecourt's textbook, c. 1235*

Of St Denis we possess only the choir and, very restored, the west front. This is of the two-tower type of Caen which now became *de rigueur* for North French cathedrals, but, against Caen, enriched by a still round-headed triple portal. Chartres followed St Denis at once. Of the cathedral of about 1145 only the west portals remain, gloriously vigorous, alert, and human in their sculpture, as against the rest of France. We can guess what the naves of St Denis and Chartres were like from the cathedrals of Sens and especially Noyon. At Noyon, the walls are enriched, as against the Norman system of arcade, gallery, and clerestory, by a low wall-passage or triforium between gallery and clerestory. This division of the wall into four zones

25. *Elevation of the nave of Noyon Cathedral, designed c. 1150*

26. *Elevation of the nave of Laon Cathedral, designed c. 1170*

instead of three does away with much that had remained inert before. The arcades have alternating supports, composite piers as major and round ones as minor divisions. In accordance with this the vaults are sex-partite as they had been in some Norman and Romanesque churches. That means that between two transverse arches ribs run across diagonally from composite to composite pier, while the shafts on the round piers are followed up by subsidiary ribs parallel with the transverse arches and meeting the diagonal ribs in the centre of the whole bay. The effect is more lively than we know in the Romanesque style (fig. 25).

However, the architects of the two cathedrals immediately following must have felt that in the walls, piers, and vaults of Noyon there was still too much left of Romanesque weight and stability. The alternating supports and sex-partite vaults especially produced square, that is static, bays. So at Laon (pl. 18a and fig. 26), after some experimenting with alternating supports, all the piers are circular, although on the upper floors an alternating between groups of five and of three thin shafts rising from the circular piers is still preserved, and there are still sex-partite vaults. The many thin shaft-rings, or annulets, round the shafts also still emphasize the horizontal. All the same, in walking along the nave the halting at every major support is avoided. That was a decisive step to take. Notre

27. *Original elevation of the nave of Notre Dame in Paris, designed c.* 1170

Dame in Paris goes yet one step further (pl. 18b and fig. 27). The shafts on the circular piers are no longer differentiated, and the shaft-rings are left out. But the wall was still, it seems, originally in four stages, with gallery and then, instead of the triforium, a row of circular windows below those of the clerestory. However, the proportions have now changed sufficiently to show what tendency lay behind these gradual modifications. The gallery arcades have coupled openings in the choir – as was the Norman tradition – but trebled, that is much slimmer, openings in the slightly later nave, and the separating colonnettes are exceedingly slender.

Still more daring than the elevation of Notre Dame is its ground plan (fig. 28). Already at Sens and Noyon a slightly

28. Paris: Notre Dame, begun c. 1163. Top half – ground floor; lower half – upper floor. The chapels between the buttresses of the nave were begun c. 1235, around the east end in 1296

centralizing tendency can be noted: at Sens by a lengthening of the chancel between transept and ambulatory, at Noyon by semicircular endings of the transepts to the north and south. Now in Paris the architect has placed his transept almost exactly half-way between the two west towers and the east end. He has adopted the most ambitious plan for nave and chancel, the one with double aisles, familiar from Old St Peter's in Rome as well as from Cluny. His transepts project very little beyond the outer aisles, and there were originally no radiating chapels at all. The present ones, as well as the present chapels between the buttresses of nave and chancel, are a later addition. The resulting spatial rhythm is much smoother than that of Romanesque cathedrals or of Noyon. It is no longer split into numerous units which one has to add up mentally, as it were, to summarize the spatial totality, but concentrated in a few, in fact

three, sections: west, centre, east. The transept acts as the centre
of the balance. The façade and the double ambulatory round
the apse are the two scales. Within the rhythm the evenness of
the narrowly spaced arcade columns is most important. It leads
you on towards the altar as forcibly as did the columns of Early
Christian basilicas.

The movement which had grown from St Denis to Noyon
and from Noyon to Paris reached maturity in the cathedrals
designed from the end of the 12th century onwards. Early
Gothic changed into High Gothic. Chartres was rebuilt after a
fire in 1194 (fig. 29). The new choir and nave at last do away
with the sex-partite vault and return to vaults with only
diagonal ribs. But whereas the Romanesque rib-vaults were
placed over square or squarish bays, the bays now are roughly
half that depth. The speed of the eastward drive is thereby at
once doubled. The piers remain circular, but they have on each
side a circular attached shaft. Toward the nave this shaft reaches
right up to where the vault starts (as the shafts of Winchester
and Normandy had already done). So the isolation of the circular column is overcome. Nothing at arcade level stops the
vertical push. And the wide and tall gallery has disappeared.
There is now only a low triforium, dividing the tall arcades
from the tall clerestory windows. These innovations constitute
the High Gothic style. The plan is less radical than that of Paris,
but has the transept also mid-way between the west front and
the choir end.

Once Chartres had introduced the new type of piers, the
three-storied elevation, and the simplified vaulting, Rheims,
Amiens, and Beauvais did nothing more than perfect it and
carry it to the boldest and most thrilling extremes (figs. 30 and
31). As in the plans so in the interiors a balance is achieved no
doubt – but not the happy, seemingly effortless and indestruc-
tible balance of the Greeks. High Gothic balance is a balance of
two equally vehement drives towards two opposite directions.
One's first impression is of breathtaking height. In Durham the
relation between width and height of nave had been 1:2.3, in
Chartres 1:2.6, in Paris 1:2.75. In Amiens it has become 1:3,
and in Beauvais 1:3.4. The absolute height in Durham had

been approximately 80 feet. In Paris it is 115 feet, in Rheims 125, in Amiens 140, and in Beauvais 157. The drive upward

29. *Elevation of the nave of Chartres Cathedral, designed c.* 1195

is just as forcible as, or, owing to the slenderness of all members, even more forcible than, was the drive eastward in Early Christian churches. And the eastward drive has not by any means slackened either. The narrowness of the arcades and the uniform shape of the piers do not seem to call for even a momentary change of direction. They accompany one on one's way, as closely set and as rapidly appearing and disappearing as telegraph poles along a railway line. There is not time at first to stop and admire them. Yet in pressing forward, the transept halts us and diverts our eyes to the right and left. Here we stop, here we endeavour for the first time to take in the whole. In an Early Christian church nothing of this kind was provided, in a Romanesque church so much of it that movement went slowly from bay to bay, from compartment to compartment. At Amiens (pl. 27 and fig. 31) there is only one such halt, and it cannot be long. Again nave and aisles, now of the chancel, close round us, and we do not come to an ultimate rest until we have reached the apse and the ambulatory, gathering with splendid energy the parallel streams of east-bound energy and concentrating them in a final soaring movement along the narrowly spaced piers of the apse and the narrow east windows up to the giddy heights of the vault ribs and vaulting bosses.

This description is an attempt at analysing a spatial experience, ignoring of course the fact that a normal 13th-century church-goer would never have been admitted to the chancel. What will have become evident from it is how spectacularly Rheims, Amiens, and Beauvais are the final achievement of an evolution which had begun back in the 11th century in Normandy and at Durham and had worked, one after another, seemingly small but very significant changes at St Denis, Noyon, Laon, Paris, and Chartres. This final achievement is, to say it once more, far from reposeful. It possesses the tension of two dominant directions or dimensions, a tension transformed by a supreme feat of creative energy into a precarious balance. Once one has felt this, one will recognize it in every detail. The piers are slender and erect, part of the upward drive. Yet they are round, firm, and shapely, with their exquisite realistic foliage (cf. pl. 34). The mouldings of the arcades are sharp and manifold with rolls and deep hollows, high lights and black but precise shadows. The clerestory is all opened up into vast sheets of glass. Yet they are subdivided by vigorously moulded shafts and by geometrical tracery. The introduction of tracery, an

30. *Elevation of the nave of Rheims Cathedral, designed c.* 1211

31. *Elevation of the nave of Amiens Cathedral, begun* 1220

invention of the Gothic style, is especially telling. Its development can be traced from Chartres to Rheims and from Rheims to Amiens in figs. 29, 30, and 31. Before Rheims tracery is just a punching of pattern into the wall, the wall itself remaining intact as a surface. At Rheims, for the first time, we find what is called bar tracery as against plate tracery. The stress now rests on the lines of the pattern, not on the surface of the wall. Each two-lighted window is crowned by a circle with a sexfoil ornament – repose at the end of forceful action. Amiens is an enrichment of Rheims, with four lighted windows and three circles instead of one. The same energetic vitality appears in the vaults. Each boss signifies Gothic balance – the firm knotting of four lines of energy, conducted by shafts and then by ribs.

This balance of high tensions is the classic expression of the Western spirit – as final as the temple of the 5th century B.C. was of that of the Greek spirit. Then it was rest and blissful harmony, now it is activity, only just for one moment held in suspense. And it requires concentrated effort to master the contrasts and partake of the balance. Like a Bach fugue, a Gothic cathedral demands all our emotional and intellectual powers. Now we find ourselves lost in the mystical ruby and azure glow of translucent stained glass, and now called back to alert attention by the precise course of thin yet adequately strong lines. What is the secret of these vast temples? Is it in their miraculous interiors with vast stone vaults at an immense height, walls all of glass, and arcades much too slim and tall to carry them? The Greek architect achieved a harmony of load and support convincing at once and for ever; the Gothic architect, far bolder constructionally, with his Western soul of the eternal explorer and inventor, always lured by the untried, aims at a contrast between an interior all spirit and an exterior all intellect. For inside the cathedral we cannot and are not meant to understand the law governing the whole. Outside we are faced with a frank exposition of the complicated structural mechanism. The flying buttresses and buttresses, though by no means without the fascination of intricate pattern, will chiefly appeal to reason, conveying a sensation similar to that of the theatre-goer looking at the stage apparatus behind the scenes.

One need hardly point out in so many words how exactly the Gothic cathedral re-echoes in all this the achievements of Western thought in the 13th century, the achievements, i.e., of classic scholasticism. Scholasticism is the name for the characteristically medieval blend of divinity and philosophy. It grew up with the Romanesque style, the centuries before the 11th having in the main not done more than simplify, regroup, and, here and there, modify the doctrines of the Fathers of the Church and the philosophers and poets of Rome. During the 12th century, when the Gothic style was created and spread, scholasticism developed into something just as lofty and at the same time just as intricate as the new cathedrals. The first half of the 13th century saw the appearance of the compendia of all worldly and sacred knowledge, St Thomas Aquinas's *Summa*, and the works of Albert the Great and St Bonaventura, the *Specula* of Vincent of Beauvais, and in poetry Wolfram's *Parsifal*.

One of these encyclopaedic tomes, the *De Proprietatibus Rerum* by the English Dominican Bartholomaeus Anglicus, written about 1240, begins with a chapter on the essence, unity, and the three persons of God. The next chapter deals with the angels, the third with Man, his soul and senses. There follow chapters on the elements and temperaments, on anatomy and physiology, on the Ages of Man, on food, sleep, and similar physical needs, on diseases, on sun, moon, stars, and zodiac, on time and its divisions, on matter, fire, air, water, on the birds of the air, the fishes of the water, the beasts of the land, on geography, on minerals, trees, colours, tools. Vincent of Beauvais, who writes about 1250, divides his work into the Mirrors of Nature, of Doctrine, and of History. And just as the Mirror of Nature starts from God and Creation, so the Mirror of History starts from the Fall of Man, and leads up to the Last Judgment. The cathedral was – besides being a strictly architectural monument of the spirit of its age – another *Summa*, another *Speculum*, an encyclopaedia carved in stone. The Virgin stood at the centre post of the centre portals of Rheims Cathedral (pl. 20). Figures were placed into the jambs of this portal representing such scenes as the Annunciation, the Visitation, the Presentation.

High up in the gables of the three portals appear the Crucifixion, the Coronation of the Virgin, and the Last Judgment. But there are also in the Gothic cathedrals the lives of Christ, the Virgin, and saints told in the stained glass of the windows, and, spread over the plinths, the jambs, the voussoirs, and up against the buttresses, saints with the attributes by which they are recognized – St Peter with the key, St Nicholas with the three golden balls, St Barbara with the tower, St Margaret with the dragon – and scenes and figures from the Old Testament, the Creation of Man, Jonah with the Whale, or Abraham and Melchisedek, and the Roman Sibyls who had foretold, it was believed, the coming of Christ, and the Wise and the Foolish Virgins, and the Seven Liberal Arts, and the months of the year with their occupations – the grafting of trees, sheep-shearing, harvesting, pig slaughtering – and the signs of the zodiac, and the elements. The profane and the sacred – a compendium of knowledge; but everything, as St Thomas puts it, 'ordered towards God'. For Jonah is represented, not because he comes into the Old Testament, but because his three days inside the whale represent the resurrection of Christ, as Melchisedek offering bread and wine to Abraham represented the Last Supper. To the medieval mind everything was a symbol. The meaning that mattered lay behind the outward appearance. The simile of the two swords, the emperor's and the pope's, was a symbolic expression of political theories. To Gulielmus Durandus the cruciform church represented the Cross, and the weathercock on the spire the preacher who rouses the sleeping from the night of sin. The mortar, he says, consists of lime, that is love, sand, that is earthly toil which love has taken upon itself, and water, uniting heavenly love and our earthly world.

All this one must keep in mind to realize how alien this world is to ours, despite all enthusiasm for the cathedrals and their sculptures. We are liable to a reaction in these vast halls which is far too romantic, nebulous, sentimental, whereas to the cleric of the 13th century everything was probably lucid. Lucid, but transcendental. That is the antagonism which defeats us in our age of agnosticism. In the 13th century the bishop and the monk, the knight and the craftsman believed firmly – though each to the measure of his capacity – that nothing exists in the world which does not come from God, and derive its sense and sole interest from its divine meaning. The medieval conception of truth was fundamentally different from ours. Truth was not what can be proved, but what conformed to an accepted revelation. Research was not conducted to find truth, but to penetrate more deeply into a pre-established truth. Hence authorities meant more to the medieval scholar than to anyone now, and hence also the faith of the medieval artist in the 'exemplar', the example to be copied. Neither originality nor the study of Nature counted for much. Even Villard de Honnecourt copied in nine out of ten of his pages. Innovations came by degrees and much less deliberately than we can imagine.

Yet the Gothic style surely was a deliberate innovation and the work of strong and self-confident personalities. Its forms allow us to assume that, and we find in fact within scholasticism, as the chief innovation of the 13th century, a marked departure from the purely transcendental attitude of the Romanesque and earlier centuries. St Peter Damiani, in the first half of the 11th century, had said: 'The world is so filthy with vices that any holy mind is befouled by even thinking of it.' Now Vincent of Beauvais exclaims: 'How great is even the humblest beauty of this world! I am moved with spiritual sweetness towards the Creator and Ruler of this world, when I behold the magnitude and beauty and permanence of His creation.' And beauty according to St Thomas Aquinas (or a close follower of his philosophy) 'consists of a certain consonance of diverging elements'.

But it is never – not yet – the beauty of the world as such that is praised. It is the beauty of God's creation. We can enjoy it wholeheartedly; for God Himself 'rejoices in all things, because everyone is in actual agreement with His Being' (St Thomas). Thus stone-carvers could now portray the loveliest leaves, the thorn, the oak, the maple, the vine (pl. 23a). When St Peter Damiani wrote, ornament was abstract or severely stylized. Now youthful life pulses in it, as it pulses in shafts and ribs. But the ornament of the 13th century is, even at its most naturalistic, neither petty nor pedantic. It is still subordinate, never forward, always ministering to a greater cause, that of religious architecture.

Yet it would not have been possible at an earlier age than that of St Francis's song to Brother Sun and Sister Earth and Brother Wind, than that of the '*dolce stil nuovo*', and the French epics of chivalry. The earliest monastic orders had lived in the seclusion of their cloisters; the new orders of the 13th century, the Dominicans and Franciscans, had their monasteries in towns and preached to the burghers. The first Crusades had been called up to liberate the Holy Land, the fourth, the one of 1203, was deflected by the Venetians to Constantinople, which they needed for the benefit of their commerce. But still in the fifth there was in the person of the French King Louis IX, St Louis, a true Christian knight, a hero in whom the ideals of religion and chivalry burned with equal ardour. Wolfram's *Parsifal* is the greatest epic of the 13th century. Here at the moment when Rheims Cathedral was begun, the young knight is taught to 'keep his soul pledged to God, without losing his hold on the world'. And he is taught that 'in joy and in grief right measure' should always be his guide. That sounds like the Greek 'Nothing in excess', but it is not. It is just as in architecture, a balance gained as the ultimate prize by him who indefatigably strives for his redemption. A noble and upright ideal worthy of the great cathedrals and the superb sculptures of their portals. At Chartres, under the name of St Theodore, one can see him, the knight of the Parsifal virtues, standing in the porch of the south transept, and at Rheims, as an unknown king, under a canopy of one of the buttresses, and on horseback at Bamberg, and again with the most beautiful young women that Western sculptors ever carved, women both vigorous and maidenly, around the choir of Naumburg cathedral.

In England the emissaries of Henry VIII and of Cromwell have destroyed the majority of what there was of cathedral sculpture. A few pieces that are left, such as a headless figure at Winchester, are of the same character and quality as 13th-century sculpture in France. But neither the façade of Wells nor the surviving statues at Lincoln and Westminster are up to the standards of Chartres and Rheims. The English are not a

sculptural race. Their architecture, however, the style which
they evolved, is just as exquisite as that of the French cathedrals,
and at the same time typically English, known under the name
of Early English.

Originally it came from France, as did the Gothic style in all
countries. The Cistercians, the new reformed order of the 12th
century, to which St Bernard belonged, favoured it. Cistercian
houses in England were among the first to use pointed arches.
Into cathedral architecture it was introduced by William of
Sens at Canterbury. Details there are French in character. What
is, however, unusual in France is the duplicating of the transepts as we find it at Canterbury and then at Lincoln, Wells,
Salisbury, and many more cathedrals. It is not a feature invented
in England. Cluny, the centre of the most influential Benedic-
tine order before the foundation of the Cistercians, had it – not
in the 10th-century shape of the church, which is illustrated
(fig. 12), but as it was rebuilt in 1095 seqq. (pl. 11b). The fact
that this duplication remained solitary in France but became so
popular in England is eminently characteristic of the different
approach to architecture in the two countries. The Gothic style
in France, as we have seen, tends all to spatial concentration.
The Early English style lacks that quality. A cathedral such as
Salisbury, with its square east end and its square double transepts (fig. 32), is still the sum, as it were, of added units, compartment joined to compartment. Looking at, say, Lincoln and
then at Rheims (pls. 21b and a), this difference comes out most
eloquently. Rheims seems vigorously pulled together, Lincoln
comfortably spread out. The same contrast can be found in the
west façades. The English ones are comparatively insignificant.
Porches, added to the naves and developed sometimes into
superb pieces of independent decorative architecture, serve as
main entrances instead. And where there are fully developed
façades, as at Wells and Lincoln, they have an existence unrelated to the interiors behind, are screens, as it were, placed in
front of the church proper, and not the logically designed outward projection of the inside system, as are French façades. It
has been said that this seemingly conservative attitude of English architects was due to the survival of so many big Norman

cathedrals, the foundations and walls of which were used in the rebuilding. But this materialistic explanation, like so many of the same kind, does not hold good. Salisbury was a new foundation. There was nothing on the site when the first stone was laid in 1220 (the same year in which Amiens Cathedral was begun), yet the ground plan is of the same type as Lincoln (fig. 32). The preference for the 'additive' plan must therefore be accepted as a national peculiarity; and once one has realized that, one will recognize its essential similarity to the

10 30 50 70 90
0 |-|-|-|-|-|-|-|-|-|-| *feet*
                    100

32. *Salisbury Cathedral, begun* 1220

Anglo-Saxon ground plans of churches such as Bradford-on-Avon (fig. 10), and also its harmony with the specifically national qualities in Early English elevations.

Canterbury cannot unreservedly be called English; Wells and Lincoln are. Wells was begun just before 1191, Lincoln in 1192. If one compares the nave of Lincoln roofed in 1233 (pl. 22a) with that of Amiens, the national contrast is obvious. Yet both cathedrals are of the aristocratic, youthful yet disciplined, vigorous yet graceful spirit of the 13th century. The bays in Lincoln are wide, while they are narrow in Amiens, the piers are of comfortable proportions; no shafts run right through from bottom to top. Those supporting the ribs of the vaults rest on corbels just above the capitals of the piers – an illogical arrangement from the French point of view. The triforium gallery has broad, low openings and pointed arches, so low that they seem round[1] – another inconsistency, a French critic would say. And most curious of all to anybody thinking in terms of Amiens or Beauvais is the vault. For while the French vault is the logical termination of the bay system, the vault of Lincoln has, besides the transverse ribs separating bay from bay, and the four cross ribs, a ridge-rib running all along the centre of the vault parallel to the arcades, and so-called tiercerons, i.e. ribs springing from the same capitals as the cross ribs, but leading up to other points along the ridge or at right angles to the ridge. Thus the vault in Lincoln assumes the shape of a sequence of stars – more decorative but less reasonable than the French system.

In all this, the Early English style appears the true representative of a national character that seems scarcely changed to this day. There is still the same distrust of the consistent and logical and the extreme and uncompromising. Now it has not been possible to discover these peculiarly English qualities in Norman architecture, and it is worth mentioning in this context that just about the middle of the 13th century there are other indications as well of an awakening of national consciousness. The Provisions of Oxford of 1258 are the first official document with a text not only in French (or Latin) but also in English. And they declare that no royal fiefs shall in future go to foreigners, and that the commanders of royal castles and ports must in future all be English. It is known that Simon de Montfort's revolt was a national movement, and that Edward I was influenced by Simon's ideas to a considerable extent. The same tendency towards national differentiation can incidentally be noticed during the same period in other European countries. It may be connected with the experiences of the Crusades. Here the knights of the West, though united in a common enterprise, must for the first time have become aware of the contrasts of behaviour, feelings, and customs of the nations.

As far as architecture is concerned, the Crusades have had, beyond this, one more immediate effect. They caused a complete reform in the planning and building of castles. Instead of

1. Though not as exaggeratedly depressed as they are at Salisbury a little later (Fig. 33).

the Norman reliance for defence on the keep, a system of concentric curtain walls with towers at intervals was now adopted. It came from the mighty castles (such as Le Crak des Chevaliers) built by the Crusaders in Syria and the Holy Land. The Crusaders took it from the Turks, who in their turn had derived it from Roman military architecture. The Tower of London, as enlarged by Henry III and his successors, is an instance of this concentric plan. What is, however, more especially important here is the fact that the new functional standard is accompanied at least in a number of cases by a new aesthetic standard. To the architects who designed the Edwardian castles of Wales the appearance of the Norman castle, with its irregular bailey and its keep on a mount in one corner, was haphazard and untidy. They rediscovered symmetry as a possible planning principle for castles – rediscovered, because Rome had known it. Just as they designed newly-founded towns (New Winchelsea, for example) on the chessboard pattern, they ventured to make of Harlech and Beaumaris completely symmetrical configurations (fig. 34). The effect, in Harlech especially, is one of overwhelming majesty. Far too few people know that here, in Wales, the most consummate masterpieces of European military architecture are to be found. For grandeur and daring of conception, only the Emperor Frederick II's slightly earlier Castel del Monte in South Italy, again a synthesis of Roman, Eastern, and Gothic elements, can be compared.

33. *Elevation of the nave of Salisbury Cathedral, designed c. 1220.*

In English religious architecture the achievement that lends itself most readily to a comparison with Harlech and Beaumaris is the 13th-century chapter-house, again something specifically English, again something hardly known abroad and – owing to the British inferiority complex in matters of art – insufficiently appreciated over here. Salisbury chapter-house of about 1275 (pl. 24) is centrally planned, an octagon with a central pillar and spacious windows filling the walls entirely except for the arcade strip just above the stone benches for the members of the Chapter. But while in France such glass walls

34. *Harlech Castle, chiefly* 1286–90

give a sensation of a rapturous union with a mysterious world beyond ours, the proportions of the windows at Salisbury, with their generously-sized tracery circles, keep the interior in safe and happy contact with the ground. A sunny breadth is achieved which makes Amiens feel both over-pointed and over-excited.

At the same time the Early English style has just as much refinement, crispness, and *noblesse* in every individual motif as the French style of the great cathedrals. It is in fact this essential similarity of detail that reminds one all the time of the ultimate identity of spirit behind French and English 13th-century architecture. To feel this, it is only necessary to look at the central pier at Salisbury or the piers of the nave arcade in Lincoln with their slender detached shafts and their resilient crocket capitals (of a type equally characteristic of *c.* 1200 in England and France, cf. fig. 20), or at the clarity and erectness of the English lancet window (English in that it presupposes a solid wall into which it is placed as against the French elimination of the whole wall), or at the masterful carving of the leaves around the capitals of Southwell chapter-house (pl. 23a), throbbing with life, yet kept under the strict discipline of architecture, economic in treatment, nowhere fussy or ostentatious, and of a precision of surface to be compared only with the classic Greek art of the Parthenon.

But the Classic is only a moment in the history of a civilization. The most progressive had reached it in France and England at the end of the 12th century. The most progressive were tired of it and embarked on new adventures shortly after the middle of the 13th. In France, however, the magnificent creative impulse soon flagged – after the Sainte Chapelle in Paris and the gigantic choir of Beauvais there was nothing for a long time with such intensity of life. England on the other hand kept up her creative energy for another century. In fact, the architecture of England between 1250 and 1350 was, although the English do not know it, the most forward, the most important, and the most inspired in Europe.

CHAPTER FOUR

The Late Gothic Style

c. 1250–c. 1500

LATE Gothic, though by the predominant use of the pointed arch still part of the Gothic style, is essentially different from the High Gothic of the great French cathedrals of Paris, Rheims, and Amiens, and the English cathedrals of Salisbury and Lincoln. It is a complex phenomenon – so complex, indeed, that it might be wise to approach it from the point of view of changes in decoration first, before trying to recognize in what way spatial changes were involved. As for decoration, the difference between early and late 13th century can clearly be seen within Lincoln Cathedral. The retrochoir, or Angel Choir (pl. 22b), was begun in 1256. It is of supreme beauty, but it no longer possesses the freshness of spring or early summer; this abundance of rich and mellow decoration has the warmth and sweetness of August and September, of harvest and vintage. But what generous fulfilment in the luxuriant foliage of the corbels and the gallery shafts and capitals, the full mouldings of the arcades and tracery of the gallery, and, above all, the two gorgeous layers of tracery up in the clerestory: one in the windows and one separating the wall-passage from the interior.

While here there is still breadth and fullness, in other equally advanced work of the same date a tendency becomes noticeable towards the more sophisticated and at the same time the more complicated. This tendency runs parallel with the dominant tendency in contemporary philosophy – the abstruse intricacies of Duns Scotus (born c. 1270) and his pupil Occam (died c. 1347) – and also with that in French architecture. But whereas the result in France is on the whole lean and retrospective, England went on inventing forms with amazing profuseness, forms merely decorative, no longer strictly architectural. The most perfect expression of this new spirit is in the kind of tracery which is called flowing as against the geometrical tracery of 1230 to about 1300. The economy of the Early English – a feature of all classic phases – is in strong contrast to the infinite variety of the Decorated. Where there had been exclusively circles with inscribed trefoils, quatrefoils, etc., there are now pointed trefoils, and ogee or double curved arches, shapes like daggers and shapes like the *vesica piscis*, and whole systems of reticulations (fig. 35).

To study this new English flow in terms of space, one must go to one west country and one east country church: the cathedral (then abbey church) of Bristol, and the cathedral of Ely. The chancel of Bristol was begun in 1298 and built chiefly during the first quarter of the 14th century (pl. 25). It differs in four significant things from all English cathedrals of the preceding period. It is an aisled hall, not a basilica – that means that its aisles are as high as its nave, so that no clerestory exists. This type of church elevation had existed in Romanesque South-Western France (see p. 49), but it had then nowhere attempted what it now does: the creation of a unified room with piers inserted, instead of the classic Gothic principle of a staggered elevation from aisle to nave. This tendency towards the unified room has its origin in the refectories and dormitories of monastic architecture and such retrochoirs as that of Salisbury. Its introduction into the body proper of the church made the Bristol architects change, with a self-assurance remarkable at such an early date, the shapes of both piers and vaults. The composite piers – an innovation which also occurs in France, Germany, and Holland – have capitals for only a few of the minor shafts, while the others run through into the vault without any caesura. As for the vaults, they have no special emphasis on the transverse arches, and appear entirely as star-shaped patterns made up of primary, secondary, and tertiary ribs, or ribs, tiercerons, and liernes, as they are called. The liernes which – that is their definition – start from neither a springer along the wall nor from one of the main bosses are a significant innovation too. Moreover, to support the weight of the nave vault, which in a basilican Gothic church is conducted

35. *Selby Abbey: east window, c.* 1325

down by flying buttresses to the roof of the aisles and then by buttresses to ground level, the aisles are crossed at the level of the springing of their vaults by curiously ingenious and yet naïve struts or bridges thrown across below the transverse arches. From their centres ribs sprout up to help in forming transverse pointed tunnel-vaults to abut the nave vault. The device may thus have been thought out for technical reasons: it is aesthetically most effective all the same. A classic Gothic interior is meant to affect us in two directions only: the façade-altar direction and the other, at right angles to it, which make us see the sheets of stained glass and the tracery on the right and the left. At Bristol our eyes are lured all the time into glimpses diagonally up and across.

The same effect can be studied on a larger scale in Wells Cathedral, where in 1338 an enormous arch or strut of similar design and function was placed between nave and crossing to support the crossing tower. It is grossly baffling, but undeniably impressive. At Bristol itself the cathedral architect has given a more playful version of the same spatial motifs in the sacristy of the cathedral. Here the ribs of the little vault are accompanied by a skeleton of secondary flying ribs starting at a lower level than the others, shooting through the air and meeting the primary ones at the central boss. The effect is again one of deliberate and pleasing confusion. Classic Gothic ribs, just like classic Gothic arches, keep strictly to the strata of space assigned to them; they never stray into others.

At Ely more than anywhere else the new attitude towards space has found an adequate form. Between 1322 and 1342 the crossing of the cathedral was rebuilt in the form of an octagon. The choice of this shape by the designer, who probably was the King's carpenter, Master William de Hurle, can have been nothing but a deliberate attempt at breaking the 13th-century's discipline of right angles. The diagonal axes, with their large windows and flowing tracery, destroy the precise dividing lines between nave, aisles, transepts, and choir which had been the groundwork in the plan and elevation of a classic Gothic church. It has been argued that the glass of Amiens or the Sainte Chapelle also breaks this logicality of the earlier Middle

Ages by opening the room towards a mysterious transcendental world. That is not so; the sheets of glass may give a diaphanous character to the enclosure, but it is an enclosure all the same. It does not really allow the eye to wander into dim, incomprehensible distances. The octagon of Ely has this very effect, an effect of surprise and ambiguity. Ely had been preceded by Siena, where the cathedral was all but completed in 1264 and has a hexagonal crossing. The effect is as surprising as at Ely, even if it appears a little accidental, owing to the irregular placing of the crossing and the haphazard shapes of the bays and vaults surrounding it.

The Lady Chapel at Ely (1321-49) achieved the same aim by subtler and more delicate means. The rectangular chapel, isolated from the main building, as only chapter-houses usually are, has all the way round an exquisite arcading with crocketed ogee arches gathered together by larger three-dimensional or nodding ogee arches (pl. 23b). Ogee-curved quatrefoils with seated figures fill the spandrels. The arches are covered with a luxuriant growth of vegetation, no longer as crisp as that of the 13th century, but with its undulations of knobbly leaves and its intricacy of minute detail, at once more sophisticated and, strangely enough, more uniform in its general appearance. This is due to a treatment that makes it impossible to isolate part from part, as one could in looking at the leaves of Southwell. Now all one sees is an incessant ripple and flow, lights and shadows whisking over bossy surfaces, fascinating but far removed from the clarity of a hundred years before.

The three-dimensional ogee arch is a motif of great significance. It does what the octagon does in Ely Cathedral, and the piers without capitals, the vaults without transverse arches, and the bridges in the aisles did in Bristol – it sets space into a motion, quicker, more complicated, and less single-minded than any to be experienced in Early English churches. Its immediate forerunner in the three-dimensional treatment of a wall is the chapter-house of York Cathedral, *c.* 1290, where the seats around the walls have not blind arcades behind, as at Salisbury (pl. 24) about fifteen years before, but are placed into tiny polygonal niches. Their forty-four times repeated projection

causes a spatial ripple too slight still to be felt as breaking the
continuity of the wall, but quite noticeable, once one is aware
of the coming of this new tendency.

But whereas in England the new experience of space in
motion expresses itself in so intricate a way, the Continent tried
to achieve a similar result by opposite means. While all is
luxuriance in England, all is plainness where in Spain, Germany, Italy, and France conscious endeavours towards a new
style were made. These endeavours were connected chiefly
with the rise of the orders of friars, the Franciscans and Dominicans (or Grey Friars and Black Friars), founded in 1209 and
1215, and spreading from 1225 onwards at a rate comparable
only to those of the Cluniac and Cistercian spreads in their
respective centuries. The 13th-century churches of the friars
were not designed to plans as standardized as those of the Cistercians. On the contrary, as early as 1252 a Dutch friar, Hum-
bertus de Romanis, complained: 'Nos autem quot domus tot
varias formas et dispositiones officinarum et ecclesiorum
habemus.' But they were all large, simple, and useful, with
little to suggest a specifically ecclesiastical atmosphere. They
did not need much in the way of eastern chapels, as many of
the friars were not priests, but they could not do without very
spacious naves to house the large congregations which came to
listen to their popular sermons.

The friars, it is known, were the orders of the people. They
scorned the secluded and leisurely existence of the other orders
on their country estates, chose busy towns to settle in and
there developed their sensational preaching technique as a
medium of religious propaganda to a degree never attempted
since the days of the Crusades. Thus all they needed was a
large auditorium, a pulpit, and an altar.

Italy built the earliest of all Franciscan churches, S. Francesco in Assisi, begun in 1228, as a vaulted aisleless room
with a vaulted transept and a polygonal chancel, very much
on the pattern of contemporary church work in Anjou.
Later the Italian Franciscans and Dominicans have aisleless halls
with timber roofs and Cistercian chancels (especially in Siena),
or aisled flat-roofed (S. Croce, Florence, 1294), or aisled vaulted

buildings (S. Maria Novella, Florence, 1278; SS Giovanni e Paolo, Venice, late 13th century; Frari, Venice, 1340). But, whether aisled or unaisled, vaulted or unvaulted, each church is always one spatial unity, with piers (often round or polygonal) merely subdividing it. In this is shown a very important new principle. In an Early or High Gothic church the nave and aisles were separate channels of parallel movement through space. Now the whole width and length of the room, thanks to the wide bays and thin supports, appears all one. The same intention led in France to the two-aisled (or two-naved, if that description is preferred) church of the Jacobins at Toulouse (*c.* 1260–1304), and in Spain to friars' churches with a wide nave, and no aisles, but chapels between the buttresses. This type appears, it seems, for the first time at St Catherine at Barcelona, begun in 1223. It then became the accepted Catalan church type, even for non-monastic churches, and even where slim supports divide off aisles (Cathedral Barcelona, begun 1298), and it also influenced France, where the most impressive late 13th-century church, the cathedral of Albi, can be explained only in Catalan terms. It was begun in 1282 and appears from outside as a mighty compact block without any of the elaborate articulation which buttresses and flying buttresses give to classic Gothic interiors.[1]

This outer plainness is typical of friars' churches in Germany (e.g. Erfurt) and England too. In England it was often a little relieved by a tower or spire over the bay between nave and chancel. Otherwise there is no structural division between the two parts at all. However, hardly any complete friars' churches survive in England, and that is probably the reason why the influence of their style on the development of the 14th century is generally underestimated. As to Germany, the interiors were at first aisleless as in Italy, and then, chiefly after 1300, halls, that is churches of the same type as Bristol, with aisles of the same height as the nave. There was a long history

1. The first of these chapels between buttresses in France are, incidentally, to be found at Notre Dame in Paris since 1235 (see plan on p. 66).

of the hall church in Germany, going back to the Romanesque style, and in one case even to the year 1015. It may thus not be necessary to suppose connections with the aisled halls of South-West France. Gothic halls were built directly the style had been taken over (Lilienfeld), inspired probably (as in England) by refectories and suchlike monastic rooms. The type spread during the second half of the 13th century. For the German 14th and 15th centuries the *Hallenkirche* is almost a matter of course, especially in Westphalia, in the brick districts of the Hanseatic coast towns, and in Bavaria, and also, after the discovery of silver, in the newly-founded, prospering towns of Upper Saxony. In its final German form, with wide arcades and wide aisles, the hall church invites the eye, even more than the narrower openings of Bristol, to wander off the main Gothic lines of vision. Diagonal vistas spread on all sides. Space seems to flow directionlessly around us while we walk in the church. Proof of the master builders' conscious development are the cases in which a choir in the new Late Gothic style was added without any aesthetic mediation to an earlier nave. This is for instance the case at St Lawrence's, Nuremberg, of 1445–72 (pl. 44). Having walked along the nave in the rigidly prescribed way of the Romanesque or earlier Gothic basilica, the entrance into the wider and higher choir with nave and aisles of identical width comes as a startling surprise. Bays are wider, piers slenderer, vaults of a rich star-like configuration (as created by the English nearly 200 years before), weighing down the vertical push of the piers. These have no capitals (again a motif of English priority), and so the streams of energy conducted upwards flew away undammed into ribs extending in all directions.[1] The sculptural decoration of the choir emphasizes its spatial freedom. The magnificent stone spire of the tabernacle rises in an

1. Some of the latest and best German churches of this period (e.g., Annaberg) have octagonal piers with concave sides – a particularly clear indication of the tendency to make the space of nave and aisles surge up from all directions against the stone divisions. The same type of piers occurs in Cotswold churches (Chipping Campden). Flying ribs as in the sacristy of Bristol, incidentally, are also a speciality of the boldest of these Late Gothic German churches.

asymmetrical position into the vault, and the huge locket of Veit Stoss's wood-carved Annunciation hangs down, joyful and transparent, into the space in front of the altar, so that you see it against the light of the central upper window. There are two rows of windows all the way round, and this, as the close pattern of the star-vault, adds weight to the horizontals. The contrast between plain outer walls with undecorated windows and the *Waldweben* inside is eminently characteristic of Late Gothic mentality, especially in Germany, a combination of mystical piety and sound practical sense, faith in a godly life within this world, the gathering of the ideas out of which Luther's Reformation was to grow. Luther was born before the tabernacle and the Annunciation were commissioned. The discrepancy between interiors of undulating flow, in which the individual may lose himself as between the trees of a forest, and exteriors of powerful solidity with unbroken walls and two rows of windows, heralds the mood of the German Reformation, torn between mystical introspection and a hearty new thrust into this world. Moreover, the new rooms of German Late Gothic had a practical advantage – the same as the aisleless halls of the Italian friars: they were evidently much better suited for listening to long sermons than the old interiors with parallel and separated avenues.

However, practical considerations alone did not create the new style, nor can it be said that the spirit of the coming Reformation alone created it. For it is just as noticeable in Spain as in Germany. In Spanish architecture of the 15th century there was a good deal of German influence. Masters from Cologne and Nuremberg were called to Burgos and established such German motifs as star-vaults and net-vaults. But these masons and stone-carvers from the North would hardly have been so successful if there had not been an indigenous Spanish trend towards the new Late Gothic expression. The star-vaults seemed no more than a variation of the theme of the Mohammedan dome with its flying ribs forming stars of many kinds. The conciseness of the classic French cross-vaults, and indeed classic French ideals altogether, had not appealed to Spaniards. As in Germany, imitation of French Gothic is rare, and as in

Germany there are wide aisles, although they are lower than the nave (that is basilican), and side chapels between the buttresses, the feature introduced by the friars. How strong the Spanish desire for unified space was is perhaps best seen at Gerona, where the cathedral had been started in the French way with a

36. *Juan Gil de Hontañon: Salamanca Cathedral, begun* 1512

choir, ambulatory, and radiating chapels in 1312. When these eastern parts were complete, work for some reason stopped, and it was not until 1416 that the then master-mason, Guillermo Boffiy, suggested the adding of a new nave. His daring suggestion was a nave, without aisles, the width of apse and ambulatory put together. There was opposition among the cathedral authorities, and so – a curiously modern idea – a commission was appointed to decide. Its members were twelve leading architects. Their answers have been preserved. Seven members were in favour of continuing the basilican scheme westward, but five were taken with Boffiy's idea. In 1417, in fact, Boffiy was committed to start on his scheme. It is a master-

piece of building technique, with a clear span of 73 feet, one of the widest vaulted rooms of medieval Europe (fig. 37). The room is somewhat bare but it has a great power, and it certainly is, with its sharp contrast of one room in the west and a system of three spatial units of staggered height and width in the east, the most convincing proof of the change of style from High to Late Gothic.

But when did the one phase end and the other begin? Our Spanish and German examples extended right through the 15th century,

37. *Guillermo Boffiy: Gerona Cathedral. The architect added to a 14th-century choir with ambulatory a nave without aisles to the width of choir and ambulatory. Begun 1417*

our examples from England were confined to the early years of the 14th. And there is indeed a notable difference between Gerona and St Lawrence in Nuremberg on the one hand and Bristol and Ely on the other. Bristol and Ely do not possess the contrast of square exterior volume and floating interior space. Nor did Britain, even at the late date of the

Nuremberg choir of St Lawrence, go to such extremes. Nevertheless British architectural style shortly after Bristol and Ely changed once more and changed most signally. The change is so obvious that, while for the Continent the terms High and Late Gothic are sufficient to indicate the chief stages, in England tradition has for more than a hundred years preferred a division into three Gothic phases: Early English, Decorated, and Perpendicular. Early English was at an end when the Angel Choir was growing. Decorated is the style of Bristol and Ely. Perpendicular corresponds to what we have seen of Late Gothic in Germany and Spain, and it is a contribution of equal national vigour. Once it had been created by a few strong-minded, clear-headed architects, it brushed aside all the vagaries of Decorated and settled down to a long, none too adventurous development of a plain-spoken idiom, sober and wideawake. People have tried to connect the coming of this new style with the Black Death of 1349. This is wrong; for it is there in all its perfection as early as 1331–37 in the south transept and as early as 1337–77 in the choir of Gloucester Cathedral (pl. 26). The thick circular piers of the Norman choir were left standing, but with their galleries hidden behind a screen of lean uprights and horizontals divided up into rows of panels. The east wall was opened into one huge window with, except for the few main partitions, nothing but a system of glazed panels. The number of horizontal divisions invalidates all that might have been left of the upward soar of earlier Gothic architecture. In this the same new tendency is visible as in the double row of windows in German churches. But while on the Continent the walls were made solid too, English Perpendicular walls remained glass screens. And just as thus the wall structure was less drastically changed than in Germany or Spain, so the spatial character of Perpendicular rooms returned – under renewed influence, it seems, of French buildings of about 1240 to 1330 – to the clarity of the High Gothic style. Basilican plans were only very rarely given up in favour of the spatially more promising aisled-hall plan of Bristol and Germany. The only fanciful feature in Gloucester, and indeed in many other Perpendicular parts of cathedral and abbey churches, is the decoration of the vaults (pl. 26b). There is as much imagination displayed in them as in the German and Spanish vaults. In fact neither of these two countries, let alone France, produced anything so complicated as the schemes of Bristol and Gloucester at so early a date. On the other hand, Perpendicular vault decoration is harsher than that of Continental Late Gothic, just as Perpendicular tracery is harsher than German, Spanish, or French tracery of about 1500 (or than English tracery of 1320). The ribs of Gloucester form patterns as abstract and as angular as the matchsticks on the walls of Earl's Barton tower three hundred years before, patterns equally remote from the luxuriance of Ely, the resilience of Lincoln, and the structural logicality of classic French rib-vaults.

Of structural logicality especially there **is** none in Perpendicular vaults. These close-knit patterns of ribs have no longer anything to do with vault construction. The main transverse ribs and cross ribs are no longer distinguishable from the innumerable tiercerons (i.e. ribs connecting the caps of the vault shafts with points on the ridge-rib) and liernes (i.e. ribs neither springing from the vault shafts nor leading to any of the main crossings). The whole is in fact a solidly built tunnel-vault with plenty of decoration applied to it. The use of the term tunnel-vault implies that the effect of Perpendicular vaults is as much an emphasis on the horizontal, as it were, lid character as the star-vaults of Germany and Spain. This interpretation is confirmed by the general substitution in English Perpendicular exteriors of low-pitched, often parapeted roofs for the higher pitch of the 12th and 13th centuries.

Gloucester is the most consistent example of the Perpendicular in English cathedrals. The naves of Winchester and Canterbury (chiefly of the later 14th century) are less uncompromising. In other cathedrals the late Middle Ages did little major work. To find English architecture of 1350 to 1525 at its best, one should visit not cathedrals and abbey churches, but manor-houses and parish churches for the happiest ensembles, and the royal chapels for the highest architectural standard. This change in the relative importance of buildings is owing to social and historical reasons.

Taking domestic architecture first, what had happened between the age of Harlech and that of, for instance, Penshurst in Kent (pl. 28a) begun, it seems, in 1341, is that half a century of internal peace had made owners of large houses in the country give up thoughts of military defence and allow themselves more domestic comforts. The extremely compact arrangement of rooms in the earlier castles was no longer necessary. Its essentials were kept – the hall as the centre of household life, with the high-table for the lord and his family at one end, the entrance and a screened-off gangway at the other, a parlour or chamber with perhaps a solar above beyond the high-table end of the hall, and kitchen, pantry, larders, buttery, etc., on the other side of the screens – but more rooms were added and the hall itself was provided with larger windows of several lights and a bay-window at the high-table end. The grandest of surviving 14th-century halls is John of Gaunt's at Kenilworth, 90 by 45 feet in size. In some houses at that time a separate dining-room must already have existed. That appears from a passage in *Piers Plowman*. It means a first step towards the desertion of the hall as the living-room and dining-room of everybody, master and men. But nearly three centuries had to pass by after Penshurst had been designed before the hall had finally become a vestibule and nothing else.

It took nearly as long to recover the principle of symmetry for the English house which had governed the plans of Harlech and Beaumaris with such splendid success. In the 14th and 15th centuries a manor-house, or, for that matter, a French *château* and a *Burg* in Germany, were picturesque agglomerations of rooms. Symmetry did not go farther than that sometimes in the 15th and early 16th centuries one straight axis ran from the gate-house to the entrance of the hall. But the hall was not the exact centre of the main block, and its entrance was eccentric anyway. The gate-house, even when it was in the middle of the outer front, did not separate identical halves (fig. 38). The results of this undisturbed growth are in Britain, as well as in France and Germany, extremely charming. But if one enquires about strictly aesthetic qualities, they are certainly not as high as those of Harlech.

A comparison between the English cathedral of the 13th century and the English parish church of the 15th shows the same changes. They are due largely to social developments. A new class had come into its own, the class responsible for the erection of the scores of splendid parish churches in Germany and in the Netherlands, and the class to which in France the business-minded royal administrators of the William of Nogaret type, in Italy the Medici and their friends and competitors, and in Northern Germany the leaders of the Hanseatic League, belonged. In England Richard Cœur de Lion had been on the throne when Lincoln and Wells were designed, and Henry III, the Saintly King as Rome called him, ruled

38. *Cothay Manor, Somerset, late 15th century*

when Salisbury and the new Westminster Abbey were designed. Simon de Montfort, a hero of the national English cause against too papal a policy, stood up against Henry III, when the Angel Choir was added to Lincoln Cathedral. Less than a hundred years later Edward III, who was crowned in 1327 and died in 1377, accepted with pleasure the honour of membership in the London Guild of the Merchant Taylors, i.e. the cloth merchants of the City. This is an eminently revealing fact, especially if it is viewed in conjunction with commercial and industrial developments in the Netherlands, Germany, Tuscany, and Catalonia. In England the age of Edward III saw a rapid development of business enterprise. Flemish weavers were called into the country, trade interests played a considerable part in the vicissitudes of the Hundred Years War.

4

Vast capitals were accumulated by men such as Dick Whittington and John Poulteney, whose country seat was Penshurst. In fact more of the manor-houses of the late Middle Ages were owned by merchants or their descendants than is usually realized. After the decimation of the old aristocracy caused by the Wars of the Roses, the proportion of *nouveaux riches* amongst the peers of the realm grew ever more rapidly, until in the council of sixteen whom Henry VIII named to reign for his little son not one was a peer of twelve years' standing.

Thus by 1500 the most active patrons of art were the king and the towns. The Crown had, between 1291 and about 1350, built St Stephen's Chapel in the Palace of Westminster which was burnt in 1834. Judging from surviving drawings it was a building of great importance. Then in the 15th century Henry VI and VII built Eton College Chapel (begun in 1441), King's College Chapel, Cambridge (1446 – 1515), Henry VII and VIII St George's Chapel, Windsor Castle (begun in 1481), and Henry VIII the Chapel of Henry VII at the east end of Westminster Abbey (1503–19). They are buildings of extremely simple exteriors and plans, but with plenty of masterfully executed decoration. The contrast is especially poignant at Cambridge. To design this long, tall, narrow box of a college chapel (pl. 30a), no spatial genius was needed. There is no differentiation at all between nave and choir. The decoration too is repetitive, the same window tracery is used twenty-four times, and so is the panel motif for the fan-vaulting. They were rationalists, the men who designed and enjoyed these buildings, proud constructors, of a boldness not inferior to that of the Catalans. Yet they succeeded – and here we are faced with the same problem as in the contemporary German churches – in combining this practical, matter-of-fact spirit with a sense of mystery and an almost oriental effusion of ornament. Standing at the west end of the nave one can hardly think of the supreme economy with which this effect of exuberance has been attained. The fan-vault in particular helps, wherever it is used, to create an atmosphere of heavy luxuriance. Yet it is an eminently rational vault, a technician's invention, one is inclined to surmise. It originated from the vault designs of chapter-houses and their development into the palm-like spread of bunches of ribs towards a heavily-bossed ridge-rib in the choir (early 14th century) and then the nave of Exeter. That had been the spatial imagination of the Decorated at its boldest moment. Then the Perpendicular came in and systematized and solidified it all, again first at Gloucester, in the east walk of the cloisters (1357–77). By giving all ribs the same length, the same distance from each other, and the same curvature, and by applying the ubiquitous panelling to the spandrels, the palm-vault of Exeter is converted into the fan-vault of Gloucester.

This system was used at Cambridge by Henry VIII's masons, men who, although at this advanced hour in the development of medieval architecture they are sometimes already mentioned by name in documents as surveyors of works and directors of works, were still by training and experience in the same category as Villard de Honnecourt and the masters of the English and French cathedrals. But as members of the king's household they now very gradually began to advance to the status of civil servants. This development went on into the 17th century. Not until then were the royal architects in France and also in England primarily civil servants.

In the 14th century a man such as Henry Yevele (died 1400) appears more as the successful London mason and contractor and distinguished member of his city guild than as a royal architect in the modern sense. We find his name coupled in one document with Chaucer's, in another with Dick Whittington's. So we imagine him in his stately fur-lined robes (which incidentally were part of his salary from the king), in his house by St Magnus, London Bridge, or one of his two manor-houses in Kent. Of work by him, the masonry on Westminster Hall (1394–1402) survives. Such men, dignitaries of their guilds and the fraternities to which they belonged, built the town-halls and guildhalls of the cities of England, the Netherlands, the cities of the Hanseatic League, and of Italy. One has to wander through such towns as Louvain, Ypres, Malines to realize to the full the might of late medieval commerce. The most impressive of Flemish halls was the Cloth Hall at Ypres (pl. 29a), begun in the late 13th century, four-square and of overwhelming dignity, but alas all but destroyed during the First World War. But the later town-halls of Bruges, Ghent, Brussels, Louvain, Oudenaarde, Middelburg, and so on are less severe but equally proud. In Italy the Palazzo della Ragione at Padua (1306, etc.) is unparalleled in sheer size, the Town Hall at Siena (1288–1309) in the regularity of its composition and the height of its tower, the Doge's Palace at Venice (1309, etc.; continued along the Piazzetta between 1423 and 1438) in splendour (pl. 29b).

As regards church building, the power of the towns appears in the predominance and the scale of the parish churches already referred to. Their towers are among the outstanding features of Late Gothic architecture, no longer groups of them, as befitted the balanced views of the High Gothic phase, but single towers shooting up to unprecedented heights. The tallest of all medieval spires is that of Ulm Münster, a parish church. Antwerp Cathedral, with its 306 feet, was a parish church too. In England Louth is 300 feet high, Boston 295. The variety of tower types in the English counties is infinite and surprising in contrast to the comparative standardization of plans and elevations – at least in churches built all at one go. Some of these cover an area larger than many a cathedral. St Mary Redcliffe at Bristol is the most spectacular of all. Prosperous small towns such as Lavenham in Suffolk and dozens of others had parish churches in which the whole local population could assemble, and the villagers from the neighbourhood still find accommodation. York has (or had before the Second World War) twenty-one surviving medieval churches besides the Minster.

Where existing churches were not entirely pulled down, they were enlarged, aisles were widened, naves heightened, new aisles or chapels added to the old, and the result is the picturesque, happy-go-lucky irregularity of plan and elevation of most English parish churches. However, while such churches may reflect most truly the history of their towns from the Anglo-Saxon to the Tudor age, they do not really reflect the aesthetic vision of any one period. What the 15th century in England desired the chief parish church of a prosperous town to look like appears in such a building as St Nicholas, King's

Lynn. The church (fig. 39) was erected as a chapel of ease from 1414 to 1419. One plan is responsible for the whole building, and that plan is as uncomplicated as those of the contemporary royal chapels. It consists of a rectangle of 162 by 70 feet, within which are comprised nave and aisles as well as aisled chancel. There is no structural articulation between west and east parts. All that interferes with the uniformity of the outline is the tower taken over from a previous building, the porch, and the slightly projecting apse. This sturdy plainness is no doubt a reflection of a change of taste which the friars' architecture had brought about. It is evidently in accordance with the style of the exteriors of German churches. But inside such churches as

39. *St Nicholas, King's Lynn, Norfolk, 1414–19*

St Nicholas, King's Lynn, or the two parish churches of Coventry (pl. 28b), or Holy Trinity, Hull, have nothing of the romanticism of Nuremberg. They stick to the traditional basilican elevation, piers are thin, mouldings wiry, and tracery is of the straightforward Perpendicular type. There are no corners left in mysterious semi-darkness, nor any surprising vistas. Where the fantasy of the Late Gothic designer shows itself in the English parish church is in wooden screens and wooden roofs. An almost inconceivable profusion of screens originally divided naves from choirs, aisle chapels from nave chapels, and the many guild chapels from the public spaces. The most lavishly decorated are in Devon on the one hand, in East Anglia on the other. But the greatest glory of the English parish churches is their timber roofs (pl. 27), roofs constructed as boldly by the carpenter as any Gothic stone vaults by masons, and looking as intricate and technically thrilling as any con-figuration of flying buttresses around the east end of a cathedral. There is a variety of types: the tie-beam roof, the arch-braced roof, the hammerbeam roof (devised for Westminster Hall by Yevele's colleague, the King's master carpenter, Hugh Her-land, in 1380), the double hammerbeam roof, and others. The most ingenious of them all is the one of the unaisled church of Needham Market, looking like a whole three-aisled building hovering over our heads without any visible support from below. The continent has nothing to emulate these achieve-ments of a ship-building nation. They are, in fact, strongly reminiscent of ships' keels upside down.

Such roofs add a quality of structural richness to English churches which they would otherwise lack. However, even they, looked at in detail, appear with their hard lines of rafters, purlins, and braces sinewy, sharp, and angular – as English in fact as the ribs of Gloucester choir and the decoration of Earl's Barton tower – directly one compares them with contem-porary work in France, Germany, or Spain and Portugal.

For even in France the 15th century had brought a belated acceptance of the principles which in England had been incor-porated in the Decorated style. Flamboyant is the French term for their Late Gothic, and some of the most enchanting ex-amples of it are to be found in Normandy, for instance the main portal, the library court, and the Tour de Beurre of Rouen Cathedral, and – in a spatially more interesting way – the church of St Maclou at Rouen, begun in 1434 (fig. 40). But even there the High Gothic east end with ambulatory and radiating chapels is still preserved, though in a modified form. The west end on the other hand is original, and in its spatial values truly Late Gothic – with the shallow polygonal plan in-stead of the classic parallelism of the three portals.

As for Spain, the briefest comparison between an English parish church or even King's College Chapel and, say, the decoration of the front of the church of St Paul's at Valladolid

(begun shortly after 1486, probably by Simon of Cologne; pl.
30b) is enough to realize the contrast between English restraint
and Spanish extremism. Substitute the St Lawrence portal of
Strassburg Cathedral (pl. 31b) for Valladolid, and you will see
Anglo-German contrasts as glaringly. It might be said that
German Late Gothic decoration is as extreme as Spanish, which
would not be surprising, since Germany and Spain, as against
France, England, Italy, are the countries of the extremes in
European civilization. However, there are obvious differences
between the Spanish and the German ways of decorating. Ever

40. *Rouen: St Maclou, begun* 1434

since Mohammedan days Spain has had a passion for filling
large surfaces with close-knit two-dimensional ornament. The
Germans share this *horror vacui*, but there is always a marked
spatial curiosity in their ornament. That connects German
Late Gothic with German Rococo, just as the flatness and
the frantic movement of the Charterhouse vestry at Granada,
which dates from the middle of the 18th century (see p. 173),
seems heralded in the details of the Valladolid façade. Valladolid has no dominant motifs. The figure sculpture is petty in
scale. Ogee arches and 'Tudor' arches (i.e. depressed pointed
arches) follow each other. The background is patterned from

top to bottom, and the patterns change with every string course. There is something of a thistly undergrowth about this ensemble which makes English Perpendicular appear strong and pure. There can be no question which of the two countries would open itself to Puritanism and which would become the stronghold of Baroque Catholicism.

The high-water mark, however, of Late Gothic frenzy was reached in Portugal during the spectacularly prosperous age of King Manuel I (1495–1521). Manueline decoration in such places as Batalha and Tomar (fig. 41) is outrageously rich, a rank growth of forms, sometimes taken, it seems, from crustacean organisms, sometimes from tropical vegetation. Much Portuguese decoration was inspired by Spain and France, but here the architecture of India, Portuguese India, is the only parallel that comes to mind. If this connection is real it is the first instance in Western history of non-European influence on European art.

However, no influence can ever act unless the one party is ready to receive the message of the other. If the countries of the Pyrenean Peninsula had not already been possessed by a passion for overdone decoration, the art of the colonies would have remained mute to them. When the Indies became Dutch, their style did indeed after a time begin to influence the furniture of Holland and helped to give it its peculiar Baroque opulence, but architects wisely kept away from it. The Dutchmen of the 17th century could never have made of it what the Portuguese could, at that particular moment, the moment just before the ornamental imagination of the late Middle Ages was harnessed into the Renaissance yoke.

The Renaissance on the other hand could never have been conceived in a country which had as recklessly indulged in ornamental vagaries as Spain and Portugal, or as daringly explored spatial mysteries as Germany. In Italy there thus exists no Late Gothic style at all – the most striking illustration of the fact that by the 15th century the present natural divisions of Europe were more or less established. The Romanesque style had been international, though regionally subdivided, just as the Holy Roman Empire and the Church of the 11th and 12th centuries had been international forces. Then, in the 13th century, France became a nation and created the Gothic style.

Germany went through the crisis of the Interregnum and decided on a national, as against the previous international, policy. The same decision was taken at the same time in England, while in Italy a wholly different development of many small town-states set in. Gothic came into Germany, Spain, England, and Italy as a French fashion. Cistercian monasteries first, and then Cologne, Burgos, and León, Canterbury and Frederick II's Castel del Monte (see p. 80) followed it closely. But already in Frederick II's Italian buildings there appear purely antique pediments side by side with the

41. *Tomar: window of chapter-house, c. 1520*

novel rib-vaults of France. The appreciative treatment of Roman motifs in Frederick II's Capua Gate is unparalleled anywhere in the North, and in the South only by Nicolò Pisano's pulpits. Nicolò Pisano was the first of the great Italian sculptors, the first in whose work the Italian character dominates over international conventions. His transformation of the current style in sculpture into something more static and more harmonious was paralleled by similar transformations of Gothic architecture. The rôle of the friars in this transformation has been mentioned. There is no *excelsior* in their wide, airy, aisleless halls. The large ones with aisles, such as S. Maria Novella and S. Croce in Florence, have such wide arcades and such shallow aisles that the static nature of the rooms is hardly disturbed. The cathedral of Florence – a cathedral, but built under the supervision of the guild of the wool merchants 'in honour of the Commune and people of Florence' – belongs to the same family (pl. 32a). Its piers with their substantial bases and heavy capitals do not point upward. The uninterrupted cornice provides a strong horizontal division. The cross-vaults are dome-shaped, and clearly isolate bay from bay. Clarity is also the expression of the dark structural members against the whitewashed surfaces of walls and vaults. To the traveller coming from the North these Italian interiors of the 14th century appear spacious, restful, and serene.

It was only here – this will now be appreciated – that the style of the Renaissance could be conceived, here, in the land of Roman traditions, of sun, blue sea, and noble hills, of vineyards and olive plantations, of pine groves, cedars, and cypress trees.

CHAPTER FIVE

Renaissance and Mannerism

c. 1420–c. 1600

THE Gothic style was created for Suger, Abbot of St Denis, councillor of two kings of France, the Renaissance for the merchants of Florence, bankers to the kings of Europe. It is in the atmosphere of the most prosperous of Southern trading republics that about 1420 the new style emerged. A firm such as that of the Medici had its representatives in London, in Bruges and Ghent, in Lyons and Avignon, in Milan and Venice. A Medici had been Mayor of Florence in 1296, another in 1376, yet another in 1421. In 1429 Cosimo Medici became senior partner of the firm. Just over one hundred years later another Medici was created the first Duke of Tuscany. But Cosimo, whom they called in Florence the Father of the Fatherland, and his grandson Lorenzo the Magnificent, were only citizens, not even, by any official title, the first of their city. To these and the other princely merchants, the Pitti, the Rucellai, the Strozzi, it is due that the Renaissance was at once wholeheartedly accepted in Florence and developed with a wonderful unanimity of purpose for thirty or forty years, before other cities of Italy, let alone foreign countries, had grown to understand its meaning.

This predisposition of Tuscany cannot be explained by social conditions alone. The cities of Flanders in the 15th century were socially of quite a comparable structure; so up to a point was the City of London. Yet the style in the Netherlands was a flamboyant Late Gothic; in England it was Perpendicular. In Florence what happened was that a particular social situation coincided with a particular nature of country and people, and a particular historical tradition. The geographical and national character of the Tuscans had found its earliest expression in

Etruscan art. They were again clearly noticeable in the 11th and 12th centuries in the crisp and graceful façade of S. Miniato (pl. 17a), and in the 14th in the spacious, happily airy Gothic churches of S. Croce, S. Maria Novella, and the cathedral of S. Maria del Fiore (pl. 32a). Now a flourishing trading republic will tend to worldly ideals, not to the transcendental; to the active, not to meditation; to clarity, not to the obscure. And since the climate was clear, keen and salutary, and the people's minds were clear, keen and proud, it was here that the clear, proud and worldly spirit of Roman Antiquity could be rediscovered, that its contrast with Christian faith did not bar its way, that its attitude to physical beauty in the fine arts and beauty of proportion in architecture found an echo, that its grandeur and its humanity were understood. The fragments of the Roman past in art and literature had been there all the time, and had never been entirely forgotten. But only the 14th century reached a point that made a cult of the Antique possible. Petrarch – the first Poet Laureate of modern times, crowned on the Capitol in 1341 – was a Tuscan; so was Boccaccio, so was Leonardo Bruni who translated Plato. And as the Medici honoured the philosophers and called them into their innermost circle, as they honoured the poets and wrote poetry themselves, so they regarded the artists in a spirit quite different from that of the Middle Ages. The modern conception of the artist and the respect due to his genius is again of Tuscan origin.

Seven years before Petrarch was crowned in Rome, the civic authorities responsible for the appointment of a new mastermason to the cathedral and city of Florence decided to elect Giotto, the painter, because they were convinced that the city architect should be a 'famous man' above all. So for the sole reason that they believed that 'in the whole world no one better could be found in this and many other things' than Giotto, they chose him, although he was not a mason at all. Now this marks the beginning of a new period in the professional history of architecture, just as Petrarch's crowning marks a new period in the history of the social status of authors. Henceforth – this is especially characteristic of the Renaissance – great architects were not usually architects by training. And henceforth great artists were honoured and admitted into positions outside their craft simply because they were great artists. Cosimo Medici is probably the first who called a painter, in recognition of his genius, divine. Later this became the attribute universally given to Michelangelo. And he, sculptor, painter, and architect, a fanatical worker and a man who never spared himself, was deeply convinced that it was his due. When he felt slighted by some of the pope's servants in an ante-room of the Vatican, he fled from Rome, deserting his post without hesitation and leaving a message that the pope could look for him elsewhere, if he wanted him. Leonardo da Vinci at the time when this happened evolved the theory of the ideal nature of art. He endeavoured to prove that painting and architecture were of the liberal arts, not arts in the trade sense of the Middle Ages. There are two sides to this theory. It demands from the patron a new attitude towards the artist, but also from the artist a new attitude towards his work. Only the artist who approached his art in an academic spirit, that is as a seeker after law, had a right to be regarded as their equal by the scholars and authors of humanism.

Leonardo has not much to say about Antiquity. But the universal fascination of Antiquity was evidently both aesthetic and social, aesthetic in so far as the forms of Roman architecture and decoration appealed to artists and patrons of the 15th century, social in so far as the study of the Roman past was accessible to the educated only. So the artist and architect who until then had been satisfied with learning their craft from their masters and developing it according to tradition and their powers of imagination, now devoted their attention to the art of Antiquity, not only because it enchanted them but also because it conferred social distinction on them. So strongly had this revival impressed the scholars from the 16th to the 19th century that they called the whole period that of rebirth, *rinascita* or Renaissance. Early writers by using this term meant the rebirth of art and letters in quite a general sense. But in the 19th century – a century of unlimited period revival – the emphasis was laid on the imitation of Roman forms and motifs. In re-examining the works of the Renaissance to-day, one must, however, ask oneself whether the new attitude towards Antiquity is really their essential innovation.

The very first building in Renaissance forms is Filippo Brunelleschi's Foundling Hospital, begun in 1419 (pl. 33a). Brunelleschi (1377–1446) was a goldsmith by training. Yet he had been chosen to complete the cathedral of Florence by adding the dome over the crossing, a masterpiece of construction and of a shape distinctly Gothic in character. At the same time, however, he designed the Foundling façade, a work of a completely different kind, consisting of a colonnade on the ground floor with delicate Corinthian columns and wide semicircular arches letting enough sun and warmth penetrate into the loggia, and a first floor with generously spaced moderately sized rectangular windows under shallow pediments corresponding exactly to the arches beneath. Medallions in coloured terra-cotta by Luca della Robbia – the famous babes in swaddling clothes sold in cheap copies of all sizes by the souvenir-dealers of Florence – are placed into the spandrels of the arcade. A subtly scaled architrave divides ground floor from first floor. Now the pediments over the windows are certainly a Roman motif. So seem to be the Corinthian columns. But arches on such slender columns are really in their expression just as different from those of, say, the Colosseum, as they are from any Gothic arcades. Their source and that of several other motifs of the façade is the Tuscan Proto-Renaissance of S. Miniato (pl. 17a), SS. Apostoli, and the Baptistery, i.e. the architecture of Florence in the 11th and 12th centuries, and nothing else. This is an eminently significant fact. The Tuscans, unconsciously of course, prepared themselves for the reception of the Roman style by first going back to their own Romanesque Proto-Renaissance.

The relation of Brunelleschi's churches to the past is very similar. Sto Spirito (pl. 32b and fig. 42), which he designed in 1435, is a basilica with round-headed arcades and a flat roof; Romanesque, one can say, in these general characteristics. The bases and capitals of the Corinthian columns, on the other hand, and the fragments of an entablature above are Roman, rendered with a correctness and understanding of their vigorous beauty that were beyond the power of the architects of the Proto-Renaissance. The curious niches of the aisles are also Roman, though treated in a very original way. But while the motifs mentioned so far can be traced back to the Middle Ages or Antiquity, the spatial expression created with their aid is wholly new and has all the serenity of the Early Renaissance. The nave is just twice as high as it is wide. Ground floor and

0   20   40   60   80   100
├──┼──┼──┼──┼──┼──┼──┼──┼──┼──┤ *feet*

42. Filippo Brunelleschi: Sto Spirito, Florence, begun 1435

clerestory are of equal height. The aisles have square bays, again half as wide as they are high. The nave consists of exactly four and a half squares, and the odd half was intended to be disposed of in a special way to be mentioned presently. Walking through the church, one may not at once consciously register all these proportions, but they contribute all the same decisively to the effect of serene order which the interior produces. It is difficult to-day to imagine the enthusiasm of the Early Renaissance for such simple mathematical relations in space. One must remember in order to appreciate it that at that very moment – about 1425 – painters in Florence discovered the laws of perspective. Just as they had no longer been satisfied with an arbitrary presentation of the space inside their pictures, so architects were now anxious to find rational proportions for their buildings. The effort of the 15th century to master space is comparable only with that of our own age, although that of the Renaissance concerned an ideal world and ours a material. The invention of printing towards the middle of the century proved a most powerful conquest of space. The discovery of America towards its end produced results nearly as important. Both must be named with the discovery of perspective as aspects of Western space enthusiasm, an attitude utterly alien to Antiquity, and one to which attention has already been drawn more than once in this book.

The feature of Sto Spirito most important in this connection is the ground plan of its eastern parts. For here Brunelleschi has departed decisively from the normal composition of Romanesque or Gothic churches. The way in which he made the transepts exactly identical with the choir, ran an aisle round all three and placed a dome over the crossing makes us feel, looking eastward, as if we were in a centrally planned building, a type usual in Roman architecture, both religious and secular, but very rare in medieval Christian churches.

Even the west end was intended to be finished in a way stressing this centralizing tendency at the expense of practical advantages. Brunelleschi had originally meant to continue the aisle round the west as round the east, north, and south ends. He would then have had to put in four instead of the customary three entrances, to comply with the four bays of aisle along the inner side of the façade. It would all have been exceedingly unusual – a sacrifice to aesthetic consistency and the desire for centralization. Indeed, during the very year in which Sto Spirito was begun, Brunelleschi had designed a completely central church, the first of the Renaissance. It is S. Maria degli Angeli (figs. 43 and 44). After three years, in 1437, the building was discontinued, and only ground-floor walls now remain. But we can read the plan and compare it with reliable engravings taken, it seems, from lost original drawings. S. Maria degli Angeli was to be wholly Roman in character and very massive, the outcome no doubt of a long stay of Brunelleschi in Rome to which we can with a good deal of certainty assign the date

1433. The light, slim columns of the other buildings are here replaced by pilasters attached to solid piers at the eight corners

43 *and* 44. *Filippo Brunelleschi: S. Maria degli Angeli, Florence, begun* 1434

of the octagon. Eight chapels surround it, each with niches hollowed out into the thickness of the walls. The dome also was to be of one piece inside and out like a Roman dome and not on the Gothic principle of an outer and a separate inner shell, still applied by Brunelleschi to Florence Cathedral. Of Romanesque or Proto-Renaissance connections there are here none left. What Roman building in particular inspired Brunelleschi we can no longer say. There were plenty of remains still in existence in the 15th century and drawn by architects, which have now disappeared.

However, one more central building, or rather part of a building, was begun shortly after S. Maria degli Angeli and

45. *Upper half: Temple of Minerva Medica, Rome, c. 250 A.M. Lower half: Michelozzo's rotunda at the east end of the SS Annunziata, Florence, begun 1444.*

completed, and this is a direct copy of an existing Roman monument. Michelozzo di Bartolommeo (1396–1472) began in 1445 to add to the medieval church of the SS Annunziata a round east end with eight chapels or niches exactly as he had seen it done in the so-called temple of Minerva Medica in Rome (fig. 45). So while in the early works of Brunelleschi we cannot emphasize too much the independence of the new forms from those of Roman antiquity, the discovery of how much could be learned from Rome to satisfy topical aesthetic needs came as early as the thirties and forties. That it appears most clearly in centrally planned buildings is eminently characteristic. For a central plan is not an other-worldly, but a this-worldly conception. The prime function of the medieval church had been to lead the faithful to the altar. In a completely centralized building (fig. 44) no such movement is possible. The building has its full effect only when it is looked at from the one focal point. There the spectator must stand and, by standing there, he becomes himself 'the measure of all things'. Thus the religious meaning of the church is replaced by a human one. Man is in the church no longer pressing forward to reach a transcendental goal, but enjoying the beauty that surrounds him and the glorious sensation of being the centre of this beauty.

No more telling symbol could have been conceived for the new attitude of the humanists and their patrons to Man and religion. Pico della Mirandola, one of the most interesting of the philosophers round Lorenzo the Magnificent, delivered an address in 1486 on *The Dignity of Man*. Machiavelli, a little later, wrote his book *The Prince* to glorify the power of Man's will, and set it as the prime moving force against the powers of religion that had up to his time interfered with practical thought. And again a little later Count Castiglione composed his *Courtier* to show his contemporaries their ideal of universal man. The courtier, he says, should be agreeable in his manners, graceful, a good *causeur*, and a good dancer, yet strong and fit, well versed in the pursuits of chivalry, riding, fencing, and jousting. At the same time he should read poetry and history, be acquainted with Plato and Aristotle, understand all the arts, and practise music and drawing. Leonardo da Vinci was the first amongst artists to live up to this ideal: painter, architect, engineer, and musician, one of the most ingenious scientists of his time, and enchanting in his personal ways. Only Christianity apparently did not occupy his mind at all. Lorenzo Valla, a Roman humanist, somewhat earlier had published his dialogue *De voluptate*, in which he openly praised the pleasures of the senses. The same Valla proved with a philological sagacity unknown before the rise of Humanism that the so-called Donation of Constantine, the document on which all papal claims to worldly domination rested, was faked. Yet he died a canon of the Lateran Cathedral in Rome. The philosophers of Florence founded an academy on Plato's model, kept Plato's supposed birthday as a holiday and preached a semi-Greek, semi-Christian religion in which Christ's love is mixed up with Plato's principle of divine love that makes us pine for beauty of soul and body in human beings. On one of the frescoes in the choir of Sta Maria Novella an inscription can be read stating that the frescoes were completed in 1490, 'when this loveliest of lands distinguished in riches, victories, arts and buildings enjoyed plenty, health, and peace'. About the same time Lorenzo the Magnificent wrote his most famous poem, which begins as follows:

> Quant'è bella giovinezza,
> Che si fugge tuttavia.
> Chi vuol esser lieto sia ;
> Di doman' non c'è certezza.

The lines are well known, and rightly so. They are here quoted in Italian, because they should be remembered in all their original medodiousness. Literally translated they mean:

> How lovely is youth,
> But it flies from us.
> If you want to be happy, be happy now;
> There is no certainty of to-morrow.

Now these men, if they built a church, did not want to be reminded by its appearance of that uncertain to-morrow and of what might come after this life has ended. They wanted architecture to eternalize the present. So they commissioned churches as temples to their own glory. The eastern rotunda of the Annunziata was intended to be a memorial in Florence to the Gonzaga, rulers of Mantua. At the same time Francesco Sforza of Milan seems to have thought of such a temple. A record of what was intended survives in a medal of about 1460 by the sculptor Sperandio (fig. 46). It seems to represent a building of perfectly symmetrical plan: a Greek cross (for the term see p. 50) to be covered with five domes, just as Périgueux and St Mark's in Venice had been three or four hundred years before. The design may be due to that mysterious Florentine sculptor and architect Antonio Filarete (died about 1470), who worked for Francesco Sforza from 1451 to 1465. His fame now rests mainly on the Milan hospital, the Ospedale Maggiore, which was begun in 1457, a vast enterprise not carried on in elevation to his designs, though in plan. The plan is remarkable in that it appears the first of those large symmetrical piles with many inner courtyards – nine at Milan – taken up in the 16th and 17th centuries for such royal schemes as the Escorial, the Tuileries, and Whitehall.

But Filarete's ambitions were for planning on a yet grander scale. He wrote a treatise on architecture, dedicated in different

46. *Projected Sforza Chapel, Milan. Plan reconstructed from Sperandio's medal, c. 1460*

47. *Antonio Filarete: projected chapel for the hospital, Milan. Reconstructed from the original drawing, c. 1455*

copies to Francesco Sforza and to one of the Medici of Florence, where the architect returned when he left Milan. Perhaps the most interesting part of the treatise is the description of an ideal town, Sforzinda; for this is the first wholly symmetrical town plan in Western history, a regular octagon with radial streets and with palace and cathedral on the square in the centre – again the central obsession of this first century liberated from the ties of medieval authority.

Thus it is not surprising to find that the churches of Sforzinda, of Zagalia (another town drawn up in the treatise), and of the hospital – this church was never built either – were meant to be of central plan. They introduce us to yet more varieties. Sforzinda and the Hospital (fig. 47) are square with a central dome and subsidiary little domed chapels in the four corners – a plan for which an Early Christian (or rather 9th century) prototype existed at Milan, the Chapel of the Holy Sepulchre at S. Satiro and a Michelozzo prototype at S. Maria delle Grazie at Pistoja (begun 1452).[1] Zagalia (fig. 48) has an octagonal central dome

48. *Antonio Filarete: church for Zagalia, reconstructed from the original drawing, c. 1455–60*

and octagonal chapels in the corners. All three churches were to be provided with four fantastically tall minarets over the four corner chapels, or somewhere between them and the centre (for the drawings are ambiguous in this).[2] A chapel actually built at S. Eustorgio in Milan in 1462 to Michelozzo's designs is square and domed and has little turrets on the four corners, but no chapels below.

Michelozzo also designed a palace for the Medici Bank at Milan. It was begun in the forms of Florentine Renaissance, but continued with the more irresponsible detail of the North Italian Gothic. The same happened to the hospital.

Evidently the Lombards were not yet capable of an understanding of the Renaissance. The cathedral of Milan was carried on in a flamboyant Late Gothic right through the 15th century.

1. Originally the type was Late Roman or Early Byzantine, cf. the late 4th century plan of the cathedral of Trier, then the plan of the Visigothic Oratory at Tarrasa, and much later that of Hosios Lucas c. 1000.

2. The Warburg Institute kindly arranged for me to have the plan of the Zagalia church and some others specially photographed from Filarete's *Codice Magliabecchiano* (Biblioteca Nazionale, Florence, II, 1, 140; già XVII, 30). The Zagalia plan is not illustrated in Lazzaroni and Muñoz's book on Filarete and has never been published before. Redrawing was necessary for reasons of clarity and has been done by Miss Margaret Tallet.

Similarly in Venice the Porta della Carta of the Doge's Palace and the Ca d'Oro belong to the 1430's and 1440's, and the first serious Renaissance structures were begun only after 1455 (Arsenal Gate, 1457, etc., Ca del Duca). In style they are Tuscan, just as Michelozzo and Filarete designed in the Tuscan style in Milan, and as the greatest of all Quattrocento architects and the one to spread the style among the art-loving and self-glorying minor rulers of Northern Italy was Tuscan.

Leone Battista Alberti (1404–72) came from a patrician Florentine family. In our context he represents yet a new type of architect. Brunelleschi and Michelangelo are sculptor-architects, Giotto and Leonardo da Vinci painter-architects. Alberti is the first of the great dilettante-architects, a man in whose life and thoughts art and architecture played just that part which it should play according to Count Castiglione's (much later) treatise. Alberti was a brilliant horseman and athlete – it is recorded that he could jump over a man's head with his two feet close together – his witty conversation was famous, he wrote plays and composed music, he painted and studied physics and mathematics, he was an expert at law, and his books deal with domestic economy as well as with painting and architecture. Alberti's *De Pittura* is the first book looking at the art of painting with a Renaissance spirit. The whole of the first part deals with geometry and perspective exclusively. The *Ten Books of Architecture* are written in Latin and modelled on Vitruvius. They prove that, while he was working in Rome as a member of the Papal civil service, he had plenty of time to study the ruins of Antiquity. It is also evident that his job allowed him to travel freely and stay away from Rome for long periods.

Before the coming of the Renaissance such a man could hardly have taken an active, constructive interest in building. But as soon as the essence of architecture was considered to be philosophy and mathematics (the divine laws of order and proportion) and archeology (the monuments of Antiquity), the theoretician and dilettante was bound to assume a new significance. Roman architecture, both system and details, must be studied and drawn to be learnt; and the system behind the styles of Antiquity was soon – with the help of Vitruvius, the newly rediscovered Roman writer on architecture – found to lie in the orders, i.e. the proportions belonging to the Doric, Ionic, Corinthian, Composite, and Tuscan columns and entablatures. By means of books on the orders foreign countries were taught the rules of classical building.

But Alberti was not a dry theorist. In him the spirit of the scholar lived in a rare and happy union with genuine imaginative and creative powers. The front of S. Francesco in Rimini (pl. 34), begun in 1446 but never completed, is the first in Europe to adapt the composition of the Roman triumphal arch to church architecture. So Alberti was much more serious than Brunelleschi in reviving the Antique. And he did not confine himself to motifs. The side of the church, opened in seven round-headed niches with heavy piers dividing them, has perhaps more of the gravity of Flavian Rome than any other building of the 15th century. Now these niches hold sarcophagi, the monuments to the humanists of Sigismondo Malatesta's court. For the east end apparently a large dome was projected, as dominating as that of the Annunziata in Florence, and again as a monument to the glory of Sigismondo and his Isotta. Sigismondo was a typical Renaissance tyrant, unscrupulous and cruel but sincerely fascinated by the new learning and the new art. The church of S. Francesco is in fact known under the name of the Temple of the Malatesta; and on its façade an inscription runs in large letters with Sigismondo's name and the date – nothing else.

Again exactly the same pride is exhibited by Giovanni Rucellai, a merchant of Florence for whom Alberti designed the second of his church fronts. Again his name appears over-conspicuously on the façade of S. Maria Novella, and when in his old age he wrote an account of his life he said of the architectural and decorative work he had commissioned for the churches of his beloved native town: 'All these things have given me, and are giving me, the greatest satisfaction and the sweetest feelings. For they do honour to the Lord, to Florence, and to my own memory.' It is this attitude that made it possible for the donors of the frescoes inside the choir of the same church to appear lifesize in the costumes of the day as if they were actors in the sacred stories. It is this attitude also that made the patricians of Florence – and the cardinals of Rome – build their Renaissance palaces. That of the Medici begun by Michelozzo in 1444 was the first (fig. 49), that of the Pitti, originally, it seems, designed by Alberti about 1458 and considerably enlarged a century later, and that of the Strozzi are the most famous. They are massive yet orderly, faced with heavily rusticated blocks and crowned by bold cornices. Their windows, symmetrically placed, are divided into two by graceful columns (a Romanesque motif again). What one expects of Renaissance delicacy and articulation is to be found chiefly in their inner courtyards. There the ground floors are opened as cloisters with the graceful arcades of the Foundling Hospital and Sto Spirito, and the upper floors are also enlivened by an open gallery of pilasters dividing the walls into separate bays, or some such feature.

Only in Rome was a severer treatment of courtyards evolved. It appears first in the Palazzo Venezia, a building begun in 1455. It is derived from the classic Roman motif of columns attached to solid piers, the motif of the Colosseum and also of the front of Alberti's S. Francesco in Rimini. Maybe it was he who suggested its resuscitation in Rome, though his name cannot be documentarily connected with the Palazzo Venezia. A most attractive compromise between the Florentine and the Roman systems appears in the Ducal Palace at Urbino (pl. 33b), another of the architecturally and altogether aesthetically most enterprising smaller courts of Italy. Here Piero della Francesca worked, the painter in whose architectural settings Alberti's spirit is so clearly reflected, and here Alberti must have appeared on his journeys. Here, moreover, we find in the 1470's Francesco di Giorgio, one of the most interesting later Quattrocento architects and one whose name will have to be mentioned in other connections again later. But the design of the courtyard and the delightful decoration inside the palace is probably due not to him, but to Luciano Laurana, who worked at Urbino between 1466 and his death in 1479. The courtyard preserves the airy lightness of the

49. Michelozzo: Palazzo Medici, Florence, begun 1444

Florentine arcades, but strengthens the corners by pilasters. Once the effect of this motif has been noticed, it makes Michelozzo's and his followers' uninterrupted sequence of columns and arches look unstable and uncomfortable. The courtyard of the Palazzo Venezia in Rome, on the other hand, appears heavy-handed in comparison with Laurana's happy balance of motifs.

Alberti himself designed one palace in Florence, the Palazzo Rucellai (pl. 35a), begun in 1446 for the same patron as the façade of S. Maria Novella. The courtyard here has no emphasis, but Alberti used pilasters in the façade and thereby introduced a splendid new means for articulating a wall.[1] There are three superimposed orders of pilasters with a free Doric treatment on the ground floor, a free Ionic on the first floor, and Corinthian on the top.

While these pilasters divide the front vertically, sensitively designed cornices emphasize the horizontal divisions. The top cornice is probably the earliest in Florence, earlier even than that of Michelozzo's Palazzo Medici. Before then projecting eaves in the medieval way had been used. The windows of the Palazzo Rucellai are bipartite as in the other palaces, but an architrave separates the main rectangle from the two round heads. The relation of height to width in the rectangular parts of the windows is equal to the relation of height to width in the bays. Thus the position of every detail seems to be determined. No shifting is possible. In this lies, according to Alberti's theoretical writings, the very essence of beauty, which he defines as 'the harmony and concord of all the parts achieved in such a manner that nothing could be added or taken away or altered except for the worse'.

Such definitions make one feel the contrast of Renaissance and Gothic most sharply. In Gothic architecture the sensation of growth is predominant everywhere. The height of piers is not ruled by the width of bays, nor the depth of a capital, or rather a cap, by the height of the pier. The addition of chapels or even aisles to parish churches is much less likely to spoil the

1. Brunelleschi had already thought along the same lines, see his never-completed Palazzo di Parte Guelfa.

whole than in a Renaissance building. For in the Gothic style motif follows motif, as branch follows branch up a tree.

One could not imagine a donor in the 14th century decreeing, as Pope Pius II did when rebuilding the cathedral of his native town (renamed Pienza to perpetuate his name), that no one should ever erect sepulchral monuments in the church or found new altars, or have wall-paintings executed, or add chapels, or alter the colour of walls or piers. For a Gothic building is never complete in that sense. It remains a live being influenced in its destiny by the piety of generation after generation. And as its beginning and end are not fixed in time, so they are not in space. In the Renaissance style the building is an aesthetic whole consisting of self-sufficient parts. A composition in the flat or in space is arrived at by grouping such parts according to a static system.

Now the Romanesque style is – as has been shown – also a static style. It is also a style in which the adding of clearly-defined spatial units is essential. How then can the difference in principle be formulated between a Norman and a Renaissance church? Walls are equally important in both, whereas the Gothic style always endeavours to invalidate them. But a Romanesque wall is primarily inert. If it is ornamented, the exact place where decoration is applied seems arbitrary. One hardly ever feels that a little more or a little less ornament, or ornament shifted to a slightly higher or slightly lower position, would make a decisive difference. In the Renaissance building this is not so. The walls appear active, enlivened by the decorative elements which in their sizes and arrangement follow laws of human reasoning. It is ultimately this humanizing that makes a Renaissance building what it is. Arcades are airier and more open than they had been. The graceful columns have the beauty of animate beings. They keep to a human scale too, and as they lead from part to part, even when a building is very large, one is never overwhelmed by its sheer size. This, on the other hand, is just what the Norman architect wishes to achieve. He conceives a wall as a whole and then keeps the expression of might and mass to the smallest detail. Hence, one need scarcely add, Romanesque sculptors could not yet rediscover the beauty of the human body. This rediscovery, and the discovery of linear perspective, had to come with the Renaissance.

50. *Leone Battista Alberti: S. Andrea, Mantua, begun* 1470

Sto Spirito, or the Palazzo Rucellai, prove this to anyone susceptible to their specific character.

To illustrate the principle of an all-pervading order which Alberti postulates in an interior as well, the plan of S. Andrea in Mantua, Alberti's last work, may be analysed (fig. 50). As in Sto Spirito, the east parts are a central composition. Alberti had in fact also made a contribution to the architects' burning problem of the completely central plan. His S. Sebastiano in Mantua (fig. 51) is a Greek cross. It was designed in 1460, that is just before

51. *Leone Battista Alberti: S. Sebastiano, Mantua, begun* 1460

or just after the Sforza Temple of Sperandio's medal. But Alberti's solution is original, whatever its date, austere and aloof, with its curiously pagan façade. No wonder that a cardinal could write of it in 1473 : 'I can't see if this is going to turn out a church or a mosque or a synagogue.' From the point of view of practical church functions such central buildings are conspicuously useless. So we find from the beginning attempts at combining the traditional longitudinal plan with aesthetically more welcome central features. Sto Spirito was one example. The most influential one, however, is S. Andrea in Mantua. Here the architect replaces the traditional nave and aisles arrangement by a series of side chapels taking the place of the aisles and connected with the nave alternately by tall and wide and low and narrow openings. The aisles thus cease to be part of the eastward movement and become a series of minor centres accompanying the spacious tunnel-vaulted nave. As to the walls enclosing the nave, the same intention is evident in the replacement of the simple basilican sequence of columns following each other without caesura by the rhythmical alternation on the *a b a* principle of the closed and the open bays. To what extent the keeping of the same proportions throughout is responsible for the deeply restful harmony of S. Andrea will be appreciated, if one realizes that the same *a b a* rhythm, identical even in details, is used as the chief motif of the façade of the church, and that the proportion of the arches of the crossing repeats that of the side chapels.

Alberti was not the only architect to experiment with such rhythmical combinations in the longitudinal church building. The North of Italy proved especially interested in the application of the principle to the church with nave and aisles, after a Florentine architect had given the first hints at Faenza Cathedral (1474). Ferrara, Parma, and other centres picked them up, and soon we see this trend of thought unite forces with that interested in central plans on the Milanese scheme of a central dome with four smaller and lower domes in the corners. Venice and the Veneto had begun to build central churches of this type shortly before 1500 (S. Giovanni Grisostomo), and in 1506 an otherwise little-known architect, Spavento, found the classic solution for its application to the basilica. S. Salvatore in Venice (fig. 52) consists of a nave of two of the Milano-Venetian units plus an exactly identical crossing. Only the transepts and apses are tacked on a little incongruously.

S. Salvatore stands historically in a similar relation to Alberti's S. Andrea in Mantua as, in the field of domestic architecture, the Cancelleria in Rome (fig. 53) stands to Alberti's Palazzo Rucellai. The Cancelleria was built in 1486-98 as the private residence of Cardinal Riario, nephew of Sixtus IV, one of the most formidable of the Renaissance popes. These popes considered themselves worldly rulers almost more than priests.

52. *Giorgio Spavento: S. Salvatore, Venice, begun* 1506

Julius II, another nephew of Sixtus IV, under whom the new St Peter's was begun, and for whom Michelangelo painted the Sistine Chapel and Raphael the *Stanze* of the Vatican, asked Michelangelo to portray him in a statue for Bologna with a sword instead of a book; for, he said: 'I am a soldier, not a scholar'. Of Alexander VI, and his nephew Cesare Borgia, it is enough to mention the names in this connection. The Palazzo Riario has a ground floor without pilasters, because it seemed more reasonable to preserve the integrity of the rustication, where only small windows were required. On the first and second floors there are pilasters, but not in the simple sequence of the Palazzo Rucellai. Again the *a b a* rhythm is used to give life and rule to the façade. It will also be noticed that, whereas Alberti's horizontal divisions had to serve as cornices and at the same time window sills, the unknown architect of the Cancelleria gives each function its clearly visible architectural expression. Moreover, the corner bays of the building are

53. *The Chancery Palace (Palazzo della Cancelleria)
in Rome, 1486–98*

slightly projected, so that to the right and the left there is no vagueness about the composition either.

The Cancelleria is the first Renaissance building of more than local importance in Rome. About the time, however, when it was completed, Rome took the leadership in architecture and

1a. Athens, The Parthenon, begun in 447 B.C.

1b. Rome, Basilica of Maxentius, *c.* A.D. 310–20

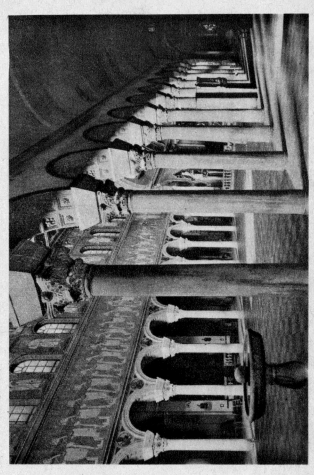

2. Ravenna, S. Apollinare Nuovo, early 6th century

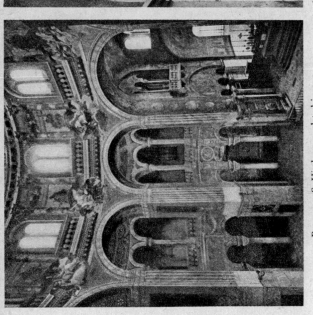

3a. Ravenna, S. Vitale, completed in 547

3b. Aachen, Cathedral (the Chapel of Charlemagne's Palace), consecrated in 805

4. S. Maria de Naranco, built as a Royal Hall shortly before 848

5b. Earl's Barton, Northamptonshire, 10th or early
11th century

5a. S. Maria de Naranco

6. Castle Hedingham, Essex, 12th century

7. Winchester Cathedral, north transept, c. 1080–90

8. Durham Cathedral, the nave, early 12th century

9. Jumièges, Abbey Church, begun *c.* 1040, consecrated in 1067

10. Toulouse, St Sernin, the nave, early 12th century

11a. Toulouse, St Sernin, from the east. Choir consecrated in 1096. The tower over the crossing dates from the 12th and 13th centuries

11b. Cluny, Abbey Church, from the east, according to Professor Conant's reconstruction, late 11th to early 12th century

12b. Périgueux, St Front, c. 1125-50

12a. Angoulême Cathedral, early 12th century

13. Vézelay, Church of the Magdalen, early 12th century

14. Autun, St Lazare, early 12th century

15a. St Gilles, west front, c. 1150

15b. Worms Cathedral, c. 1175–1250

16. Milan, S. Ambrogio, probably second quarter of the 12th century

17a. Florence, S. Miniato al Monte; ground floor second half of the 11th century, upper parts later

17b. St Denis, Choir Ambulatory, 1140-44 (The pier on the right is of c. 1235)

18b. Paris, Notre Dame, nave designed *c.* 1185. The east bay shows a reconstruction of the original arrangement of the windows

18a. Laon Cathedral, nave, last quarter of the 12th century

19. Amiens Cathedral, begun 1220

20. Rheims Cathedral, the west front, begun *c.* 1225

21a. Rheims Cathedral, from the north, begun in 1211 ; chancel, transepts, and nave 13th century, towers 15th century

21b. Lincoln Cathedral, chiefly 1190–1280. Upper parts of towers 14th century

22a. Lincoln Cathedral, nave, roofed 1233

22b. Lincoln Cathedral, the Angel Choir, begun in 1256

23b. Ely Cathedral, from the Lady Chapel, 1321–49

23a. Southwell Minster, capital from the chapter-house, late 13th century

24. Salisbury Cathedral, chapter-house, *c.* 1275

25. Bristol Cathedral, chancel aisle, 1298–1332

26a. Gloucester Cathedral, chancel, 1337–77

26b. Gloucester Cathedral, the vault of the chancel

27. Swaffham, Norfolk, timber roof, 1454 or later

28a. Penshurst Place, Kent, begun *c.* 1341

28b. Coventry, St Michael's, 15th century (destroyed in the Second World War)

29a. Ypres : Cloth Hall, c.1260-1380 (mostly destroyed in the First World War)

29b. Venice : The Doge's Palace : the façade on the right 1340-1419, that on the left added from 1424

30a. Cambridge, King's College Chapel, begun 1446, mainly early 16th century

30b. Valladolid, St Paul's, c. 1490–1515. Designed by Simón de Colonia

31a. Nuremberg, St Lawrence, chancel, 1445–72 (severely damaged in the Second World War)

31b. Strassburg Cathedral, portal of St Lawrence by Jakob of Landshut, 1495

32b. Filippo Brunelleschi: Sto. Spirito, Florence, begun 1435

32a. Florence Cathedral, begun 1296, built chiefly from 1357 onwards. Principal architects: Arnolfo di Cambio and Francesco Talenti

33a. Filippo Brunelleschi : Foundling Hospital, Florence, begun 1419

33b. Luciano Laurana (?) : Courtyard of the Ducal Palace, Urbino, c. 1470–75

34. Leone Battista Alberti : S. Francesco, Rimini, begun 1446

35a. Leone Battista Alberti : Palazzo Rucellai,
Florence, 1446–51

35b. Raphael : Palazzo Vidoni Caffarelli, Rome,
c. 1515–20

36b. Antonio da San Gallo : Palazzo Farnese, Rome, 1530–46. The top floor by Michelangelo.

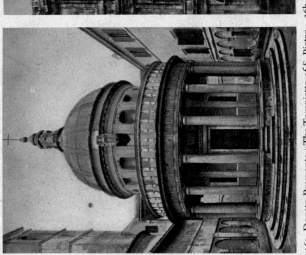

36a. Donato Bramante : The Tempietto of S. Pietro in Montorio, Rome, 1502

37. Michelangelo: Anteroom to the Laurenziana Library, Florence, begun in 1526

38a. Baldassare Peruzzi : Palazzo Massimi alle Colonne, Rome, begun 1535

38b. Guilio Romano : The architect's own house at Mantua, *c.* 1544

39a. Andrea Palladio : Palazzo Chiericati, Vicenza, begun in 1550

39b. Andrea Palladio : Villa Rotonda, outside Vicenza; begun *c.* 1567

40a. Giorgio Vasari : The Uffizi Palace, Florence, begun in 1570

40b. Giacomo Vignola : Church of the Gesù, Rome, begun in 1568

41. Michelangelo : The dome of St Peter's in Rome, designed in 1558–60, completed by Giacomo della Porta, 1588–90

42. St Peter's in Rome, with the front and nave by Carlo Maderna, 1607–c. 1615, and the colonnades by Bernini, begun in 1656. The Vatican Palace appears on the right

43b. Francesco Borromini : S. Carlo alle Quattro Fontane, Rome, the front, begun in 1667

43a. Francesco Borromini : S. Carlo alle Quattro Fontane, Rome, begun in 1633

44. Pietro da Cortona : S. Maria della Pace, Rome, begun in 1656

45a. Gianlorenzo Bernini : Altar of S. Teresa at S. Maria della Vittoria, Rome, 1646

45b. Gianlorenzo Bernini : The Scala Regia in the Vatican Palace, Rome, c. 1660–70

46. Luis de Arévalo and F. Manuel Vasquez : Sacristy of the Charterhouse
(Cartuja), Granada, 1727–64

47a. Narciso Tomé : The Trasparente in Toledo Cathedral, completed in 1732.

47b. Cosmas Damian and Egid Quirin Asam : S. John Nepomuk, Munich, 1730–c. 1750

48. Johann Balthasar Neumann : Vierzehnheiligen, 1743–72

49a. Matthaus Daniel Poppelmann : The Zwinger at Dresden, 1709–19 (badly damaged in the Second World War)

49b. Jakob Prandtauer : the Monastery of Melk on the Danube, 1702–36

50. Johann Balthasar Neumann : Staircase in the Electoral Palace at Bruchsal,
designed 1730 (badly damaged in the Second World War). Ground floor

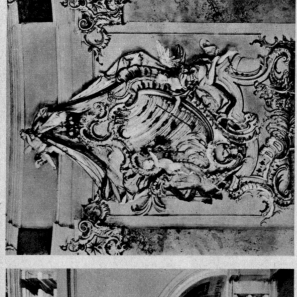

51a. Johann Balthasar Neumann: Staircase in the Electoral Palace at Bruchsal, designed 1730. Half-way between ground floor and upper floor

51b. Johann Michael Feichtmayr : Stucco cartouche, Bruchsal, 1752

52a. Cambridge: King's College Chapel, stalls, c. 1532–36

52b. Blois: The Castle, wing of Francis I, 1515–c. 1525

53a. Burghley House, Northants, centre pavilion in the courtyard, 1585

53b. Pierre Lescot: South-west pavilion in the Louvre courtyard, Paris, 1546

54a. Longleat, Wiltshire, begun in 1567

54b. Inigo Jones : Queen's House, Greenwich, begun in 1616

55a. Jacob van Campen : The Mauritshuis, The Hague, 1633–5

55b. François Mansart : The Orléans wing of Blois Castle, 1635–8

56a. Claude Perrault : The Louvre, Paris, east front, begun in 1665

56b. John Wood the Elder : Prior Park, near Bath, begun in 1735

56c. John Wood the Younger : Royal Crescent, Bath, begun in 1767

57b. Sir Christopher Wren : St Paul's Cathedral, London, 1675–1710

57a. Jules Hardouin-Mansart : St Louis des Invalides, Paris, 1675–1706

58b. Sir John Vanbrugh : Blenheim Palace, begun in 1705

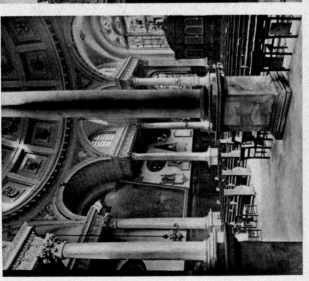

58a. Sir Christopher Wren : St Stephen's Walbrook, London, 1672-8

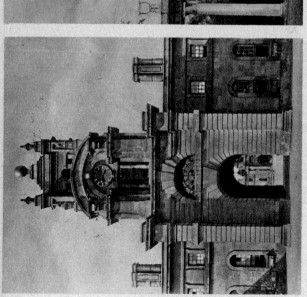

59a. Sir John Vanbrugh : Blenheim Palace, gate pavilion of the kitchen wing, 1708–9

59b. Robert Adam : Syon House, near London. The entrance screen, 1773

60a. Blenheim Palace from the air. The grounds laid out by Lancelot Brown

60b. Robert Adam : Syon House, near London. The Library, designed *c.* 1765

61a. Friedrich Gilly : Plan for a National Theatre, Berlin, 1798

61b. Sir John Soane : Design for the architect's own house, Lincoln's Inn Fields, London, 1813

62a. Sir Charles Barry and A. W. N. Pugin : The Houses of Parliament,
London, begun in 1835

62b. Sir Robert Smirke : The British Museum, London, 1823–47

63a. Sir Charles Barry : The Reform Club, London, begun in 1837

63b. Charles Garnier : The Opera, Paris, 1861–74

64. Walter Gropius : Model Factory at the Werkbund Exhibition, Cologne, 1914

art out of the hands of Florence. This moment marks the beginning of the High Renaissance. The Early Renaissance was essentially Tuscan. The High Renaissance is Roman, because Rome was at that time the only international centre of civilization, and the High Renaissance has an ideal classicity which made it internationally acceptable and in fact internationally canonic for centuries. Rome's place in the history of the Renaissance style corresponds exactly to that of Paris and the cathedrals around Paris in the history of the Gothic style. We do not know to what part of France the architects of Notre Dame, Chartres, Rheims, and Amiens belonged by birth and upbringing, but we do know that Donato Bramante came from Lombardy, Raphael from Umbria, and Michelangelo from Tuscany. These are the three greatest architects of the High Renaissance, and none of them – again the case we have met before – was an architect by training. Bramante was originally a painter, so was Raphael, and Michelangelo was a sculptor.

Bramante was the oldest of them. He was born in 1444 near Urbino. There he grew up while Piero della Francesca painted, Laurana worked at the Ducal Palace, and Francesco di Giorgio was busy writing a treatise on architecture – the third of the Renaissance, after Alberti's and Filarete's – in which incidentally he took a close interest in central planning. Some time between 1477 and 1480 Bramante went to Milan. His first building there, the church of S. Satiro, presupposes a knowledge of Alberti's S. Andrea in Mantua, a building started only a few years before. It looks as if Bramante had studied the plans carefully. His own church had no space for a chancel, and so – delighted to make a daring show of his knowledge of linear perspective – he feigned one in flat relief. If you stand in the right position, the trick comes off to perfection.

The same church, S. Satiro, has a sacristy, centrally planned; and S. Maria delle Grazie, Bramante's next architectural work in Milan, has an east end also on a central plan, very similar incidentally to Alberti's S. Sebastiano in Mantua. But when S. Maria delle Grazie was begun in 1492, another artist, the most universal that ever lived, and one who has to influence considerably the slightly older Bramante, had already lived at

7

Milan for nine years. Leonardo had gone to Milan in 1482 as
an engineer, a painter, a sculptor, a musician – as anything
and everything, but not as an architect. Yet in his fertile mind
architectural problems moved all the time. In Florence he had
already sketched the plans of Brunelleschi's Sto Spirito and
S. Maria degli Angeli, and in Milan he looked carefully at
the specifically Milanese solutions proposed by Filarete. The

54. *Leonardo da Vinci: design for a church. Redrawn
from the MS. Paris, Institut de France, BN 2037, folio 56*

outcome was drawings in his sketch-books showing several
kinds of complex central structures, for instance one with a central octagon and eight chapels, each of the Milanese plan with
centre dome and little square corner bays (fig. 54). So here we
find as against the central schemes worked out by Renaissance
architects before Leonardo not a major contrasted with a number of radiating minor members, but a system of three grades
each subordinate to the one above. Another project was to
prove even more important for the future. It appears in
Leonardo's Paris Manuscript B and consists of a combination

of a major Greek cross with minor Greek crosses in the corners (fig. 55). Bramante must have seen this, and remembered it years after he had left Milan and moved to Rome.

Apart from what Bramante had learnt from Leonardo, the change from the Milanese to the Roman atmosphere, which took place in 1499, altered his style decisively. His architecture assumed at once an austerity far beyond anything in Milan. This appears already in his first Roman designs, the cloister for S. Maria della Pace and the Tempietto of S. Pietro in Montorio. At S. Maria della Pace the courtyard has piers and attached columns in the Roman way on the ground floor, and an open gallery on the first whose slim columns support a straight architrave instead of arches. At S. Pietro in Montorio Bramante appears even graver. The Tempietto of 1502 is the first monument of the High as against the Early Renaissance – truly a

55. *Leonardo da Vinci: sketch for a church. Redrawn from the MS. Paris, Institut de France, B, folio 57 v*

monument, i.e. more a sculptural than a strictly architectural achievement (pl. 36a). It was built to mark the spot on which St Peter was supposed to have been crucified. One can thus call it an enlarged reliquary. In fact the intention had been to alter the courtyard in which it stood into a circular cloister to house the little temple. The first impression of the Tempietto after the churches and palaces of the 15th century is almost forbidding. The order of the colonnade is Tuscan Doric, the earliest modern use of this severe, unadorned order. It supports a correct classical entablature, again a feature that adds weight and strictness. There is, moreover, except for the metopes and the shells in the niches, not a square inch of decoration on the whole of the exterior. This in conjunction with the less novel but equally telling simplicity of the proportions – the ratio between width and height of the ground floor is repeated in the upper floor – gives the Tempietto a dignity far beyond its size. Here for once the classic Renaissance has achieved its conscious aim to emulate classic Antiquity. For here is – beyond motifs and even beyond formal expression – a building that appears as nearly pure volume as a Greek temple. Space – that all-important ingredient of Western architecture – seems here defeated.

But Bramante did not stop there. Only four years after he had accomplished the ideal Renaissance expression of architectural volume, he set out to reconcile it with the ideal Renaissance expression of space, as it had been evolved by the 15th-century architects from Brunelleschi to Leonardo da Vinci. In 1506 Julius II commissioned him to rebuild St Peter's, the holiest of Western churches. St Peter's still survived then essentially in its Constantinian form (see p. 24). Nicholas V, the first pope in sympathy with humanism and the Renaissance, had begun rebuilding it outside the old east end in a way so similar in character to Alberti's S. Andrea in Mantua that Alberti can perhaps be assumed to be the originator of the design. But nothing more than the foundations had been laid when Nicholas V died in 1455, and nothing further happened. Julius II's St Peter's was to be a building on a strictly central plan, an amazing decision, considering the strength of the tradition in favour of longitudinal churches on the one side and the immense religious significance of St Peter's on the other. With the pope adopting this symbol of worldliness for his own church, the spirit of Humanism had indeed penetrated into the innermost fortress of Christian resistance.

Bramante was over sixty when the foundation stone was laid of the new St Peter's (fig. 56). It is a Greek cross, with four apses, so extremely symmetrical that on the plan nothing indicates which of the apses was to hold the high altar. The main dome was to be accompanied by minor domes over corner chapels and by towers in the corners further out still. All this was clearly in the Milanese and Leonardo traditions. But Bramante amplified his rhythm by enlarging the corner chapels into

Greek crosses so that each of them has two apses of its own, the other two being cut off by the arms of the major Greek cross. Thus a square ambulatory is created framing a huge central dome, designed to be hemispherical like the dome over the Tempietto. Four corner turrets complete the exterior into a

0 40 80 120 160 200
├──┼──┼──┼──┼──┼──┤ *feet*

56. Donato Bramante: original plan for St Peter's in Rome, 1506

square with projections for only the main apses. So far Bramante's scheme was not more than a magnificent development of 15th-century ideas. What is new and entirely of the 16th century is the modelling of the walls and above all the piers supporting the central dome, the only parts of Bramante's plan that were executed and are still partially visible. In them nothing is left of the human scale and gentle modelling of Early Renaissance members. They are massive pieces of masonry, boldly hollowed out as if by the sculptor's moulding hand.

This conception of the plastic potentialities of a wall, in its origin Late Roman, and first rediscovered (though less massively used) by the late Brunelleschi of S. Maria degli Angeli, was to be of the greatest importance for the future development of Italian architecture.

The immediate future, however, belonged to Bramante the master of classic harmony and greatness, not to Bramante the herald of the Baroque. Raphael (1483–1520) was the architect to follow most closely the Bramante of the Tempietto, and the new courts of the Vatican (1503 seqq.), Bramante's other Roman masterpiece. Of Raphael's architectural works few are actually documented. Amongst the buildings attributed to him on good evidence is the Palazzo Vidoni Caffarelli in Rome (pl. 35b), a very near descendant of the Palazzo Caprini, which Bramante had designed just before he died in 1514 and which Raphael had bought in 1517. It is now altered out of recognition. The Palazzo Caffarelli is also no longer as Raphael intended it to be. It was at a later date considerably enlarged in width and height. Here again the change of scale which marks the High Renaissance is noticeable. Balance and harmony are still the aims, but they are now combined with a solemnity and greatness unknown to the 15th century. Tuscan Doric columns replace the pilasters of the Palazzo Rucellai and the Cancelleria, and the happy *a b a* rhythm is contracted into a weightier *a b* with a new accent on the *a* by the duplication of the columns, and on the *b* by the straight architraves over the windows. The design of the rustication on the ground floor also emphasizes the horizontality, i.e. the gravity, of the composition.

The development from the Early to the High Renaissance, from delicacy to greatness and from a subtle planning of surfaces to a bold high relief in the modelling of walls encouraged an intensified study of the remains of Imperial Rome. Only now was their drama fully understood. Only now did humanists and artists endeavour to visualize and perhaps recreate the Rome of the ruins as a whole. Raphael's Villa Madama as originally planned, with a circular courtyard and manifold apsed and niched rooms, is the boldest attempt at emulating the grandeur of Roman baths. Its delicious decoration is derived immediately from such remains of Imperial Rome as Nero's Golden House. These remains had been found below ground – hence the name Grottesche given to this kind of ornament favoured by Raphael and his studio. It is thus, considering plan and decoration of the Villa Madama, evidently more than co-incidence that Raphael was appointed in 1515 by Leo X, the Medici pope, to be Superintendent of Roman Antiquities, that he had Vitruvius translated by a humanist friend for his private use, and that he (or in all probability he) drew up a memorandum to the pope advocating the exact measuring of Roman remains, with ground plans, elevations, and sections separate, and the restoration of such buildings as could be '*infallibilmente*' restored.

Here precisely archeology in the academic sense begins, re-presentative of an attitude quite different from that of the 15th-century admirers of Roman architecture. It produced scholars of ever wider knowledge and ever deeper appreciation of Antiquity, but artists of weakened self-confidence, classicists where Bramante and Raphael had been classics.

At this point a warning must be sounded against confusion between the three terms classic, classical, and classicist. The dif-ference between classic and classical has been pointed out on p. 50. If classic is the term denoting that rare balance of con-flicting forces which marks the summit of any movement in art, and if classical is the term for anything belonging to or de-rived from Antiquity, what then is classicist? A definition is far from easy. In our context it can be arrived at only in a some-what roundabout way.

Neither classic nor classicist are terms which signify historic styles such as Romanesque, Gothic, and Renaissance. They co-incide rather with aesthetic attitudes. However, in so far as aesthetic attitudes as a rule change with historic styles, the two sets of terms can often be co-ordinated. In England the position until a relatively short time ago was that the term Renaissance was used to cover the art from the 15th right up to the early 19th century. But there had been so many fundamental changes of styles during these more than three hundred years that the term covering such a long period could not stand for any

distinct aesthetic characteristics. Thus, on the example of the
Continent, it was gradually divided up into Renaissance and
Baroque, the Baroque to cover the work of such artists as Bernini, Rembrandt, Velasquez. However, since our knowledge
of, and susceptibility to, distinctions in aesthetic expression have
grown considerably within the last fifty years or so, it is becoming more and more patent that Renaissance and Baroque
do not really define the qualities of all art of importance in the
15th, 16th, and 17th centuries. The contrast between Raphael
and Bernini or Rembrandt is evident, but art of the period between roughly 1520 or 1530 and 1600 or 1620 does not fit into
the categories of the Renaissance or the Baroque. So a new
name was introduced about twenty or twenty-five years ago:
Mannerism, a name which was not specially coined, but which
in a derogatory sense had already been used to characterize certain schools of 16th-century painting. The name in its new
sense is only now becoming known in this country. It has much
to recommend it. It certainly helps to make one see the important differences between art of the High Renaissance and art of
the later 16th century.

If balance and harmony are the chief characteristics of the
High Renaissance, Mannerism is its very reverse; for it is an unbalanced, discordant art – now emotional to distortion (Tintoretto, El Greco), now disciplined to self-effacement (Bronzino).
The High Renaissance is full, Mannerism is meagre. There is
luxuriant beauty in Titian, stately gravity in Raphael, and
gigantic strength in Michelangelo, but Mannerist types are
slim, elegant, and of a stiff and highly self-conscious deportment. Self-consciousness to this extent was a new experience
to the West. The Middle Ages, and the Renaissance too, had
been much more naïve. Reformation and counter-Reformation broke up that state of innocence, and this is why Mannerism is indeed full of mannerisms. For the artist now for the first
time was aware of the virtues of eclecticism. Raphael and
Michelangelo were recognized as the masters of a Golden Age,
the equals of the Ancients. Imitation became a necessity in quite
a new sense. The medieval artist had imitated his masters as a
matter of course, but he had not doubted his own (or his

time's) ability to surpass them. This confidence had now gone. The first academies were founded, and a literature on the history and theory of art sprang up. Vasari is its most famous representative. Deviation from the canons of Michelangelo and Raphael was not ostracized, but it assumed a new air of the capricious, or the demonstrative, or the daring: forbidden pleasures. No wonder that the 16th century saw the sternest ascetics and the first writers and draughtsmen to indulge in the hidden sins of pornography (Aretino and Giulio Romano).

So far only names of painters have been mentioned because the qualities of 16th-century painting are at least a little more familiar than those of architecture. The application of the principles of Mannerism to architecture is only in its very tentative stages on the Continent and in America; in England it has not even been attempted. Yet if we now turn to buildings and compare the Palazzo Farnese (fig. 57 and pl. 36b) with the Palazzo Massimi alle Colonne (pl. 38a) as the most perfect examples of High Renaissance and Mannerist palace architecture in Rome, the contrast between their emotional qualities will at once be visible. The Palazzo Farnese was designed in 1530 by Antonio da San Gallo the Younger (1485–1546). It is the most monumental of Roman Renaissance palaces, an isolated rectangle of about 150-feet frontage, facing a square. The façade has strongly emphasized quoins, but no rustication. The ground-floor windows are provided with straight cornices, those on the first floor with alternating triangular and segmental pediments, supported by columns (i.e. so-called *aediculae*), a Roman motif revived during the High Renaissance. The top floor and the overpowering top cornice were added later and in a different spirit (see p. 151). The symmetry and spaciousness of the interior are worth noting, especially the magnificent central entrance with the tunnel-vaulted passage leading into the courtyard. This (pl. 36b) possesses the cloistered ground floor of all Renaissance palaces, now, in accordance with the Bramante tradition, with Tuscan Doric columns and a correct frieze of metopes and triglyphs instead of the light columns of the Tuscan 15th century. The first floor has no gallery, but noble, pedimented windows set into blank arcades, and an Ionic order. This is correct according to Roman usage (Theatre of Marcellus): the sturdier Tuscan Doric must be on the ground floor, the elegant Ionic on the first, and rich Corinthian on the second. In this (but only in this) the later second floor of the Palazzo Farnese follows the archeological example.

57. Antonio da San Gallo: Palazzo Farnese, Rome, begun 1530

The Palazzo Massimi by Baldassare Peruzzi of Siena (1481–1536), a member of the Bramante-Raphael circle in Rome, begun in 1535, disregards all the canons of the Ancients. Nor does it really show much regard for the achievements of Bramante and Raphael. Both the Palazzi Vidoni and Farnese were logical structures in which the knowledge of any one part gives a clue to the whole. The entrance loggia of the Palazzo Massimi, with its coupled Tuscan Doric columns and its heavy cornice, is in no way a preparation for the upper floors. Both the Palazzi Vidoni and Farnese are modelled into a generous though not over-charged relief. In the Palazzo Massimi there is a poignant contrast between the deep darkness of the ground-floor loggia and the papery thinness and flatness of the upper parts. The first-floor windows are shallow in relief compared with what the High Renaissance regarded as appropriate, the second- and third-floor windows are small and have curious leathery surrounds. They are in no way differentiated in size or importance as they would have been in the Renaissance. Moreover a slight curve of the whole façade gives it a swaying delicacy, whereas the squareness of the Renaissance front seemed to express powerful solidity. The Palazzo Massimi is no doubt inferior to the Palazzi Vidoni and Farnese in dignity and grandeur; but it has a sophisticated elegance instead which appeals to the over-civilized and intellectual connoisseur.

Now this brings us back to the fact that classicism is an aesthetic attitude first appreciated during this phase of Mannerism. The Early Renaissance had rediscovered Antiquity and enjoyed a mixture of detail copying and a naïve licence in the reconstruction of more than details. The High Renaissance was in their use of Roman forms hardly more accurate, but the Antique spirit was for a brief moment truly revived in the gravity of mature Bramante and Raphael. After their death imitation began to freeze up initiative. Classicism is imitation of Antiquity and even more of the classic moment of the Renaissance, at the expense of direct expression. The attitude culminated, needless to say, during the late 18th and early 19th centuries, in that phase of classicism *par excellence* which is on the Continent often called Classicism pure and simple, but which in England goes under the name of Classic Revival. The idea of copying a whole Antique temple exterior (or a whole temple front) for Western use is the quintessence of classicism. The 16th century did not go quite so far. But it did conceive that blend of academic rigidity with distrust of emotional freedom which made the latter-day all-out revival possible.

A pupil of Raphael, Giulio Romano (1494–1546), artist-in-chief to the Duke of Mantua, designed a house for himself about 1544 (pl. 38b). It is a striking example of Mannerist classicism – apart from being one of the earliest architect's houses on such an ambitious scale. The façade is again flatter than would have pleased the High Renaissance. Detail, e.g. in the window surrounds and the top frieze, is hard and crisp. There is a proud aloofness, an almost arrogant taciturnity and a stiff formality about the building that reminds one at once of the Spanish etiquette accepted everywhere in the later 16th century. Yet the apparent general correctness is broken by an occasional, as it were, surreptitious licence here and there (one such licence in Giulio Romano's work as a draughtsman has been mentioned before). The smooth band above the windows of the rusticated ground floor seems to disappear behind the keystones of the windows. The entrance has a most illicit depressed arch, and the pediment on top with no base to it is nothing but the main string course at sill height of the first-floor windows lifted up by the effort of the arch. These windows themselves are recessed in blank arcades like those of the Palazzo Farnese, but as against the logical and structurally satisfying surrounds and pediments there, one flat ornamental motif runs without hiatus along sides, top, and pediments. It is exquisite, but very self-conscious, just like the contemporary sculpture of Benvenuto Cellini.

This style, first conceived in Rome and Florence, appealed almost at once to North Italy and the transalpine countries. Giulio Romano was the first to show it north of the Apennines; Sammicheli, though fifteen years older, followed, partly under direct Roman influence, partly under the influence of Giulio's early Mantuan masterpiece, the Palazzo del Té of 1525–35, and reshaped the appearance of Verona in this spirit of Mannerist classicism. At Bologna Sebastiano Serlio, a pupil of Peruzzi, though six years his senior, and twenty-four years older than Giulio, preached it. In 1537 he began to publish a first part of a treatise on architecture which proved a source of lasting inspiration to classicist minds on the other side of the Alps. Serlio himself went to France in 1540 and was almost at once made 'peintre et architecteur du roi'. The so-called school of Fontainebleau, where Serlio and the Italians Primaticcio and Niccolò dell' Abbate worked, is the transalpine centre of Mannerism. Spain accepted the new style even earlier – a violent reaction against the violence of her Late Gothic. Charles V's new and never finished palace on the Alhambra at Granada (begun in 1526 by Pedro Machuca) looks, with its vast circular colonnaded inner court and the motifs of its 207-foot-long façade, as though it were based on the Raphael of the Villa Madama and Giulio Romano, somewhat provincially interpreted. England and Germany were slower in succumbing to the dictatorship of classicism. The style was not in all its implications appreciated before the second decade of the 17th century (Inigo Jones and Elias Holl, see pp. 201 and 204), and then not so much in its problematical Giulio Romano-Serlio form as in that created by the happiest and most serene of all later 16th-century architects, Andrea Palladio (1518–80).

Palladio's style, though it first followed Giulio, Sammicheli, and Serlio, and as far as possible Vitruvius, the obscure and freely misinterpreted Roman authority on architecture, is highly personal. His work must be seen at and around Vicenza. He designed no churches there (though his San Giorgio Maggiore and Il Redentore in Venice are amongst the few really relevant churches in the Mannerist style, as will be shown later). What he was called upon to do was almost exclusively the designing of town and country houses, *palazzi* and *ville*, and it is significant that the far-reaching effect of his style can quite adequately be demonstrated without any analyses of his churches. For from the Renaissance onwards secular architecture became as important for visual self-expression as religious architecture, until during the 18th century the ascendancy of domestic and public buildings over churches was established. For the Middle Ages, in a book such as the present, little had to be said on castles, houses, and public buildings. Of Renaissance examples here discussed, half were secular. This will remain the proportion for the next two hundred years in the Roman Catholic countries. In those converted to Protestantism secular architecture was dominant at an even earlier date.

Palladio's buildings, despite their elegant serenity, would hardly have had such a universal success if it had not been for the book in which he published them and this theory of architecture. Palladio's *Architettura* took its place by the side of Serlio's, and later superseded it, especially after its revival in England early in the 18th century. His style appealed to the civilized taste and the polite learning of the Georgian gentry more than that of any other architect. Palladio is never dry or demonstratively scholarly. He combines the gravity of Rome with the sunny breadth of Northern Italy and an entirely personal ease not achieved by any of his contemporaries. In his Palazzo Chiericati (pl. 39a), begun in 1550, the Tuscan Doric and correct Ionic order of the Bramante tradition, with their straight entablatures, are unmistakable. But the freedom in placing what had been confined to the courtyards of Roman palaces into the façade, thus opening up most of the façade and retaining only one solid piece in the centre of the first floor surrounded on all sides by air, is all Palladio's. He was especially fond of colonnades in his country houses, where he used them to connect a square main block with far out-reaching wings (fig. 58).

The contrast between solid and diffused had a great fascination for him. In one of his most complete schemes, the Villa Trissino at Meledo on the Venetian mainland (fig. 58), the house is almost completely symmetrical. The most extreme case, still existent and well preserved, of such extreme symmetry is the Villa Capra, or Rotonda, just outside Vicenza (pl. 39b, begun *c.* 1567), an academic achievement of high perfection and one specially admired by Pope's England. As a house to live in it has nothing of the informal snugness of the Northern manor-house, but it has nobility and, with its slender Ionic porticoes, its pediments, its carefully placed few pedimented windows, and its central dome, it appears stately without being pompous. Now to get the totality of a Palladian countryside composition one has to add to such a nucleus the curved colonnades and low outbuildings by which the villa takes in the land around. This embracing attitude proved of the greatest historical consequence. For here for the first time in Western architecture landscape and building were conceived as belonging to each other, as dependent on each other. Here

58. *Andrea Palladio: Villa Trissino at Meledo.*

for the first time the chief axes of a house are continued into nature; or, alternatively, the spectator standing outside sees the house spread out like a picture closing his vista. It is worth mentioning that in Rome at about the same time Michelangelo

planned a comparable vista for the Palazzo Farnese which he
had been commissioned to finish. He suggested that the palace
should be connected with the Farnese gardens on the other
side of the Tiber.

It may seem odd to us that the Farnese family should have
gone to Michelangelo the sculptor to complete their palace
after San Gallo's death. But it must be remembered that Giotto,
Bramante, and Raphael were painters, and that Brunelleschi
was a goldsmith. All the same, the story of how Michelangelo
became an architect is worth telling, because it is equally characteristic of him and his age. He had as a boy been apprenticed to
a painter, until, when Lorenzo the Magnificent had discovered
him, given him lodgings in his palace, and drawn him into his
private circle, he was sent to learn in a freer, less medieval way
the art of sculpture from Lorenzo's favourite sculptor, Ber-
toldo. His fame rested on sculpture. His huge David, the
symbol of the civic pride of Renaissance Florence, he began at
the age of twenty-six. A few years later Julius II commissioned
him to prepare plans for an enormous tomb which the Pope
wanted to erect for himself during his lifetime. Michelangelo
regarded it as his *magnum opus*. The first scheme provided for
more than forty life-size or over life-size figures. The famous
Moses is one of them. Architecture of course was also involved,
though only as an accompaniment. However, when Julius had
decided to rebuild St Peter's to Bramante's design, he lost
interest in the tomb and forced upon Michelangelo the task of
painting the ceiling of the Sistine Chapel instead. Michelangelo
never forgave Bramante for having, as he suspected, caused
this change of mind. So for nearly five years – as he worked
without an assistant – he had to stick to painting.

Then he returned to the tomb of Pope Julius, and perhaps in
connection with conceptions that had passed through his mind
when thinking of how architecturally to relate large figures
with the wall against which they were going to stand, he began
to take an interest in the plans of the Medici family to complete their church of S. Lorenzo in Florence by at last adding a
façade. The church was Brunelleschi's work. Michelangelo in
1516 designed a façade two stories high, with two orders and

ample accommodation for sculpture. The commission was given to him, and for several years he worked in the quarries – a work he loved. Then, however, in 1520, the Medicis found too many difficulties in the transport of the marble and cancelled the contract. But they made at once another one with Michelangelo for the erection of a family chapel or mausoleum by S. Lorenzo. This was in fact begun in 1521 and completed, though less ambitiously than originally planned, in 1534. The Medici Chapel is thus Michelangelo's first architectural work, and the work, it must be added, of one never initiated into the secrets of building technique and architectural drawing. It has already – though again chiefly conceived as background for sculpture – all the characteristics of his personal style. Architecture without any support from sculpture is to be found in his work for the first time in another job for the Medicis at S. Lorenzo, the library and the anteroom to the library (pl. 37). The library was designed in 1524, the anteroom (with the exception of the staircase for which the model was supplied as late as 1557) in 1526.

The anteroom is high and narrow. This alone gives an uncomfortable feeling. Michelangelo wanted to emphasize the contrast to the long, comparatively low and more restful library itself. The walls are divided into panels by coupled columns. At the ground-floor height of the library itself the panels have blank windows and framed blank niches above. The colour scheme of the room is austere, a dead white against the sombre dark grey of columns, window niches, architraves, and other structural or decorative members. As for the chief structural members, the columns, one would expect them to project and carry the architraves, as had always been the function of columns. Michelangelo reversed the relations. He recessed his columns and projected his panels so that they painfully encase the columns. Even the architraves go forward over the panels and backward over the columns. This seems arbitrary, just like the relations between ground-floor loggia and flat façade above or between second- and third-floor windows, in the Palazzo Massimi. It is certainly illogical, because it makes the carrying strength of the columns appear wasted. Moreover,

they have slender corbels at their feet which do not look substantial enough to support them and in fact do not support
them at all. The thinness of the Massimi front characterizes the
blank windows with their tapering pilasters, fluted without
any intelligible reason in one part only. The pediment over the
entrance to the library is held only by the thin line around the
door, raised into two square ears. The staircase tells of the same
wilful originality; but the sharpness of detail which Michelangelo developed in the 'twenties is now replaced by a heavy,
weary flow as of lava.

It has often been said that the motifs of the walls show
Michelangelo as the father of the Baroque, because they express the superhuman struggle of active forces against overpowering matter. I do not think that anybody who examines
without prejudice his sensations in the room itself would sub-
scribe to this statement. There seems to me no expression of
struggle anywhere, though there is conscious discordance all
the way through. This austere animosity against the happy and
harmonious we have seen already, although hidden under a
polished formalism, in Giulio Romano. What Michelangelo's
Laurenziana reveals is indeed Mannerism in its most sublime
architectural form and not Baroque – a world of frustration
much more tragic than the Baroque world of struggles between mind and matter. In Michelangelo's architecture every
force seems paralysed. The load does not weigh, the support
does not carry, natural reactions play no part – a highly artificial system upheld by the severest discipline.[1]

In its spatial treatment the Laurenziana is just as novel and
characteristic. Michelangelo had exchanged the balanced proportions of Renaissance rooms for an anteroom as tall and
narrow as the shaft of a pit, and a library proper, reached by a
staircase, as long and narrow as a corridor. They both force us,
even against our wills, to follow their pull, upward first and

1. But to Jacob Burckhardt, the Swiss historian of the 19th century
and the discoverer of the Renaissance in the sense in which we understand the style to-day, the anteroom of the Laurenziana is but 'an incomprehensible joke of the great master' (*Geschichte der Renaissance in
Italien*, 7th edition, 1924, p. 208; written in 1867).

then forward. This tendency to enforce movement through space within rigid boundaries is the chief spatial quality of Mannerism. It is well enough known in painting, for instance in Correggio's late Madonnas, or Tintoretto's Last Suppers with the figure of Christ at the far, far end. The most moving of all examples is Tintoretto's painting of the Finding of the Body of St Mark (Brera, Milan, *c.* 1565). Nowhere else is Mannerist space so irresistible. In architecture this magic suction effect is introduced into Giulio Romano's extremely severe cathedral at Mantua with its double aisles, the inner one with tunnel-vaults, the outer one and the nave flat. The uninterrupted rhythm of its monotonous columns is as irresistible as that of an Early Christian basilica. In secular architecture its most familiar and easily accessible example is no doubt Vasari's Uffizi Palace in Florence (pl. 40a). It was begun in 1560 to house Grand Ducal offices. It consists of two tall wings along a long narrow courtyard. The formal elements are familiar to us : lack of a clear gradation of stories, uniformity coupled with heretical detail, long, elegant, and fragile brackets below double pilasters which are no pilasters at all, and so on. What must be emphasized is the finishing accent of the composition towards the River Arno. Here a loggia, open in a spacious Venetian window on the ground floor and originally also in a colonnade on the upper floor, replaces the solid wall. This is a favourite Mannerist way of linking room with room, a way in which both a clear Renaissance separation of units and a free Baroque flow through the whole and beyond are avoided. Thus, Palladio's two Venetian churches terminate in the east, not in closed apses, but in arcades – straight in S. Giorgio Maggiore (1565), semicircular in the Redentore (1577) – behind which back rooms of indistinguishable dimensions appear. And thus Vasari, together with Vignola (1507–73), designed the Villa Giulia, the country *casino* of Pope Julius III (1550–55), as a sequence of buildings with loggias towards semicircular courts and with vistas across the entrance through the first loggia towards the second, through it towards the third and through that into a walled back garden (fig. 59).

For the garden of the 16th century is still walled in. It may

have long and varied vistas, as you also find them at the Villa
Este in Tivoli or at Caprarola, but they do not stretch out into
infinity as in the Baroque at Versailles. Neither do the low
colonnades on the ground floors of Mannerist buildings, such
as the Palazzo Massimi and the Uffizi, indicate infinity – that
is, a dark, unsurveyable background of space, as a Rembrandt
background. Back walls are too near. The continuity of the
façade is broken by such colonnades – that is what the Renaissance would have disliked – but the layer of opened-up space

59. *Giorgio Vasari, Giacomo Vignola, and Bartolommeo Ammanati: the villa of Pope
Julius III, Rome, begun 1552*

is shallow and clearly confined in depth. Palladio's Palazzo
Chierigati is the most perfect example of this screen technique
in palace architecture, although, in its serenity, different from
Florentine and Roman Mannerism and particularly from
Michelangelo. Palladio's palace may have a certain coolness
too, but it is not icy as the Laurenziana.

This frozen self-discipline is not usually connected with the
genius of Michelangelo and therefore needs special emphasis,
emphasis above all because textbooks sometimes still treat
Michelangelo as a master of the Renaissance. The truth is that
he belonged to the Renaissance for only a very few years of
his early career. His Pietà of 1499 may be a work of the High
Renaissance. His David may be in the spirit of the Renaissance
too. Of his Sistine Ceiling this can be said only to a limited
extent; and of his work after 1515 hardly at all. His character

made it impossible for him to accept the ideals of the Renaissance for long. He was the very opposite of Castiglione's *Courtier* and Leonardo da Vinci: unsociable, distrustful, a fanatical worker, negligent in his personal appearance, deeply religious, and uncompromisingly proud. Hence his dislike for Leonardo, and for Bramante and Raphael, a dislike made up of contempt and envy. We know more of his character and his life than of those of any artist before. The unprecedented adoration for him caused the publication of two biographies while he was still alive. Both are based on a systematic collecting of material. It is good that it should be so; for we feel we must know much about him to understand his art. In the Middle Ages the personality of an architect could never to that degree have influenced his style. Brunelleschi, though clearer to us as a character than the architects of the Gothic cathedrals, is still surprisingly objective in his forms. Michelangelo was the first to turn architecture into an instrument of individual expression. The *terribilità* that frightened those who met him fills us with awe immediately we are faced with any work of his, a room, a drawing, a piece of sculpture, or a sonnet.

For Michelangelo was a consummate poet too, one of the profoundest of his age; and in his poems he gives to posterity a reckoning of his struggles. The fiercest of them was that between a platonic ideal of beauty and a fervent faith in Christ. It is in the most concentrated form the struggle between the age of the Renaissance in which he lived when he was young, and that of the Counter-Reformation and Mannerism that began when he was about fifty years old, just before the sack of Rome in 1527. Now new stricter religious orders were founded, the Capuchins, the Oratorians, and above all the Jesuits (1534). Now new saints arose, St Ignatius Loyola, St Teresa, St Philip Neri, St Charles Borromeo. In 1542 the Inquisition was reintroduced, in 1543 literary censorship. In 1555 the Emperor Charles V abdicated and retired to the silence of a Spanish monastery. A few years later his son, Philip II, began his bleak and enormous palace of the Escorial, more a monastery than a palace. Spanish etiquette stood for a discipline as rigid as that of the early Jesuits and the Papal court of the same

decades. In Rome nothing seemed left of the Renaissance
gaiety. The Venetian ambassadors wrote home that even the
carnivals were cold and lean. Paul V, the strictest of the popes,
had meat on his table only twice a week.

Michelangelo too had always been exemplarily sober and
self-denying. He trained himself to need little sleep, and used to
sleep with his boots on. While at work he sometimes fed on
dry bread, eaten without putting his tools aside. He felt his
duties to his genius more heavily than the light-hearted architects of the Renaissance – and he could therefore venture to
reply to a critic who objected to his having represented
Giuliano de Medici on his tomb beardless, though he wore a
beard in life: 'Who in a thousand years will care for what he
looked like?' a saying utterly impossible before the Renaissance had freed artists. For while the Middle Ages did not de-
mand portrait likeness, because it is part of what is merely
accidental in human nature, and while the early Renaissance
had enjoyed portrait likeness, because it had only just discovered the artistic means for attaining it, Michelangelo refused
to comply with it, because it would have hemmed in his
aesthetic freedom. Yet his religious experience was of the most
exacting, and it grew more so as he grew older and the century
grew older, until he, the greatest sculptor of the West, and the
most admired artist of his age, gave up painting and sculpture
almost entirely. Architecture alone he still carried on, and he
refused to accept a salary for his work at St Peter's.

The final break seems to have come after he had passed his
seventieth year. Between the Medici buildings of the mid-
twenties and 1547 he seems to have designed and built only the
fortifications of Florence in 1529 – an engineering job, we
would say, but a type of job in which Leonardo da Vinci and
San Gallo, his predecessor in most of his Roman works, also
excelled. In 1534 he had left Florence for good and gone to
Rome. In 1535 Paul III appointed him Superintendent of the
Vatican Buildings, an all but nominal appointment at first. In
1537 he was consulted about a more stately rebuilding of the
municipal palaces on the Capitol; but nothing materialized.
Then in 1546 San Gallo died, and now Michelangelo was called

upon almost at once to complete the Palazzo Farnese, re-design St Peter's, and replan the Capitol. The Capitol is an early example of town-planning in the sense that a group of buildings is conceived together with the square between them and the approach to them. Bernardo Rossellino (Alberti's executant at the Palazzo Rucellai and the resident architect of Nicholas V's new St Peter's) had preceded Michelangelo in this, when he designed for Pope Pius II the square, cathedral, and palace of Pienza (*c.* 1460), and Venice was busy throughout the first half of the 16th century in making of her Piazza and Piazzetta the most inspired (and the freest) piece of Renaissance town-planning.

In Michelangelo's *œuvre* town-planning could not play so important a part. To him architecture was too direct an emotional experience and too much an expression in terms of the structural shaping of stone. There is thus more to grip our sympathy in the Palazzo Farnese and St Peter's than in the Capitol. At the Palazzo Farnese we shall now easily discover his Mannerism in the second-floor details (pl. 36b). The triplicating of the pilasters and especially the odd discordant framing of the windows with corbels on the sides not supporting anything and special corbels immediately above, on which the segmental pediments rest, are Michelangelo's personal expression, individual to an unprecedented extent and impossible before the breaking up first of the transcendentally ordered world of the Middle Ages and then of the aesthetically ordered world of the Renaissance.

Michelangelo's architectural masterpiece, the back and the dome of St Peter's, are also an expression of revolt against Bramante and the spirit of the Renaissance, although they are not to the same extent Mannerist. When Michelangelo was appointed by Paul III, the Farnese Pope, to be architect of St Peter's, he found the church essentially left as it had been at Bramante's death. Raphael and San Gallo had designed naves to comply with the religious demands of the first post-Renaissance generation. But they were not begun. Michelangelo returned to the central plan, but he deprived it of its all-governing balance (fig. 60). He kept the arms of the Greek cross, but where Bramante (fig. 56) had intended sub-centres repeating on a smaller scale the motif of the main centre, Michelangelo cut off the arms of the sub-centres, thus condensing the composition into one central dome resting on piers of a dimension that Bramante would have refused as colossal, i.e. inhuman, and a square ambulatory round. As for the exterior, he altered Bramante's plans in exactly the same spirit, replacing a happily

60. *Michelangelo Buonarroti: plan for the completion of St Peter's in Rome,* 1546

balanced variety of noble and serene motifs by a huge order of Corinthian pilasters supporting a massive attic and by strangely incongruous windows and niches surrounded by aedicules and smaller niches of several sizes – a mighty yet somewhat discordant *ensemble.* At the west end, Michelangelo wanted to add a portico of ten columns with four columns in front of the middle ones. This – it was never built, because Maderna after 1600 added a nave – would have destroyed Bramante's ideal symmetry, and in fact the classic ideal of symmetry altogether; for the duplication of the centre columns is of course an utterly

un-antique conception. Bramante's cupola was to be a perfect
hemisphere, Michelangelo's (pl. 41) – if we can take it (in spite
of the emphatic denial by some scholars) that its present shape
is Michelangelo's and not della Porta's who completed it in
1588–90 – is elongated and with the projecting coupled columns
of the drum, the ribs up the dome and the coupled columns and
concave top of the lantern a revision in very personal Renaissance forms of the essentially Gothic design of Brunelleschi's
Florentine dome. Now the triumphant soar of this dome is not
Mannerist. This superhuman victory of gigantic forces against
huge masses points towards the Baroque. To admit that does
not mean invalidating the thesis that Mannerism was the predominant tendency of later 16th-century architecture. It
merely means admitting the vastness of Michelangelo's genius.
He – and the same is true of the other greatest masters of his
generation, of Raphael and Titian – in growing out of, and
beyond, the Renaissance conceived the styles of both the 16th
and 17th centuries. The 16th followed his manner and turned
it into Mannerism, the 17th appreciated the *terribilità* of his con-
flicts and made Baroque out of it. So the eternal city is crowned
not by a symbol of Renaissance worldliness, as Julius II had
visualized it, but by an overwhelming synthesis of Mannerism
and Baroque, and at the same time of Antiquity and Christianity.

It was Michelangelo's last three-dimensional work of such
violence. He was seventy-two when he designed it. The
eighteen years that were left to him he spent in meditation on
life after death. 'Let there be no more painting, no more carving,' he says in one of his late sonnets, 'to soothe the soul
turned towards that Divine Love which opened His arms
from the cross to receive us.'

> 'Nè pinger nè scolpir fia più che quieti
> L'anima volta a quell' Amor Divino
> C'aperse, a prender noi, 'n croce le braccia.'

He carved after this only three more groups, all three Entomb-
ments of Christ. One of them was for his own tomb, one he
left unfinished, or rather sublimated to so immaterial a form

that it can no longer be regarded as sculpture in the Renaissance sense. His late drawings too are spiritualized to a degree almost unbearable in an artist who had done more than any before him to glorify the beauty and vigour of body and movement. And one of his last architectural plans – a fact not widely enough known – was to design the Roman church of the newly-founded, severely counter-reformatory order of the Jesuits. He offered to take charge of the building without any fee, just as he had refused to accept a salary as architect of St Peter's.

The Gesù was not begun until four years after Michelangelo's death. It has perhaps exerted a wider influence than any other church of the last four hundred years (fig. 61). Giacomo Vignola (1507–73), the architect, following probably Michelangelo's ideas, combines in his ground plan the central scheme of the Renaissance with the longitudinal scheme of the Middle Ages – an eminently characteristic fact. The combination as such is not new. Alberti had done the same a hundred years before at S. Andrea in Mantua (fig. 50). The façade too (fig. 62) seems to take up a theme that Alberti had conceived. The problem for architects of the Renaissance, and after the Renaissance, was how to project the dimensions of tall nave and lower aisles on to the exterior without abandoning the orders of classical architecture. Alberti's solution was to have a ground floor on the triumphal arch system and a top floor the width of the nave only but with volutes, i.e. scrolls, rising towards it from the entablature in front of the lean-to roofs of the aisles. This method was adopted by Vignola in his design for the Gesù façade (though with the fuller and less harmonious orchestration of his age), and then by della Porta, who substituted a new design for Vignola's. It has been repeated innumerable times and with many variations in the Baroque churches of Italy and the other Roman Catholic countries.

As for the interior (fig. 61) Vignola keeps Alberti's interpretation of the aisles as series of chapels opening into the nave. He does not, however, concede them as much independence as the Renaissance architect considered necessary, always anxious as he was to let every part of a building be a whole. The extreme width of the nave under its powerful tunnel-vault degrades the chapels into mere niches accompanying a vast hall, and it has been suggested that the choice of this motif was due to Francesco Borgia, the Spanish General of the Jesuit Order, and thus ultimately to the traditions of the Gothic style in Spain (see p. 92) as already represented in Rome by the Catalan church of S. Maria di Monserrato (1495). If the suggestion is accepted,

61. *Giacomo Vignola: Church of Jesus (Gesù), Rome, begun 1568*

there is here yet another instance of the post-Renaissance return to medieval ideals – another, after the revival of Catholic faith which showed itself in the new Saints and the new Orders, after the Gothic curve of the dome of St Peter's and the reintroduction of a longitudinal emphasis in the Gesù plan. In the Gesù this emphasis on the eastward drive is obviously deliberate. The tunnel-vault and above all the main cornice, running all the way through without a break, take it up most eloquently in the elevation. There is, however, one element in Vignola's design that it would be impossible to find in the same sense in any medieval church: the light. In the cathedral of the

62. *Giacomo Vignola's design for the front of the Gesù*

13th century the stained-glass windows glow by means of light penetrating, but light itself is not a positive factor. Later on, in the Decorated style, light begins to model walls with their ogee-arched niches and play over filigree decoration, but it is never a major consideration of architectural design. In the Gesù, on the other hand, certain important features are introduced into the composition exclusively in order to make light-effects possible. The nave is lit from windows above the chapels – an even, subdued light. Then the last bay before the dome is shorter, less open, and darker than the others. This contraction in space and lightness prepares dramatically for the majestic crossing with its mighty cupola. The floods of light streaming down from the windows of the drum create that sensation of fulfilment that Gothic architects achieved in so much less sensuous a way.

The decoration of the Gesù appears sensuous too, luxurious though sombre. However, it is not of Vignola's day. He would have been more moderate, with smaller motifs and a shallower relief; this is certain from what we know of late 16th-century decoration. Thus the effect of the medieval movement towards the east would have been much stronger, with less to deflect attention from the cornice and the mighty tunnel-vault. The redecoration was done in 1668–73. It belongs to the High Baroque, whereas the building is, to say it again, Mannerist, with neither the equanimity of all High Renaissance, nor the expansive vigour of all Baroque.

CHAPTER SIX

The Baroque in the Roman Catholic Countries

c. 1600–*c.* 1760

MANNERISM, it has been pointed out, was originally a noun connected with 'mannered' and nothing else. Some twenty years ago it changed its meaning and became the term for a specific historic style in art, the post-Renaissance style of the 16th century, particularly in Italy. The same process had taken place about fifty years earlier with regard to Baroque. Baroque had originally signified odd, especially of odd shape. It was therefore adopted to describe an architectural style which to the classicist appeared to revel in odd, extravagant shapes, that is, the style of Italy during the 17th century. Then, chiefly in the 'eighties of the last century and chiefly in Germany, it lost its derogatory flavour and became a neutral term to designate the works of art of that century in general.

We have seen the Baroque style first heralded in the massive forms and the gigantic *excelsior* of the dome of Michelangelo's St Peter's. We have then seen that these efforts of Michelangelo towards the Baroque remained exceptional and that he himself in other works of architecture gave way to the pressure of Mannerism. It was only after Mannerism had completed its course that a new generation at the beginning of the 17th century, especially in Rome, tired of the forced austerity of the late 16th, rediscovered Michelangelo as the father of the Baroque. The style thus introduced culminated in Rome between 1630 and 1670, and then left Rome, first for the north of Italy (Guarini and Juvara in Piedmont) and then for Spain and Portugal and Germany and Austria. Rome, after the late 17th century, turned back to its classical tradition, partly under the influence of Paris. For the Paris of Richelieu, Colbert, and

Louis XIV had become the centre of European art, a position which until then Rome had held unchallenged for well over 150 years.

The popes and cardinals of the 17th century were enthusiastic patrons, eager to commemorate their names by magnificent churches, palaces, and tombs. Of the severity of fifty years before, when the Counter-Reformation had been a militant force, nothing was left. The Jesuits became more and more lenient, the most popular saints were of a lovable, gentle, accommodating kind (such as St Francis de Sales), and the new experimental science was promoted under the very eyes of the popes, until in the 18th century Benedict XIV could accept books which Voltaire and Montesquieu sent him as presents.

However, a general decline in the religious fervour of the people can hardly be noticed before 1660 or even later. Not the intensity of religious feelings, only their nature, changed. Art and architecture prove that unmistakably. We can here analyse but a few examples, and it is therefore advisable not to choose the most magnificent, say the nave and façade of St Peter's, as Carlo Maderna designed them in 1606, and as they were completed in 1626, but the most significant.

Maderna was the leading architect of his generation in Rome. He died in 1629. His successors in fame were Gianlorenzo Bernini (1598–1680), Francesco Borromini (1599–1667), and Pietro da Cortona (1596–1669). Bernini came from Naples, Maderna and Borromini from the north of Italy, the country round the lakes, and Cortona, as his name shows, from the south of Tuscany. As in the 16th century, so there were in the 17th only very few Romans amongst the great men of Rome. In architecture the influx from Lombardy had a considerable effect on the appearance of the city. A breadth and freedom were introduced in distinct contrast to Roman gravity. Thus Maderna's ground plan of the Palazzo Barberini (fig. 63) – its façade is by Bernini and a good deal of its decorative detail by Borromini – is of a kind wholly new in Rome, but to a certain extent developing what Northern Italian palaces and villas (especially those of Genoa and its surroundings) had done in the later 16th century. As against the austere blocks of the Florentine and Roman palaces (cf. the Palazzo Farnese, fig. 57), the Barberini Palace has a front with short wings jutting forward on the right and the left as so far done

63. *Carlo Maderna (and Gianlorenzo Bernini?): Palazzo Barberini, Rome, begun 1628.*

only in villas near Rome, and a centre opened in wide loggias. Bramante's design of the Damasus Court in the Vatican with colonnades on all stories is, one might say, cut into two, and only one half remains. The colonnades are now part of the façade. This exposing to the public of what had until then been kept private is eminently characteristic of the Baroque, as will be seen presently. The main staircase of the Barberini Palace also is wider and more open than those of the 16th century, the oval second staircase is a typical Serlio-Palladio motif, and the semicircular niche to the entrance hall in the centre, as well as the oval saloon to which it leads, are forms that the architect might have found in Roman churches and in the ruins of Imperial Rome, but that in domestic architecture are also distinctly in the spirit of Palladio (and the Lombards too).

It is important to remember that when Bernini with his South Italian impetuosity won the first place in Roman sculpture and architecture, this infiltration of North Italian elegance had already done its work. His noble colonnades in front of St Peter's (pl. 42) have something of the happy openness of Palladian villa architecture, in spite of their Roman weight and their Berninesque sculptural vigour. For Bernini was the son of a sculptor and himself the greatest sculptor of the Baroque. He incidentally also painted, and as for his reputation as an architect, it was so great that Louis XIV invited him to Paris to design plans for an enlargement of the Louvre Palace. Bernini was as universal as Michelangelo, and nearly as famous. Borromini, on the other hand, was trained as a mason, and, since he was distantly related to Maderna, found work in a small way at St Peter's when he went to Rome at the age of fifteen. There he worked on, humble and unknown, while Bernini created his first masterpiece of Baroque decoration, the bronze canopy under Michelangelo's dome, in the centre of St Peter's, a huge monument, nearly 100 feet high, and with its four gigantic twisted columns the very symbol of the changed age, of a grandeur without restraint, a wild extravagance, and a luxury of detail that would have been distasteful to Michelangelo.

The same vehemence of approach and the same revolutionary disregard of conventions characterize Borromini's first important work, the church of S. Carlo alle Quattro Fontane (pl. 43a), begun in 1633. The interior is so small that it would fit into one of the piers which support the dome of St Peter's. But in spite of its miniature size it is one of the most ingenious spatial compositions of the century. It has been said before that the normal plan for longitudinal churches of the Baroque was that of the Gesù: nave with side chapels, short transepts, and dome over the crossing. It was broadened and enriched by the following generations (S. Ignazio, Rome, 1626 seqq.). But the centralized ground plan was not given up either. It was only the predominance of the circle in central churches which the Baroque discarded in Rome. Instead of the circle the oval was introduced, already in Serlio's Book V, i.e. in 1547, and then in Vignola's S. Anna dei Palafrenieri (fig. 64), a less finite form,

0 10 20 30 40 50 feet

64. *Giacomo Vignola: S. Anna dei Palafrenieri Rome, begun c.* 1570

and a form that endows the centralized plan with longitudinal elements, i.e. elements suggestive of movement in space. An infinite number of variations on the theme of the oval was developed first by the architects of Italy and then by those of other countries. They constitute the most interesting development of Baroque

church architecture, a development belonging in Italy chiefly to the second half of the 17th century. Serlio and Vignola place the longer axis of the oval at right angles to the façade. This is repeated by most of the others, but S. Agnese in Piazza Navona (fig. 65), begun in 1652 (by Carlo Rainaldi and provided by Borromini with its North Italian two-tower façade), consists of an octagon in a square, with little niches in the corners, and extended by identical entrance and choir chapels in west and east, and by considerably deeper north and south transeptal chapels so as to produce an effect of a broad oval parallel to the façade, with masonry fragments sticking into its outline. Bernini had placed a real oval in the same position in his oratory at S. Filippo Neri (no longer existent) in 1634 and again in his late church of S. Andrea al Quirinale, 1678 (fig. 66). Vignola's composition was taken up by Maderna at S. Giacomo al Corso, 1594, and by Rainaldi at S. Maria di Monte Santo, 1662. This, incidentally, is one of the two identical churches by the Porta del Popolo, marking the start of three radiating streets towards the centre of Rome.

The oval even captured France, especially by the efforts of Louis Levau, as we shall see later. Meanwhile by far the most brilliant paraphrase on the oval theme is Borromini's S. Carlo. The church can serve better than any other to analyse what tremendous advantages the Baroque architect could derive from composing in ovals instead of rectangles or circles. Whereas all through the Renaissance spatial clarity had been the governing idea, and the eye of the spectator had been able to run unimpeded from one

65 and 66. *Carlo Rainaldi: S. Agnese, Rome, begun 1652, and Gianlorenzo Bernini: S. Andrea al Quirinale, Rome, begun 1678.*

part to another and read the meaning of the whole and the parts without effort, nobody, standing in S. Carlo, can at once understand of what elements it is made, and how they are intertwined to produce such a rolling, rocking effect. To analyse the ground plan (fig. 67) it will be best not to set out from the oval at right angles to the façade which, broadly speaking, the church seems to be, but from the domed Greek cross of the Renaissance. Borromini has given the dome absolute supremacy over the arms. Their corners are bevelled off so that the walls under the oval dome read like an elongated lozenge opening out into shallow chapels, the dwarfed arms of the original Greek cross. The chapels on the right and the left are fragments of

67. *Francesco Borromini: S. Carlo alle Quattro Fontane, begun* 1633. *Front,* 1667

ovals. If completed, they would meet in the centre of the building. The entrance chapel and the apsidal chapel are also fragments of ovals. They just touch the side ovals. Thus five compound spatial shapes merge into each other. We can stand nowhere without taking part in the swaying rhythm of several of them. The Late Gothic churches of Germany had achieved a similar wealth of spatial relations, but by means of forms that seem wiry when compared with the undulating walls of S. Carlo. Michelangelo is responsible for this turn of architecture towards the plastic. Space now seems hollowed out by the hand of a sculptor, walls are moulded as if made of wax or clay.

Borromini's most daring enterprise in setting whole walls into motion is the façade of S. Carlo which was added in 1667, the year of his death (pl. 65). The ground floor and its cornice give the main theme: concave – convex – concave. But the first floor answers by a concave – concave – concave flow, complicated by the insertion of a kind of flattened-out miniature oval temple set into the centre concavity so that this bay seems convex as long as one does not look up to its top part. Such relations in volume and space sound dry when described; when seen, however, there is *brio* and passion in them, and also something distinctly voluptuous, a swaying and swerving as of the naked human form. Watch how the two west towers of S. Agnese stand away from the main front of the church, separated by the convex curves of the two sides of the façade centre, or how in Pietro da Cortona's S. Maria della Pace (1656–57) the front is spread out with straight wings on the ground floor, but a sweeping convex curve on the first floor out of which the centre of the façade reaches forward, ending in a semicircular portico on the ground floor and a slightly set back shallower convex curve on the first floor (pl. 44). Columns and pilasters crowd together on it in a way that makes the composition of Vignola's Gesù front seem restrained in the extreme.

In fact the majority of Roman Baroque façades kept to the basic composition of Vignola and endowed it with a new meaning only by way of an excessive abundance of columns jostling against each other, and the most unconventional use and motives of decoration (fig. 68). One can follow this Baroque development of the Gesù front from Maderna's S. Susanna of *c.* 1596–1603 to the younger Martino Lunghi's SS Vincenzo ed Anastasio of 1650 (fig. 68) and to the excesses of Borromini's S. Carlo façade. Here the curious oval windows on the ground floor should be observed with the palm leaves that surround them, and with a crown above, and some sort of a Roman altar in relief beneath, and so, motif for motif, up the façade until the ogee arch at the top is reached, and the polygons and odd shapes and diminishing sizes that decorate the cupola inside. Every one of these details is senseless, unless they are seen together and as parts of a super-ordinate decorative whole.

To understand the Baroque it is essential to see it in this perspective. We are too much used to looking at decoration as something that may or may not be added to architecture. In fact all architecture is both structure and decoration, decoration for which the architect himself, or the sculptor, the painter, the glass-painter may be responsible. But the relation of decoration to structure varies in different ages and with different nations. In the Gothic style of the cathedrals all decoration served the mason's work. Then

68. *Martino Lunghi the Younger: SS Vincenzo ed Anastasio, Rome,* 1650

ornamental sculpture, late in the 13th and early in the 14th century, seemed to overgrow sculpture. Then, again somewhat later, figure sculpture and painting freed themselves from the supremacy of architecture altogether. A monument like Verrocchio's Colleoni in Venice, standing free in a square without any architectural support, would have been inadmissible in the Middle Ages. Just as novel was the conception of easel painting as such, painting independent of the wall against which it was going to be placed. The Renaissance accepted the independence of the fine arts, but was able to hold them together within a building, because of the principle of relatively independent parts that governed all Renaissance composition. Now however, in the Baroque, that principle had been abandoned. Again, as in Gothic architecture, parts cannot be isolated. We have seen that at S. Carlo. But the Baroque, although believing in the unity of all art, could not restore the supremacy of structure. Architects of the 17th century had to accept the claims of the sculptor and painter, and in fact often were sculptors and painters. Instead of the Gothic relation of super-ordinate and subordinate, there is now a co-operation of all the arts. The result was still that 'Gesamtkunstwerk' (total art) which Wagner, in his operas, after it had been wilfully destroyed at the end of the Baroque, endeavoured in vain to recover for the 19th century. In the works of Bernini and Borromini, what binds architectural, ornamental, sculptural, and pictorial effects into indivisible unity is the decorative principle common to all.

Now this decorative creed could leave no room in the minds of patrons and artists of the Baroque to be squeamish about honesty in the use of materials. As long as the effect was attained, what could it matter whether you attained it with marble or with stucco, with gold or with tin, with a real bridge or a sham bridge such as we find sometimes in English parks? Optical illusion is in fact (to Ruskin's grave displeasure) amongst the most characteristic devices of Baroque architecture. Bernini's Royal Staircase, the *Scala Regia* in the Vatican Palace (pl. 45b and fig. 69), illustrates this at its most suggestive. It was built during the same 'sixties which saw Borromini's façade of S. Carlo rise from the ground and the colonnades in front of St Peter's (pl. 42). As they are a masterpiece of stage setting, seemingly raising the height and weight of Maderna's façade, and at the same time making the loggia of the Papal benedictions and the *Porta Santa* visible to everybody amongst the tens of thousands who would stand in the forecourt on the occasion of great celebrations, so is the Scala Regia designed with a supreme knowledge of scenic effects. It is the main entrance to the palace. Coming from the colonnades, one reaches it along a corridor. The corridor ends in about fifteen or twenty steps, and then there is a slight break just at the point where one enters at right angles from the galilee porch of St Peter's. So here two main directions meet. They had to be joined and connected up. It was a master-stroke of Bernini to place opposite the entrance from the church an equestrian monument to the Emperor Constantine. Coming up from the

69. *Gianlorenzo Bernini: The Royal Staircase (Scala Regia) in the Vatican Palace, Rome, c. 1665*

corridor it appears on the right and forces us to halt, before we enter the Royal Staircase itself. The sudden appearance of the white prancing horse against a storm-swept drapery lit by windows above serves to conceal the otherwise unpleasant change of direction.

The *Scala Regia* had to be fitted into an awkwardly-shaped area between church and palace. It is long, comparatively narrow, and has irregularly converging walls. Bernini turned all this to advantage by means of an ingenious tunnel-vaulted colonnade of diminishing size. The principle is that of vistas on the Baroque stage. Streets there were made to appear long by the use of exaggerated perspective. In the same way Borromini treated the niches at S. Carlo (pl. 43a and b) and the windows on the top floor of the Palazzo Barberini. Such scenic illusions were not entirely new. They are to be found in Bramante's early works in Milan. Michelangelo too in his design for the Capitol in Rome had placed the palaces on the sides at such an angle as to increase the apparent height of the Senate House. Light is another means for dramatizing the ascent up the Royal Staircase. On the first landing halfway up it falls in from the left, on the second in the far distance a window faces the staircase and dissolves the contours of the room. Finally there is the decoration, the splendid angels, e.g. with their trumpets holding up the Pope's arms, to complete this gorgeous overture to the Vatican Palace.

Angels, genii, and such-like figures, preferably in realistic colouring, are an essential part of Baroque settings. Not only do they serve to cover up structural joints and to hide the contraptions 'behind the scenes' which make these illusions work, but they also act as intermediaries between the real space in which we move and the space created by the artist. The Baroque does not want to keep the border line visible between audience and stage. Such terms from the world of the theatre – or should one rather say the world of the opera, which was an Italian invention of the 17th century – come to mind with good reason. However, there is more than a mere theatrical trick in this flow from reality into illusion and from illusion into reality. Bernini's famous chapel of St Teresa in the church of S. Maria della Vittoria in Rome proves that (pl. 45a). The chapel, which dates from 1646, is faced with dark marbles, their gleaming surfaces of amber, gold, and pink reflecting the light in ever-changing patterns. In the middle of the wall in front of the entrance is the altar of the saint. It is flanked by heavy coupled columns and pilasters with a broken pediment, placed on the slant so that they come forward towards us and then recede to focus our attention on the centre of the altar, where one would expect to find a painting, but where there is a niche with a sculptural group, treated like a picture and giving an illusion of reality that is as startling to-day as it was three hundred years ago. Everything in the chapel contributes to this *peinture vivante* illusion. Along the walls on the right and the left there are also niches opened into the chapel walls, and there Bernini has portrayed in marble, behind balconies, members of the Cornaro family, the donors of the chapel, watching with us the miraculous scene, precisely as though they were in the boxes, and we in the stalls of a theatre.

The boundary line between our world and the world of art is in this most ingeniously effaced. As our own attention and that of the marble figures is directed towards the same goal, we cannot help giving the same degree of reality first to them as to ourselves, and then to the figures on the altar too. And Bernini has used all his mastery in the modelling of St Teresa and the angel to help in that deception. The heavy cloak of the nun, the fluffiness of the clouds, the light drapery of the youthful angel and his soft flesh are all rendered with an exquisite realism. The expression of the saint in the miracle of the union with Christ is of an unforgettable voluptuous ecstasy. She faints as though overwhelmed by a physical penetration. At the same time she is raised into the air, and the diagonal sweep of the group makes us believe the impossible. Beams of gold – they are gilt metal shafts – conceal the back wall of the niche, and an opening high up behind the entablature glazed with a yellow pane models the scene with a magical light.

The chapel of St Teresa is the most daring example of such illusionism in Rome. It is in fact an exception. Rome has never really believed in extremes. Bernini was a Neapolitan; and Naples was Spanish. To experience the thrills of extremes and excesses one must indeed go to Spain, or else to Portugal, or of course Germany. To these countries the Baroque came late, but it was taken up with tremendous fervour. Italy has no examples of such orgiastic interpenetration of reality and fiction as can be seen in some few Spanish and many more South German churches of the early 18th century.

The most outstanding example on Spanish soil is Narciso

Tomé's *Trasparente* in Toledo Cathedral (pl. 69 and fig. 70).
The cathedral is a 13th-century building in the style of classic
French Gothic. It has a high altar with a vast Late Gothic rere-
dos. Catholic orthodoxy objected to people walking along the
ambulatory behind the Blessed Sacrament. So an ingenious
plan was worked out by which the Sacrament could be seen
and would be respected from the ambulatory as well. It was
placed in a glass-fronted receptacle – hence the name *Trasparente* – and an altar scenery was built up around it of unheard-
of pomp. The work was completed in 1732. Attention was
focused on to the Sacrament by richly decorated columns.
They are linked up with large outer columns by cornices
curved upwards. These curves and the relief scenes in perspective on the panels below give the illusion – in the same way
as Bernini's colonnade in the *Scala Regia* – that the distance
from front to back of the altar is far deeper than it really is.
Moreover, the glass-fronted opening is surrounded by angels
to cover all structural props. By the clouds of angels our eyes
are led up to where the Last Supper is acted – at a fantastic
height – by figures of polychromatic marble. Higher up still is
the Virgin soaring up to Heaven. To enhance the effect of a
miraculous apparition, the whole scene is floodlit from behind
where we stand while we stare at it, lit, that is, in the way special
stage lighting is operated to-day. What the ingenious architect
has done is to take out the masonry between the ribs of half a
Gothic vault of the ambulatory – the engineering skill of the
13th century allowed him to do so without weakening the
construction – spread groups of angels around the opening, and
then erect above it a dormer with a window, invisible from
below, which lets in a flood of golden light past the angels and
the bay of the ambulatory in which we stand, on to the altar
with its figures and the Sacrament. And when, to discover this
source of magic light, we turn round, away from the altar, we see
in the dazzling light beyond the angels Christ Himself seated on
clouds, and prophets and the Heavenly Host surrounding Him.

Such spatial extremism, the pulling of a whole room into
one vast stupefying ornament, is, it has been said before,
exceptional in Spain. What Spain and Portugal excelled in was

70. *Narciso Tomé* : *Trasparente in the cathedral of Toledo, completed 1732*

this same extremism expressing itself in the piling of ornament on to surfaces. This ornamental mania had been a Spanish heritage ever since Mohammedan times, the Alhambra, and the Late Gothic of such works as the front of St Paul's at Valladolid (pl. 30b), but never yet had it taken quite such fantastic shapes as it now did in the so-called Churrigueresque style, named after its chief exponent José de Churriguera (1650–1725). The immediate inspiration of the barbaric scrolls and thick mouldings of, for instance, the Sacristy of the Charterhouse at Granada (1727–64; pl. 46; by Luis de Arévalo and F. Manuel Vasquez) must have been native art of Central or South America, as the immediate inspiration of the Manueline style in Portugal has been found in the East Indies. It is in fact in Mexico that the Spanish architects celebrated the wildest of all orgies of over-decoration.

The *Trasparente* stands on a higher aesthetic level no doubt than the incrustations of the Churrigueresque, though morally, especially to the Ruskinian morality of Late Victorian England, they may both be equally objectionable. Southern Germany in the 18th century was almost as fond of ornament for ornament's sake as Spain. There again the tradition leads back to the Middle Ages. But as it has been shown that German Late Gothic was fonder of spatial complexity than the late Gothic of any other country, so the exploitation of space became now the central problem of German Late Baroque, a problem occasionally solved with the knock-out technique of the *Trasparente*, but more often by purer strictly architectural means.

Two architects only out of the many working between 1720 and 1760 can here be introduced: Cosmas Damian Asam (1686–1739) and Johann Balthasar Neumann (1687–1753).

Cosmas Damian Asam was a painter and decorator, his brother Egid Quirin (1692–1750) a sculptor. The two as a rule worked together, not considered as anything but competent craftsmen and not apparently considering themselves as anything else either. They, and in common with them the majority of the German 18th-century architects, were not really architects in the Renaissance or modern sense. They were brought up in villages to know something about building, and that was enough. No big ideas about professional status entered their heads. In fact the sociological position of architecture in Germany before the 19th century was still medieval, and most of the patrons were still princes, bishops, abbots, just as they had been three hundred years earlier. Neumann belongs to another category, one that had not existed in the Middle Ages or the Renaissance. Its source is the France of Louis XIV, as will be shown later (see p. 214). He had started in the artillery force of the Prince-Bishop of Würzburg. There he had shown a keen interest in mathematics and fortification. Michelangelo too, it will be remembered, had worked on defence engineering, and some of the other leading 16th-century architects in Italy, e.g. Sammicheli, had been distinguished military engineers. The Prince-Bishop singled out young Neumann for architectural work, made him his surveyor of works, and sent him to Paris and Vienna to discuss the plans for his new palace at Würzburg with his opposite numbers there, the French king's and the Emperor's architects, and to learn from them. Thus his most famous work, the palace at Würzburg, is only partly his; but his experience grew, and the Bishop appreciated him more and more. He was made a captain, then a major, then a colonel, but he had no longer any duties of active service and could devote all his time to architecture. He did all the designing and supervising for the Bishop that had to be done, and was soon also asked to design palaces and churches for other clients.

Thus churches of the 18th century in Germany may originate from very different *milieus*: the workshop of the medieval craftsman or the drawing-board of the technically skilled courtier. Differences in architectural character may often be explained in this way. Asam churches are naïve, Neumann's are of an intellectual complexity equal to Bach's. Spatial effects, however, are as important in the Asams' as in Neumann's work. But the Asams stick to the more ostentatious devices of optical illusion (raising them, it is true, to a high emotional pitch), while Neumann composes his configurations of space scorning easy deceptions.

At Rohr near Regensburg the Asams, instead of a High Altar, placed in the chancel of the church a showpiece, cruder than

Bernini's St Teresa, and twice as melodramatic: the Apostles, life-size figures standing round a life-size Baroque sarcophagus, and the Virgin rising to Heaven supported by angels to be received into a glory of clouds and cherubs high above. Wild gesticulation and dark glowing colour all help to inflame the passions of faith. The chancel at Weltenburg, another church near Ratisbon, is the stage for a more mysterious apparition: a silver St George on horseback wielding a flame-shaped sword and riding straight towards us out of a background of dazzling light which is let in from concealed windows. The dragon and the princess stand out as dark golden silhouettes against all this glitter. Rohr was built in 1718–25, Weltenburg in 1717–21. They are early works of the Asams.

In their best later work they endeavoured to achieve more than a *Trasparente* effect. Egid Quirin owned a house at Munich; when he approached the age of forty he began to think of a monument that he might proudly leave behind after his death. So he decided in 1731 to build on a site adjoining his house a church as his private offering. The church was built from 1733 to about 1750 and dedicated to St John Nepomuk. It is a tiny church (pl. 47b) less than thirty feet wide, relatively tall and narrow with a narrow gallery all the way round, a ground-floor altar and a gallery altar. The gallery balancing on the fingers of pirouetting termini or caryatid angels sways forward and backward, the top cornice surges up and droops down, the colour scheme is of sombre gold, browns, and dark reds, glistening in sudden flashes where light falls on it, light which comes only from the entrance, that is from behind our backs, and from concealed windows above the cornice. The top east window is placed in such a way that a group of the Trinity appears against it; God holding the Crucifix, and the Holy Ghost above, the whole again surrounded by angels – wildly fantastic, yet of a superb magic reality. What raises St John Nepomuk above the level of Rohr, Weltenburg, and the *Trasparente* is the co-operation of strictly architectural composition with the merely optical deceptions to achieve an intense sensation of surprise which may turn easily into religious fervour.

But sensational it is all the same, sensational in a literal sense: no artists before Bernini, the Asams, and Tomé have aimed at such violent effects. And are they therefore debauched, unscrupulous, and pagan as our Pugins and Ruskins have made them out? We should not accept their verdicts uncritically, lest we might deprive ourselves of a good deal of legitimate pleasure. We may indeed, up here in the North where we live, find it hard to connect Christ and the Church with this obtruding physical closeness of presentation. To the Southerner, in Bavaria, in Austria, in Italy, in Spain, where people live so much more with all their senses, it is a genuine form of religious experience. While in the North during the lifetime of Bernini, the Asams, and Tomé, Spinoza visualized a pantheism, with God pervading all beings and all things, Rembrandt discovered the infinite for painting in his treatment of light and his merging of action into undefined but live background, and Newton and Leibniz discovered it for mathematics in their conception of the calculus, the South had its more concrete realization of an all-embracing oneness and a presence of the infinite in the architects' and decorators' unification of real and fictitious worlds, and in their spatial effects stepping beyond the bounds of what the beholder can rationally explain to himself. And Neumann's work proves conclusively what architectural purity and subtlety can be achieved by such spatial magic, provided the visitor to his buildings is able to follow his guidance. We of the 20th century do not usually find it easy to concentrate on spatial counterpoint, just as our audiences in church and concert no doubt hear musical counterpoint less distinctly than those for whom Bach wrote. The parallelism is in fact striking, in quality too. The best German 18th-century architecture is up to the standard of the best German 18th-century music.

Take Neumann's pilgrimage church of Vierzehnheiligen in Franconia, built from 1743 to 1772 (pl. 48 and figs. 71 to 73). The first impression on entering this vast, solitary pilgrimage church is one of bliss and elation. All is light: white, gold, pink. In this the church testifies to its later date than that of St John Nepomuk. Asam's work is still Baroque in the 17th-century sense, Neumann's belongs to that last phase of the Baroque which goes under the name Rococo. For the Rococo is not a separate style. It is part of the Baroque, as Decorated is part of the Gothic style. The difference of Baroque and Rococo is only one of sublimation. The later phase is light, where the earlier was sombre; delicate, where the earlier was forceful; playful, where the earlier was passionate. But it is just as *mouvementé*, as vivacious, as voluptuous as the Baroque. One connects the term Rococo chiefly with France and the age of Casanova on the one hand, Voltaire on the other. In Germany it is not intellectually or sensually sophisticated – it is as direct an expression of the people's aesthetic instinct as late Gothic architecture and decoration had been, and one can see from the devotion to-day of the peasants in these German Baroque – and the Italian Baroque – churches that their style is not a style of interest only to a privileged set of virtuosi.

Yet the style of Vierzehnheiligen is not an easy style. It is not enough to be overwhelmed by it, as anyone may be in Asam churches; it asks for an exact understanding – which is a job for the expert: architects' architecture, as the fugue is musicians' music. The oval central altar in the middle of the nave may well please the rustic worshippers who kneel round this gorgeous object, half a coral reef and half a fairy sedan chair. Having taken in this glory of confectionery, the layman will then look up and see on all sides glittering decoration, surf and froth and rocket, and like it immensely. But if he starts walking round, he will soon find himself in utter confusion. What he has learned and so often seen of nave and aisle and chancel seems of no value here. This confusion of the lay mind, a keen thrill of the trained, is due to the ground plan, one of the most ingenious pieces of architectural design ever conceived (figs. 71–73). The church, if one looks at it from outside, has apparently a nave and aisles, and a centrally-planned east end with polygonal ends to transepts and choir. In fact the choir is an oval, the transepts are circular, and the nave consists of two ovals following each other so that the first, into which one enters immediately one has passed the Borrominesque undulating front, is of the size of the choir oval and the second

71, 72, and 73. Balthasar Neumann: *Vierzehnheiligen in Franconia, begun 1743. Section (without west towers), plan on ground-floor level, plan of vaults*

considerably larger. It is here that the altar of the fourteen saints stands. Here then is the spiritual centre of the church. So there arises an antagonism of great poignancy between what the exterior promises as the centre and what the interior reveals to be the centre – namely between the crossing where nave and transepts meet, and the centre of the principal oval. As for the aisles they are nothing but spatial residues. Walking along them, one feels painfully behind the scenes. What matters alone is the interaction of the ovals. At vault height they are separated by transverse arches. These, however, are not simple bands across from one arcade column to the one opposite. They are three-dimensional, bowing to each other, as the nodding arches had done on a small scale in the 14th century. This has the most exciting and baffling effect at the crossing. Here in a church of the Gesù type – and Vierzehnheiligen appears from outside to belong to this type – one would expect a dome, the summit of the composition. Instead of that, there lies, as has been said before, just at the centre of the crossing, the point where choir oval and central oval meet. The two transverse arches struck from the piers of the crossing bend, the western one eastward, the eastern westward, until they touch each other in exactly the same place as the ovals, purposely emphasizing the fact that, where a normal Baroque church would have had the crest of the undulating movement of the vaults, Vierzehn-heiligen has a trough – a most effective spatial counterpoint. Yet another spatial complication is incidentally provided by the insertion of a second minor transept farther west than the main one. Side altars are placed in it, just as altars stand against the east end of the church and against the east piers of the crossing. The latter are set diagonally so as to guide the eye towards the splendid high altar – a decidedly theatrical effect.

This is one of the chief objections against such churches. Its validity has already been queried. Besides, why did architects and artists so fervently strive to deceive and create such intense illusion of reality? What reality was the Church concerned with? Surely that of the Divine Presence. It is the zeal of an age in which Roman Catholic dogmas, mysteries, and miracles were no longer, as they had been in the Middle Ages, accepted as truth by all. There were heretics, and there were sceptics. To restore the first to the fold, to convince the others, religious architecture had both to inflame and to mesmerize. But it is brought forward as another argument against Baroque churches that they seem worldly as compared with the churches of the Middle Ages. Now it is true that the character of Baroque decoration in a church and a palace is identical. But is not exactly the same true of the Middle Ages? The idea behind the identity is perfectly sane. By the splendour of the arts we honour a king; is not supreme splendour due to the King of Kings? In our churches to-day and in those churches of the Middle Ages which the 19th century restored, there is nothing of this. They are halls with an atmosphere to concentrate the thoughts of a congregation on worship and prayer. A church of the Baroque was literally the house of the Lord.

Still, there is no denying the fact that we, observers or believers, never feel quite sure where in a church such as Vierzehnheiligen the spiritual ends and the worldly begins. The ecstatic *élan* of the architectural forms at large is irresistible, but it is not necessarily a religious *élan*. There was, it is true, a real mania in Southern Germany and Austria between 1700 and 1760 for building vast churches and monasteries. However, not all this building was done entirely *ad majorem Dei gloriam*. Did a monastery like Weingarten near the lake of Constance really need these far-stretched, elegantly curved outbuildings which appear in a rebuilding scheme of 1723 (fig. 74)? This scheme was never carried out; but others – e.g. at Klosterneuburg, St Florian, and Melk, all three on the Danube – were. Melk was begun in 1702 by Jacob Prandtauer (died 1726); it is in many ways the most remarkable of the three (pl. 49b), shooting up out of the rocks, steep above the river. The church with its undulating front, its two many-pinnacled towers and its bulbous spires is set back. Two pavilions of the monastery buildings, housing the marble hall and the library, jut forward to its right and left converging as they approach the front bastion. They are here connected by lower roughly semicircular wings. Between these, exactly in line with the church, is an oddly Palladian arch to keep the vista open from the west

portal towards the river. It is an exquisite piece of visual cal-
culation – a late and subtle development of Palladio's so much
simpler connecting of villa and landscape, and evidently the
work of the century which discovered landscape gardening
(see pp. 231 *seqq.*).

But, to return to our question, while the towering church on
the cliff – a Durham of the Baroque – may rightly be considered a monument of militant catholicism, the palaces for

74. *Plan for the rebuilding of the monastery of Weingarten,* 1723

abbot and monks with their richly ornamented saloons and
their terraces are amenities of this world, on exactly the same
level, and planned and executed in exactly the same lavish
manner, as the contemporary palaces of the secular and clerical
rulers of the innumerable states of the Holy Roman Empire or
the country palaces of the English aristocracy, or Caserta, the
palace of the King of Naples, or Stupinigi, the palace of the
Duke of Savoy and King of Sardinia.

One of the most irresponsible of these schemes is the
Zwinger in Dresden, built by Mathäus Daniel Pöppelmann
(1662–1736) for the Elector Augustus the Strong, athlete,
glutton, and lecher. The Zwinger (pl. 49a) – very badly damaged in 1944 and in course of restoration now – is a combined

orangery and electoral grandstand for tournaments and pageants. It was not supposed to stand on its own, as it does now, attached only to the 19th-century picture gallery; it was meant to form part of a palace stretching across to the River Elbe. It consists of one-storied galleries with two-storied pavilions between. The galleries are comparatively restrained in design, but the most exuberant decoration is lavished over the pavilions. The gate pavilion especially is a fantasy unchecked by any consideration of use. The ground-floor archway has instead of a proper pediment two bits of a broken pediment swinging away from each other. The first-floor pediment is broken too, but nodding inward instead of outward. The whole first floor is open on all sides – a kiosk or gazebo, as it were, and above its attic swarming with figures of putti is a bulbous cupola with the royal and electoral emblems on top.

If those who can admire a Gothic Devon screen feel repelled by the Zwinger, they either do not really look at the object before them, or they look at it with the blinkers of puritanism. What an exultation in these rocking curves, and yet what a grace! It is joyful, but never vulgar; vigorous, boisterous perhaps, but never crude. It is of an inexhaustible creative power, with ever new combinations and variations of Italian Baroque forms placed against each other and piled above each other. The forward and backward motion never stops. Borromini appears massive against this swiftness of movement through space.

As in every original style, the same formal intention seems, in the German Rococo, to model space and volume. The three-dimensional curve is the *leitmotif* of the period. It appears at Vierzehnheiligen as it appears in the Zwinger, and it pervades buildings from their main theme of composition down to the smallest ornamental details. Nowhere else perhaps can this be seen as convincingly as in one of Neumann's secular masterpieces, the staircase of the Bishop's Palace at Bruchsal (pl. 50, 51a and fig. 76). The palace itself is not by Neumann. It was in quite an advanced state when in 1730 Neumann was called in to redesign the staircase.

The palace, one of the most deplorable of all war casualties, consisted of a rectangular centre block or *corps de logis* and lower projecting wings, i.e. the Palladian scheme which had

75. *Enrique de Egas: staircase in the Holy Cross Hospital, Toledo, 1504–14*

spread from Northern Italy to England and also to France, where it has been modified and then, in its revised shape with the space between the wings treated as a formal *cour d'honneur*, taken over by Germany. In the centre of the *corps de logis* is the staircase, an oval room, larger than any other in the palace. This alone is a most significant fact.

In the Middle Ages staircases had mattered little. They were nearly always tucked away – a purely utilitarian part of the building. Newel staircases taking up as little space as possible were the rule. The very latest phase of the Gothic style with its new appreciation of space had sometimes tried to endow them with spatial expression, emphasizing the delights of ever-changing axes. The culmination is such French staircases as that of Blois (pl. 52b)[1] and the splendid interior double-newel staircase – two parallel spirals within the same well – in the centre of the symmetrical palace of Chambord. But the staircase at Chambord may well be derived from an idea of Leonardo da Vinci, who died at Amboise, only 25 miles from Chambord, in the very year in which the château was begun. There are such double and even quadruple and octuple staircases amongst his sketches. However, Leonardo, as in his painting and sculpture, has a freedom and a sense of movement in his spatial conceptions that was quite unique in the Italian Renaissance. He alone reached out to combine Gothic and Renaissance ideals in a new unity closely approaching the Baroque.

Otherwise the Italian Renaissance was on the whole not favourable to developments of the staircase. It is too dynamic a motif to meet with the approval of Renaissance architects. Alberti says this of staircases: 'Scalae, quo erunt numero pauciores . . . quoque occupabunt minus areae . . . eo erunt commodiores' ('The less staircases there are in a building and the less space they take up, the better'). Thus the standard Renaissance staircase is one of two flights running up first to the intermediate landing between solid walls, then turning by 180 degrees and reaching the upper floor by the second flight also between solid walls. Such staircases, as they occur from Brunelleschi's Foundling Hospital to the Palazzo Farnese and beyond, are really only vaulted corridors running up at an angle.

1. Their origin was the famous late 14th-century *Vis du Louvre* in Paris.

A more imaginative treatment is rare in 15th-century Italy. Nothing survives that would be worth mentioning. But Francesco di Giorgio, whose treatise written in the 'seventies has been mentioned before, apropos the history of central planning, illustrates suggested plans of palaces, and in two of these shows staircases of new types – and, indeed, of types which were to become of the greatest importance for the centuries to come.

Their introduction into real architecture, however, or at any rate their popularization, was due to a more restless country than Italy : Spain. The first and most important of these new types is the square newel staircase, with three straight flights of steps around a spacious open well and the landing on the fourth side. This type occurs for the first time after Francesco de Giorgio in Enrique de Egas's part of S. Juan de los Reyes at Toledo (completed 1504), the Hospital of the Holy Cross also at Toledo and also by Egas (1504–14; fig. 75), and in Michele Carlone's castle of Lacalahorra (1508–12). A few years later Diego Siloée erected the magnificent Escalera Dorada inside the cathedral of Burgos, developed essentially on a T-plan, i.e. starting with one straight flight and then forking at the landing at an angle of 90 degrees to the left and right. The derivation of this plan from Bramante's outdoor staircase in the vast Belvedere Court of the Vatican has been proved, but again Francesco de Giorgio had come before Bramante (no doubt influencing him). He suggests the same type of staircase for a Palazzo di Republica – in exactly the same position, incidentally, in which much later such staircases were popular in Genoese palaces.

Meanwhile, however, Spain had introduced yet another type, the grandest of all, and in this case no Italian precedent has so far been discovered. It is the type known as the Imperial Staircase. It runs in a large oblong cage, starting with one straight arm and then, after the landing, turning by 180 degrees and leading up to the upper floor with two arms to the left and right of, and parallel with, the first arm (or starting with two and finishing with one). This type appears to my knowledge for the first time in Juan Bautista de Toledo's and Francisco de Herrera's Escorial (1563–84). It is eminently characteristic that

these staircases, in which space is experienced most vividly by
those who ascend them or descend them, were developed outside Italy. If we examine the best 16th-century staircases in Italy,
we find that Bramante's delightful Vatican staircase is of the
traditional newel type, though with a wide open well and of
gentle rise and generous measurements. Serlio and Palladio

76. *Bruchsal, Episcopal Palace. The central staircase by Balthasar Neumann,*
1732

followed Bramante in this, although they knew and used
the square three-flight type. However, their hearts were not
in staircase design. Their only innovations are the newel staircase elongated into an oval shape (Maderna incidentally kept to
this in the Barberini Palace (fig. 63)) and the flight of stairs cor-
belled out of the wall without any inner support on the side of
the open wall. The Baroque of the 17th century, especially in
France, only enriched the current types (see page 223). That
of the Escorial became in many variations the hall-mark of

princely magnificence. Neumann's Würzburg staircase with its Tiepolo paintings belongs to it.

But the staircase at Bruchsal is unique. Words can hardly re-evoke the enchanting sensation experienced by anybody who has had the good fortune to walk up one of its two arms, when it still existed undamaged by war. The arms started in the rectangular vestibule. After about ten steps one entered the oval. On the ground floor it is a sombre room, painted with rocks in the rustic manner of Italian grotto imitations. The staircase itself then unfolded between two curved walls, the outside wall solid, that on the inside opened in arcades through which one looked down into the semi-darkness of the oval grotto. The height of the arcade openings of course diminished as the staircase ascended. And while you walked up, it grew lighter and lighter around you, until you reached the main floor and a platform the size of the oval room beneath. But the vault above covered the larger oval formed by the outer walls of the staircase. Thus the platform with its balustrade separating it from the two staircase arms seemed to rise in mid-air, con-nected only by bridges with the two principal saloons. And the vast vault above was lit by many windows, painted with the gayest of frescoes and decorated with a splendid fireworks of stucco. The spatial rapture of the staircase was in this decora-tion transformed into ornamental rapture. It culminated in the cartouche over the door leading into the Grand Saloon (pl. 51b). The cartouche was not Neumann's design. It was by a Bavarian stuccoist, Johann Michael Feichtmayr. The contract was made in 1752. These Bavarian stuccoists nearly all came from the same village of Wessobrunn, where boys were as a matter of course trained to become proficient in stucco work, just as the decorators of Romanesque churches so often came from certain villages round the North Italian lakes, the makers and vendors of plaster-of-Paris statuettes in the 19th century from Savoy, and the onion-men of to-day from Brittany. Feichtmayr travelled about from job to job, and, when he worked for a monastery, still received wages and board just as the workmen did seven hundred years ago. Neumann must have met him on some job and have recognized his immense wealth of ornamental inventiveness. He appears at Vierzehn-heiligen as well as at Bruchsal. In his stucco ornament not one part is symmetrical. The main composition is a zig-zag, from the alluring young angel on the right, up to the cupid or cherub higher up on the left, and up again to the cherub at the top. The forms in detail seem to be incessantly changing, splashing up and sinking back. What are they? Do they represent anything? Sometimes they look like shells, sometimes like froth, sometimes like gristle, sometimes like flames. This kind of ornament is called *rocaille* in France, where it was invented in the 1720's by Meissonier, Oppenord, and a few others of provincial or semi-Italian background. It has given the Rococo style its name, and rightly so; for it is a completely original creation, not dependent on anything of the past, as the ornament of the Renaissance had been. It is abstract art of as high an expressional value as any that we are offered to-day so much more pretentiously.

Bruchsal with its perfect unity of space and decoration was the high water mark of the Baroque style. It was also its end. For only a few years after it had been completed and Neumann had died, Winckelmann published his first books, initiating the Classical Revival in Germany. Between Neumann's world and that of Goethe there is no link. The men of the new world no longer thought in terms of churches and palaces. No church designed anywhere after 1760 is amongst the historically leading examples of architecture. Napoleon built no palaces.

The English nobility, it must be admitted, did; right into the Victorian age. But they had nothing of the unreflecting attitude of the Baroque. This change from a style binding for all and understood by all to a style for the educated only did not take place in Germany and Italy until 1760. In France and Britain it had come about earlier. But then neither France nor Britain (nor the north of Germany, Holland, Denmark, and Scandinavia) had ever accepted the Baroque with all its implications. Their world – it is in many respects *the* modern world – is that of Protestantism. In Roman Catholic countries medieval traditions lived and flourished down to the 18th century. In the North the Reformation had broken that happy unity. But it had also opened the way for independent thinking and feeling. The Protestant countries (and one should include here the France of the Gallicans, Jansenists, and Encyclopaedists) had created Puritanism, Enlightenment, the modern predominance of experimental science, and finally the Industrial Revolution in the material and the symphony in the spiritual world. What the cathedral had been to the Middle Ages, the symphony was to the 19th century.

CHAPTER SEVEN

Britain and France from the 16th to the 18th Century

AT the time of Bruchsal and the *Trasparente*, large houses of Palladian or Neo-Classical style appeared all over England, houses such as Prior Park, near Bath, Holkham Hall, Stowe, and Kenwood. In France meanwhile the classic grandeur of Versailles had given way to the Neo-Classical delicacy of the Place de la Concorde and the Petit Trianon. Evidently the development of architecture after the end of the Gothic style had been very different in Western Europe from that in Central Europe.

Yet in Britain, France, the Netherlands, Spain, and Germany, the position had been virtually the same early in the 16th century. In all these countries artists at the same moment turned their backs on their Gothic past, attracted by the same new style, the Italian Renaissance. Everywhere during the 15th century the fascination of Humanism, of Roman literature, and the clarity and suppleness of the classic Latin style had been experienced by scholars. The invention of printing helped to spread the new ideals, and many patrons arose among princes, noblemen, and merchants. A few of these, when for some reason or other they found themselves in Italy, were converted to Italian art as well, as soon as they had understood its humanistic character. How forceful the sensation must have been it is hardly possible for us to appreciate. One keeps forgetting that it was still a time of scanty and slow communications. Perpendicular to the English, Flamboyant to the French, and their national versions of Late Gothic to the Spaniards and Germans were the only architecture they knew. Now all of a sudden, when Charles VIII of France set out on his campaign against Italy in 1494, marched right across the country and captured Naples, or when Dürer, the greatest of German painters, went to Venice in the same year as a young man of twenty-three, they were faced with a style that made all they had known appear confused, crabbed, and petty. At the same time, however, these airy, spacious halls, these bold square palaces, these columns, balusters, and round-headed arches, these garlands and laurel wreaths and cupids were so disconcertingly novel that it took even the most progressive many years to digest them. Charles VIII, under whom the French Army had first invaded Italy, died in 1498. Hardly any work of his reign survives in France in which Italian motifs occur. He had, however, called Italian workmen into the country, and from about 1500 onwards we find them entrusted with a good deal of decorative architectural work. Similarly in Spain some of the noble families, notably the Mendoza, had been converted to the new style, and Renaissance portals or courtyards appear here and there already in the 'eighties (Cogolludo, Valladolid, etc.), and more often between 1500 and 1510 (e.g. the Hospital of the Holy Cross at Toledo, see p. 183). During the next decade, or more precisely in 1506, Dürer went to Venice a second time, now to start embellishing his pictures and engravings with Italian ornament. Again only one or two years later Quentin Matsys, the leading artist of Antwerp, introduced Southern motifs into his works. And in 1509 Henry VII had an agreement drawn up with an Italian sculptor, Giulio Mazzini, called Paganino, who then worked at the French court, to carve his tomb. The job did not materialize, but in 1512 Henry VIII found another Italian, Pietro Torrigiani, a fellow-student of Michelangelo in Florence, to design the tomb for his father. As Torrigiani carved it, so it now stands in Henry VII's Chapel in Westminster Abbey (fig. 77), a stranger in the midst of the wonders of Gothic ingenuity that surround it. No more poignant contrast can be imagined than that between Perpendicular panels and these medallions surrounded by wreaths, Perpendicular piers and these daintily ornamental pilasters, Perpendicular mouldings and the Antique mouldings of this base and this cornice, or Perpendicular foliage and the smiling beauty of these roses and acanthus friezes.

One should however keep in mind that, when France,

England, Spain, and Germany discovered the loveliness of this style and made a fashion of it, it was already a style of the past in Italy. What the architecture of 1520 was like in Rome has been shown. Bramante, Raphael, and their followers had discarded most of that pretty ornament and turned towards a grave classic ideal. For this, time was not ripe yet – in France for some twenty years, and in Britain for nearly a hundred.

77. *Pietro Torrigiani: tomb of Henry VII at Westminster Abbey, designed in* 1512

Early Renaissance was in full blossom this side of the Alps, when on the other side art and architecture had already passed the summit of High Renaissance. Michelangelo's Medici Chapel and Laurenziana with their Mannerist discords are earlier than the most exquisite piece of Italian decoration surviving in England, the stalls of King's College Chapel, Cambridge, of *c.* 1532–36 (pl. 78). Again the contrast between the only slightly older chapel itself and this addition from abroad is striking. And as the one was in the idiom with which everybody had grown up, while the other seemed to speak a foreign language, it is understandable that English patrons wavered between admiration and bewilderment. Very few were prepared to go the whole way (more in fact in France, where there was less of a racial contrast than in England), and those who did had to rely on craftsmen from Italy, because the English or even the French mason could not at once get into a manner so novel both technically and spiritually.

Now of Italians there were more and more who found their way into France and were welcomed by Francis I, but few who travelled on to Britain. Leonardo da Vinci died in France, Primaticcio came in 1532, Serlio in 1540. They were all painters and not trained for building in the medieval sense. They only designed, and for the execution of their designs had to rely on the native master masons. A deep antagonism developed at once between the Italians and the competent traditional craftsmen of France to whom these Italian intruders were mountebanks and jacks-of-all-trades. So the new ideal of the artist-architect entered France in this interesting form of a struggle between the builder and the decorator.

However, the contrast does not often appear in actual buildings. For – again probably thanks to racial affinity – the French master masons very soon adopted the Italian vocabulary and used it to produce an essentially original style neither Gothic nor Renaissance. Two stages can be distinguished: the first that of the Loire school, the second that of Lescot's work at the Louvre. The wing of Francis I at Blois (pl. 52b) was built between 1515 and about 1525. Every motif used in its decoration is of the North Italian Early Renaissance. On the other hand the fact that it is a newel staircase and that its vertical supports are scarcely disguised buttresses is medieval. Yet the emphasis on horizontal divisions, the even stronger emphasis on the top cornice, the comfortably gradual ascent of the staircase, and the arcaded galleries along the whole garden front prove that the designer of Blois, a Frenchman for all we know, had a feeling for what the Renaissance meant.

The attitude of English architects was characteristically different. Hampton Court had been begun in 1515 for Cardinal Wolsey. In 1529 Wolsey thought it wise to make a

9

present of the palace to his king. Henry added to it, amongst other parts, the Great Hall (fig. 78). Now the palace with its courtyard and gate towers is just as completely in the

78. *Hampton Court: Great Hall, detail from the hammerbeam roof, 1533.*
Probably by James Needham

Gothic tradition as the hall with its hammerbeam roof. Of the Italian Renaissance there is nothing but a limited number of ornamental details, the medallions with the heads of Roman emperors on the gate towers and the putti and foliage in the spandrels of the hall roof. They are competently done, but no attempt is made to bridge the gulf between English construction and Italian decoration.

So while the first stage in the process of assimilation had been identical in Britain and France, their ways separated at the second already. The distance widened at the third. In the 'thirties two or three of the most talented French architects of the younger generation, Philibert Delorme (*c.* 1515–70), Jean Bullant (*c.* 1515–80), and perhaps Pierre Lescot (*c.* 1510–78), had gone to Rome, where they had devoted their time to the study of Antiquity and the Renaissance, and in 1545 Serlio had begun to publish parts of his treatise on architecture in French at Lyons. Thus the façade of the Louvre towards the court designed by Lescot in 1546 is both classical and French (pl. 53b). Italian forms are handled with ease and at the same time with a freedom which proves that they had become the architect's natural idiom. The central motif especially is beyond a doubt of Italian origin: the triumphal arch motif with coupled columns in superimposed orders and niches between each pair. The motif goes back to Bramante, if not further, and was also used by Bullant at Ecouen (*c.* 1550) and by Delorme at Anet (also *c.* 1550). The pediments on brackets above windows and the garlands held by cupids are also of Italian stock, but there is an agility in the presentation, a polish and a graceful splendour, that are French in the extreme. The segmental pediment especially, so sharply drawn and yet so smooth, with the two female figures holding with an inimitable rhetorical ostentation the shield with Henri II's crowned initial, would be impossible in Rome, where at that time Michelangelo placed his mighty cornice on the Farnese palace; impossible also in Northern Italy, where Palladio built the first of his serene villas and palaces, and utterly impossible in both Spain and England.

For Spain after her early welcome of the severest Italian 16th-century classicism (see page 141) had almost at once relapsed into the ornamental vagaries of her past. The austerity of the Escorial, Philip II's vast castle-monastery, with its seventeen courts and its 670 feet of frontage without any decoration, is exceptional. What meets the traveller everywhere is the

Plateresque, a wildly mixed style of Gothic, Mohammedan, and Early Renaissance ingredients, spread over façades and

79. *Salamanca: portal of the university, c.* 1525–30

inner walls as irresponsibly as ever. The Renaissance had evidently not yet been grasped in its meaning (fig. 79).

Almost the same happened in the Netherlands and Germany.

An international centre such as Antwerp might put up a town
hall (1561–65, by Cornelis Floris, fig. 80), tall, grave, square,
of considered proportions, and with a three-bay centre of
proud Italian display. The motif of the coupled columns with
Ionic correctly placed on top of Tuscan and Corinthian on top
of Ionic and the niches between may have been seen by the
architect in France rather than Italy, or else it may come from
Serlio. The date of the Antwerp Town Hall is too early to
make it probable or even possible that another of the popular

0 20 40 60 80 100 *feet*

80. *Cornelis Floris: Antwerp Town Hall, 1561–65*

and soon apparently indispensable Books of Orders or general
Books of Architecture served as a model: Hans Blum's *Five
Orders* of 1550, Ducerceau's *Livre d'Architecture* of 1559,
Vignola's *Rule of the Five Orders* of 1562, Bullant's *Règle
Générale des Cinque Manières* of 1564, Delorme's *Architecture* of
1568, or Palladio's *Architecture* of 1570. How characteristic of
the ruling style of Mannerism this sudden outcrop of books on
theory is has been pointed out before. It must however be emphasized here to what extent France shared in the new zest for
publication. Germany, in the person of the humble Blum,
made her voice heard, and England took part too, in a somewhat homespun way, with John Shute's *Chief Groundes of*

Architecture, published in 1563, and with John Thorpe's drawings at the Soane Museum in London, done no doubt with an
eye to publication but never printed. They were worked on
late in the 16th and even in the first years of the 17th century,
and Thorpe derived as much inspiration from French and
Italian books as he did from the fantastic ornamental pattern
books of the Netherlands, especially those by Vredeman de
Vries which came out in 1565 and 1568.

These pattern books summed up what is the most remarkable contribution of Flanders and Holland to the style of Mannerism, a novel language of ornament known as bandwork or
strapwork. Floris in his town hall handles it with discretion. It
hardly appears in the towering gable with its obelisks, scrolls,
and caryatid pilasters, the finishing flourish to this ponderous
building, and a motif entirely in the Northern medieval tradition. But in the smaller town halls, guild halls, and market halls,
and the private houses of the Netherlands these gables, the
leitmotif of the 16th and early 17th centuries, are overcrowded
with strapwork. The provincial decorator-architects were not
prepared to give up any of the exuberance to which the Flamboyant of the 15th century had accustomed them. And instead
of making up an *olla podrida* of Gothic and Renaissance, such as
the Spanish did in their Plateresque, they were headstrong and
imaginative enough to invent something for themselves. For
invention these forms must be called, even if they can be traced
back to such Mannerist detail as that round the top windows of
the Palazzo Massimi (pl. 38a), and to the work of the Italian
decorators at Fontainebleau. They consist chiefly of somewhat
stocky thick-set curves of fretwork or leather-strap appearance
(fig. 81), sometimes flat, but more often three-dimensional and
contrasted with naturalistic garlands and caryatids. The popu-
larity of the strapwork style soon spread into the adjacent
countries – not to France of course, but to Germany as well as
England.

To understand Elizabethan and Jacobean architecture in
England one has to be familiar with the three sources just mentioned: the Italian Early Renaissance, the Loire style in France
and the strapwork decoration of Flanders. This wide-awak

interest in so many foreign developments is the aesthetic equivalent of England's new international outlook since Queen Elizabeth, Gresham, and Burghley. However, one has also to remember all the time that a strong Perpendicular tradition, the tradition of the picturesque, asymmetrical, stone-gabled manor-house with its mullioned windows and its extreme ornamental restraint, was still alive. Thus English architecture between 1530 and 1620 is a composite phenomenon, with French and Flemish elements prevailing where we are near the court, and English traditions as soon as we get away from it. Much of it is derivative, both in the sense of imitation and of conservatism, but occasionally a new expression is developed as original and as nationally characteristic as Lescot's Louvre.

81. *Typical Flemish and Dutch strapwork ornament of the later 16th century (from the Rhineland County Hall, Leiden, 1596–98)*

Burghley House, near Stamford, is the work of William Cecil, Lord Burghley, Queen Elizabeth's trusted adviser and friend. It is a mighty rectangle of about 160 by 200 feet with an inner courtyard. The central feature of this courtyard is a three-storied pavilion, dated 1585 (pl. 53a). It is again designed on the French triumphal arch motif with the typically French niches between the coupled columns. It has three orders, correctly applied; but on the third floor between the Corinthian columns there sits an utterly incongruous English mullioned and transomed bay window (the English have at no time been happy without bay windows) and above that the pavilion shoots out bits of strapwork and obelisks – a crop of Flemish decoration. The analysis of style is confirmed by documentary evidence. We know that no architect in a modern sense was wholly responsible for the building. Lord Burghley himself must have made a good many of the suggestions embodied in the design. He represents a coming type: the architectural dilettante. In 1568 he wrote to Paris for a book on architecture, and some years later he wrote again specifying one particular French book which he desired. On the other hand it is also certain that workmen for Burghley came from the Netherlands and that a certain amount of work was actually done at Antwerp and then shipped to England. Thus Flemish as well as French motifs are easily accounted for. What is harder to understand is why this happy-go-lucky mixing up of foreign phrases with the English vernacular (the chimney stacks are coupled Tuscan Doric columns complete with entablature) does not appear disjointed. The England of Queen Elizabeth – this is all that can be said by way of an explanation – possessed such an overflowing vitality and was so eager to take in all that was sufficiently adventurous and picturesque and in some cases mannered that it could digest what would have caused serious trouble to a weaker age.

However, while Burghley (and Wollaton Hall of 1580 and the entrance side of Hatfield of 1605–12) are spectacular and stimulating enough, the real strength of English building lay in less outlandish designs. One of the earliest, if not the earliest, in an unmistakable Elizabethan style is Longleat in Wiltshire, begun in 1567 (pl. 54a). Here you find strapwork only very inconspicuously on the top balustrade. The portal is small and in the Italian style; with its Tuscan Doric columns it appears surprisingly restrained. Ornament is sparingly used. The effect is one of sturdy squareness. The roof is flat, the hundreds of many-mullioned, many-transomed windows are straight-headed, and the bay windows project only slightly and have straight sides. This English squareness and the predominance of large expanses of window create sometimes, for instance at Hardwick Hall and even more in the garden side of Hatfield House, a curiously modern, that is 20th-century, effect. More often these large windows, the windows of Perpendicular tradition, are combined with the plain customary English triangular gables. Small houses of this type are still as asymmetrical as of old, larger houses are symmetrical at least in plan, of Ⅼ or Ⅎ shape or, if larger, still developed round courtyards. There is a great deal of difference between Longleat and Burghley, but it took a William Cecil and a Raleigh, a Shakespeare and a Spenser, and many clear-minded, hard-headed, and strong-bodied businessmen to make up the England of Elizabeth. Yet it is one England, of one spirit and one style in building, vigorous, prolific, somewhat boastful, of a healthy and hearty soundness which, it is true, is sometimes coarse and sometimes dull – but never effeminate and never hysterical.

Compared with the gulf that separates buildings like Burghley House (or Audley End of 1603–16, or Hatfield House) from Inigo Jones's supreme achievements, the Queen's House at Greenwich, designed in 1616, though not completed until immediately before the Civil War, and the Banqueting House in Whitehall of 1619–22, the change in English architecture between 1500 and 1530 seems almost negligible. Only now England experienced what France had experienced before the middle of the 16th century, and experienced it far more startlingly, because Inigo Jones transplanted whole buildings of purely Italian character into England, where such men as Lescot, Delorme, and Bullant had only transplanted features and – up to a point – the spirit that stood behind them.

Inigo Jones (1573–1652) began, it seems, as a painter. At the age of thirty-one he appears as a designer of costumes and stage-settings for one of the masques which were a favourite entertainment of the court at that period. He became soon the accepted theatrical designer to the royal family. Plenty of drawings for masques exist. They are brilliantly done, the costumes of that fantastic kind which the Baroque connected with ancient history and mythology, the stage-settings nearly all in the classical Italian style. Jones had, perhaps, been in Italy about 1600, interested probably more in painting and architectural decoration than in architecture proper. Then, however, the Prince of Wales made him his surveyor, i.e. architect, as did a short time later the Queen, and, in 1613, the King. So he went back to Italy, this time, we know from his sketch-books, to study Italian buildings seriously. His ideal was Palladio: an edition of Palladio annotated by Jones is preserved.

Looking back from the Queen's House (pl. 54b) – a villa in the Italian sense, out at Greenwich – to Palladio's Palazzo Chiericati (pl. 39a), the close connection of style is evident, though nothing is copied. In fact we find nowhere in Jones's work mere imitation. What he had learned from Palladio and the Roman architects of the early 16th century is to regard a building as a whole, organized throughout – in plan and elevation – according to rational rules. But the Queen's House has not the weight of the Roman Renaissance or Baroque palace. It was originally even less compact than Palladio's country houses, for it was not a complete block, as it is now, but consisted of two rectangles standing to the right and the left of the main Dover Road and connected with each other only by a bridge (the present centre room on the first floor) across the road – a curious, if not unique, composition of a spatially most effective openness. In contrast to this freedom in general plan, the strictest symmetry governs the grouping of the rooms. Now in Elizabethan country houses we find the decision already taken to tidy up façades into more or less complete symmetry. One may even come across blocked windows and similar contrivances to force into outward symmetry what could not be made to match inside. For wholly symmetrical plans were still rare by 1610, although the trend towards them is unmistakable. In this Inigo Jones is the logical successor to the Jacobeans. But if one takes his elevations, their dignified plainness is in stronger contrast to the Jacobean animation by windows of varying sizes, bay windows, rounded and polygonal, dormer windows, gables, and high-pitched roofs. The centre portion of the Queen's House with the loggia projects slightly: that is the only movement of the wall surface. The ground floor is rusticated, the top floor smooth. A balustrade sets the façade off against the sky. The windows are thoughtfully proportioned. There is no ornament anywhere but the delicately moulded cornices above the first-floor windows.

This was a principle with Inigo Jones. He wrote on Jan. 20, 1614: 'Ye outward ornaments oft to be sollid, proporsionable according to the rulles, masculine and unaffected.' The character of the Queen's House could not be better described. And Jones knew that in building thus he was holding up an ideal not only in opposition to contemporary Britain but also to contemporary Rome, i.e. the Baroque. 'All thes composed ornaments,' he added, 'the which Proceed out of ye aboundance of dessigners and wear brought in by Michill Angell and his followers in my oppignion do not well in solid Architecture.' Yet he did not despise ornament altogether. He uses it inside the Queen's House and, with luxurious exuberance, in the so-called double-cube room at Wilton House. Even there, however, there is nothing crowded. The form of his wreaths and garlands of flowers and fruit is compact. They fit into clear-cut panels, and never overgrow the structural divisions of a room. Again, Jones was fully aware of the contrast between his simple exteriors and his rich interiors. He wrote: 'Outwardly every wyse man carrieth a graviti in Publicke Places, yet inwardly hath his imaginacy set on fire, and sumtimes licenciously flying out, as nature hirself doeth often times stravagantly', and demands the same attitude in a good building. And once more the way in which he puts his observation is personal to a degree inconceivable in an architect in England in Elizabethan and Jacobean days. For Inigo Jones is the first English architect in the modern sense. He achieved in this country what the earliest artist-architects had achieved in Italy at the beginning of the Renaissance. And as one is interested in Alberti or Leonardo da Vinci as individuals, so the genius of Inigo Jones makes one deplore over and over again how little is known of his personality.

Of Jones's other works – and those attributed to him with some degree of certainty – only two more can be mentioned. One is Lindsay House in Lincoln's Inn Fields, because with its rusticated ground floor and its giant order of pilasters above, supporting entablature and top balustrade, it is the prototype for a whole series of representational English town houses down to the Royal Crescent at Bath (pl. 56c) and Nash's

Regent's Park terraces. The other is the layout of Covent Garden, with its tall houses, dignified and unadorned, open in galleries on the ground floor, which Jones had taken from a *piazza* at Leghorn (in fact Covent Garden was known in Evelyn's and Pepys's time as the Piazza), because it is the first of the regularly-planned London squares. Its west side was centred on the small church of St Paul's with its low, very grave, Antique portico, a design inspired by the Italian 16th-century books on architecture and the earliest classical portico of detached columns erected in the North.

Now here, though only for a moment, a church has to be mentioned. For about a hundred years church architecture had all but stopped in Britain. And in France, although there are a number of interesting 16th-century churches with curious mixtures in varying proportion of Gothic conceptions with Southern detail (for instance St Eustache and St Etienne du Mont, both in Paris), they are not amongst the historically leading works. The same might also be said of the 17th century, or at least its beginning. Paris now took over the Gesù scheme of façade and interior (see pp. 154–155), the scheme which, as has been said before, became more widely popular than any other during the period between 1600 and 1750 (Jesuit Novitiate Church begun 1612, now destroyed; St Gervais façade 1616 by Clément Métézeau; Church of the Feuillants begun 1624(?) by François Mansart).

The parallelism between this French development based on Vignola and the English one based on Palladio need not be specially stressed. It was part of the universal tendency of the north of Europe early in the 17th century. In Germany at exactly the same time Elias Holl (1573–1646) built his Palladian Augsburg Town Hall (1610–20). And in palace architecture in France Salomon de Brosse (*c.* 1550/60–1626) at the request of Marie de' Medici incorporated into his monumental plan for the Luxembourg Palace, begun in 1615, motifs of the Mannerist parts of the Pitti Palace in Florence. The plan of the Luxembourg consists of an H-shaped *corps de logis* with lower wings along a *cour d'honneur* and a screen wall on the front side. The central axis is strongly marked by the entrance pavilion in the screen wall and the centre pavilion of the *corps de logis*.

Such grand symmetrical schemes, more rigidly formal as a rule than Elizabethan and Jacobean compositions, are characteristic of France. They were originally (that is early in the 16th century, at the time when the Loire *château* of Chambord was designed in perfect symmetry with thick round towers) a fusion of symmetrical discipline in medieval castles and in Italian Renaissance palaces. With Delorme's plan of 1564 for the Tuileries (devised no doubt under the influence of the Escorial) the grand scale was reached. The Tuileries were to have a 200-foot front and five courts. A little later, under Charles IX, a yet bigger project was drawn up by Jacques Androuet Ducerceau (c. 1510–85), who has so far been mentioned only as a writer on architecture. Charleval in Normandy was intended to be a large square with a square inner courtyard and a *cour d'honneur* in front, possessing on the right and left service wings each again with two courts. The size intended was over 1000 by 1000 feet, far more than that of the Escorial. From such schemes Charles I's and Charles II's ideas for a gigantic Whitehall palace were derived, the ideas which were first put on paper by Inigo Jones and then in exactly as Italian a style by John Webb, his pupil.

But before 1650 or 1660 Jones and Webb were almost alone in pursuing such Southern ideas. The popular style in England after the Jacobean and often still side by side with the Jacobean was a homely Dutch style with curved and pedimented gables (Kew Palace, etc.). To this corresponds in France the style of Henri IV still lingering on into the 'thirties of the 17th century, a style of brick buildings with stone quoins and window dressings, best illustrated by the architecture of the Place des Vosges in Paris (1605–12) and by Richelieu's little town of Richelieu, founded in 1631 and designed with his palace by Lemercier (c. 1585–1654). The palace, long since destroyed, was modelled on the Luxembourg pattern and thus already a conservative work when it was completed.

For in monumental French architecture Richelieu's period and even more that of Mazarin are characterized by a broad

new influx of Italian ideas – and that now meant ideas of the
Baroque – and by the way they were developed in the hands of
a few leading architects into a classic French style which corresponds in terms of building to that of Poussin in painting, of
Corneille in drama, and of Descartes in philosophy. There is
no parallel in England to this phase, though from 1660 onwards parallelism, if in very different national idioms, is again
patent.

François Mansart (1598–1664) is the first great protagonist,
Louis Levau (1612–70) the second. Mansart's two *magna opera*

82. *Jacques Lemercier: Church of the Sorbonne, Paris, 1635–42*

were built between 1635 and 1650: the Orléans wing at Blois
and the country house of Maisons Lafitte. The *cour d'honneur* at
Blois especially (pl. 55b; on the extreme right a corner of
Francis I's wing is just visible) is a masterpiece of civilized re-
ticence, elegant, not very warm-hearted, yet far from pedan-
tically correct with its two-storied triumphal arch and the
remarkably original little semicircular third-storied pediment
above. The links backward with Lescot's age are as evident as
the links forward with the smooth perfection of the Rococo
hôtel. The curved colonnades especially convey that distinct
feeling of Rococo. The way in which they smooth over the

angular break at the corners is very French and very accomplished. A similar interior effect is achieved at Maisons Lafitte by the oval rooms in the wings. These were new to France; an Italian motif introduced, it appears, by Mansart and Levau. Of its Italian use in churches and palaces (Palazzo Barberini) enough has been said. Its most prominent occurrence in France is in the mighty, very Italian and very Baroque fancy palaces

83. *Louis Levau: Church of the Collège des Quatre Nations (now Institut de France) Paris, 1661.*

published in Antoine Lepautre's (1621–91) *Desseins de plusieurs palais* in 1652 – the parallel to Puget's sculpture – in Louis Levau's church of the Collège des Quatre Nations (now Institut de France) of 1661 and in his country house of Vaux-le-Vicomte, begun in 1657. The church of the Collège des Quatre Nations (fig. 83) is, broadly speaking, a Greek cross, but the arms and the corners between the arms are designed with considerable freedom and differ widely from each other. The dominant features of the church are the oval centre with its dome and an oval atrium. Oval also is the effect of the earlier Sorbonne Church (fig. 82) by Jacques Lemercier (1635–42),

84. *Louis Levau: Vaux-le-Vicomte, begun 1657*

where a Greek cross is combined with a circular centre but with a great deal of deliberate stress on one axis of the cross as against the other. There is just as much spatial ingenuity in these plans as in those of contemporary Italy, although their detail appears cold and restrained against the Baroque of Rome.

Vaux-le-Vicomte (figs. 84 and 85) is in many ways the most important French building of the mid-17th century. It was begun by Levau for Colbert's predecessor Fouquet and is surrounded by gardens in which the great Le Nôtre first experimented with ideas later to be developed so spectacularly at Versailles. Lebrun, Louis's *Premier Peintre*, also worked at Vaux before he started at Versailles.

In the house itself (as at Maisons and some others before) the traditional plan of the Luxembourg is given up for that of the Palazzo Barberini, with very much shorter projecting wings, and the centre pavilion is occupied by a domed oval saloon, again on the pattern of the Barberini Palace. In the wings the roofs have still the high pitch

85. *Louis Levau: Vaux-le-Vicomte, begun 1657*

characteristic of the French 16th and early 17th centuries, but slender Ionic pilasters appear in one giant order for both stories. Giant orders were nothing new. We have found them in Inigo Jones and before. Palladio had had them and France herself occasionally too (Bullant at Ecouen, Ducèrceau at Charleval, etc.). But in this particularly light and elegant manner they are curiously similar to those which since about 1630 Holland had favoured.

Holland just at that time attained the leadership of Western commerce, and she was much envied and imitated by both Colbert and the English. She also led in science and could boast more men of artistic genius than at any other period in her national existence. In architecture her development had led her from a gay and jolly style of 1600, parallel to Henri IV's style and the Jacobean, to a new classicism, parallel to Mansart's in France and Inigo Jones's in England. The Mauritshuis at The Hague, built by Jacob van Campen in 1633-35 (pl. 55a), has a correct pediment on correct giant pilasters, and giant pilasters also along its sides. In this it may well have influenced France and Vaux in particular, but its intimate size for a princely residence, its unpretentious plain brick walls and its all-pervading feeling of solid comfort are very Dutch and quite different from anything French of that period.

England, on the other hand, could sympathize with these North-Western qualities of the Dutch. And her architecture since 1616 was indeed greatly influenced by the buildings of van Campen, Post, and Vingboons, and by Vingboons's engraved publications of 1648, 1674, and 1688. However, architects, amateurs, and scholars, and especially the Stuart court, were not blind to either the glamour or the real achievements of the Paris of Colbert and Louis XIV. There was trading success on the one hand, the grandeur of absolute monarchy on the other. Hence representational architecture tended towards the Parisian, domestic architecture towards the Dutch. In Sir Christopher Wren's work inspiration from both sources can be traced. He must have studied engravings of Dutch architecture with great care, and he went to Paris personally, when he had realized that the designing and supervising of buildings was to be his main job in life. For Wren (1632-1723) – this is again characteristic of Renaissance and Baroque – had not been trained as an architect or a mason. Nor was he a painter or sculptor or engineer. He represents yet another type, a type not so far met with in this book.

Wren's father had been Dean of Windsor, his father's brother Bishop of Ely. He was sent to Westminster School. At the age of fifteen, after he had finished school, he was made an assistant demonstrator in anatomy at the College of Surgeons. Then he went up to Oxford. His main interest was science, in that curious mixed and vague sense which science still had in the mid-17th century. During the time he was at college, 'that miracle of a youth', as John Evelyn called him, put before the authorities fifty-three inventions, theories, experiments, and mechanical improvements. Some of them seem trifling now, others aimed right at the central problems of astronomy, physics, and engineering. In 1657 he was made professor of astronomy in London, in 1661 in Oxford. It was the moment when experimental science was just coming to the fore everywhere in Europe. In Paris the Royal Academy of Science was established. The Royal Society in London started its activities even earlier. Wren was one of its founders and most distinguished members. Newton calls him together with Huygens and Wallis 'huius aetatis geometrarum facile principes'. His most important scientific work is on cycloids, the barometer, and Pascal's problem. In his inaugural lecture in London he revealed a prophetic vision of nebulae as the firmaments of other worlds like ours. In 1664 he illustrated Willis's *Anatomy of the Brain*. Again in 1663 he presented to the Royal Society a model for a building which he had designed at the request of Oxford University, the Sheldonian Theatre, completed in 1669. Its roof is an ingenious piece of timber engineering, but its architecture is awkward, evidently the work of a man with little designing experience. The same can be said of his second work, Pembroke Chapel, Cambridge, of 1663–66. An even earlier connection with building construction is indicated by Charles II's request to him to fortify Tangier. So architecture, engineering, physics, and mathematics go hand in hand in the development of Wren's mind. The resolution to specialize in architecture may have been brought about by the Fire of London in 1666. Wren found himself a member of the Royal Commission for the rebuilding of the city, and very soon also the elected designer of the many new churches to be built in the city, including St Paul's. In 1669 the King made him Surveyor-General. His only important journey abroad took him not to Italy, but to Paris. That is a very significant fact. At the time of Inigo Jones's *Wanderjahre*, Paris could not have been more than a station on the way to Rome. Now Wren, in a letter, called Paris 'a School of Architecture, the best probably at this Day in Europe'. The most important it certainly was. While Wren was in Paris, Louis XIV, who intended to rebuild the east parts of the Louvre, had invited Bernini to come and contribute designs. He did so, but his plans, a colossal square on the Roman pattern with giant orders of detached columns on the outer and the courtyard fronts, and with a vigorous top cornice crowned by a balustrade, plans which Wren succeeded in examining for only a precious few minutes, were dropped as soon as the great man left. They were replaced by the famous east front with the colonnades which Claude Perrault (1613–88) designed in 1665.

The choice of Perrault was characteristic. He was an amateur and a distinguished doctor. His brother was a lawyer and courtier, had in 1664 been made Inspector-General of the King's buildings, and later wrote a mediocre poem called *Le Siècle de Louis le Grand*. In the history of French literature he is known chiefly as one of the leaders in the *Querelle des Anciens et des Modernes*. Boileau defended Antiquity, Perrault a contemporary style – which of course did not really mean more than a certain amount of freedom in applying the rules of the ancients.

Claude Perrault's Louvre front (pl. 56a) goes beyond Mansart and Levau in several ways. It represents the change from Mazarin to Colbert, or from early to mature Louis XIV. It has a disciplined formality to which Perrault's knowledge of Bernini's project contributed two important motifs. Bernini as well as Perrault have flat balustraded roofs, and Bernini as well as Perrault model their fronts without any marked projections or recesses of wings. Both these features were new in France. Otherwise, however, Perrault is wholly national. French in feeling, though very original and so un-academic that his less adventurous contemporaries never forgave him, are the slim coupled giant columns of the main story raised up on the tall, smooth, podium-like ground floor. French are the segment-headed windows, and French (of direct Lescot derivation) the oval shields with garlands hanging down from them.

The whole is of a grandeur and yet a precise elegance that the 17th century, in spite of Blois and Maisons, had never before achieved, and that the architects of Louis XIV's later years never surpassed. Perrault has summed up to perfection the various, sometimes seemingly contradictory tendencies of the *siècle de Louis XIV*, the gravity and *raison* of late Poussin, Corneille, and Boileau, the restrained fire of Racine, the lucid grace of Molière, the powerful sense of organization of Colbert.

It is necessary for an appreciation of this style to remember the atmosphere in which it grew, the struggles first between Protestantism and Catholicism in the 16th century, Henri IV's decision to return to the Roman Church, because, as he put it, 'Paris is worth a mass', then the spreading of religious indifference, until it became all-powerful in the policy of Richelieu, the cardinal, and Father Joseph, the Capuchin, who fought Protestants in France but favoured them abroad, in both cases purely for reasons of national expediency. For the centre of their thoughts and ambitions was France, and a strong and prosperous France could be created only by first building up a rigorously centralized administration. Now the only visible symbol of the might of the state could be the person of the king. Absolutism was therefore the appropriate form of government for whoever was in favour of a national policy. Thus Richelieu prepared the ground for absolutism, Mazarin followed, and Colbert, the indefatigable, competent, and tenacious bourgeois, made a system of it. He organized France with an unheard-of thoroughness: mercantilism in industry and commerce, royal workshops, royal trading companies, close supervision of roads, of canals, of afforestation – of everything.

Art and architecture were an integral part of the system. A flourishing school of painting, sculpture, and the applied arts stimulated export and at the same time enhanced the glory of the court. Architecture was useful to create work and again to celebrate the greatness of king and state. But there should be no licence; style had to conform to standards set by the prince and his minister. Thus academies were founded, one for painting and sculpture, another for architecture, the earliest of a modern type, both educational and representational, and the most powerful that have ever existed. And when artists had gone through these schools and gained distinction, they were made royal sculptors or royal architects, drawn nearer and nearer to the court, honoured and paid accordingly, but made more and more dependent on the will of Louis and Colbert. It was in Paris at that time that the principle of architecture as a department of the civil service was established. The French and English kings had had their royal master-masons ever since the 13th century. But they were craftsmen, not civil servants. Also the competencies of the various surveyors, inspectors, and whatever they were called later on were never clearly defined. Michelangelo had been Superintendent of the Papal Buildings; but nobody would have considered such an appointment a full-time job. Now the architectural office developed, and a system of training at the drawing board and on the jobs.

Jules Hardouin-Mansart (1646–1708) was the perfect type of the official French architect, competent, quick, and adaptable. In his church of St Louis des Invalides (pl. 57a and fig. 86) of 1675–1706 he achieved, just as Perrault did, that specific combination of grandeur and elegance which is not to be found anywhere outside France. The composition, externally and internally, is meant to be taken as an improvement on Lemercier's Sorbonne and Levau's Collège des Quatre Nations. The interior, except for the oval chancel, is more academically balanced, that is less dynamic in its spatial relations, than the works of Hardouin-Mansart's predecessors. But the dome is constructed so that in looking up one sees through a wide opening in the inner cupola on to the painted surface of a second cupola, lit by concealed windows – a wholly Baroque spatial effect. Examining the façade one will now become aware of its Baroque qualities too, in spite of its seemingly correct portico with Doric and Ionic orders. The free rhythmical spacing of the columns (taken from Perrault) should be

noted, and the graded advance in plan towards the centre: first
step from the walls to the columns of the wings, second step to
the columns on the sides of the portico, and third step to the
four middle columns. Not only the Greeks but also Palladio
and even Vignola would have deprecated this strongly.

Sir Christopher Wren did not. His St Paul's Cathedral of
1675–1710 (pl. 88 and fig. 87), though apparently so much a

86. *Jules Hardouin-Mansart: St Louis des Invalides, Paris*

monument to Classicism, is in fact just as much a blend of
the classical and the Baroque as the Dôme des Invalides. The
dome of St Paul's, one of the most perfect in the world, is
classical indeed. It has a more reposeful outline than Michelangelo's and Hardouin-Mansart's. The decoration, with a
colonnade round the drum, is also characteristically different
from the projecting groups of columns and broken entablatures of St Peter's and the segment-headed windows – so remarkably domestic-looking – and the slim, graceful shape of
the lantern of St Louis's. But, looking more closely, even there
the alternation of bays where columns flank niches with bays
where they stand in front of loggias introduces an element
of unclassical variety. The lantern, too, is at least as bizarre as
Mansart's. And as for the façade of St Paul's, begun in 1685, it

is, with the coupled columns which Wren (just as Hardouin-
Mansart) took over from Perrault's Louvre façade, and the two
fantastic turrets on the sides (designed after 1700), a decidedly
Baroque composition. The side elevations are dramatic, though
of a secular, palace-like effect. The windows have even a framing of sham-perspective niches of the S. Carlo and Palazzo
Barberini type (see pl. 43a). Inside there is a poignant contrast

87. Sir Christopher Wren: St Paul's Cathedral, London, 1675–1710

between the firmness of every part and the spatial dynamics of
the whole. The dome is as wide as nave and aisles together – a
motif which Wren may have remembered from Ely or from
engravings of such Italian buildings as the Cathedral of Pavia.
It adds splendour and surprise to the whole composition. The
diagonally-placed piers are hollowed out into colossal niches.
Niches also set the outer walls of the aisles and choir aisles into
an undulating motion. With a similar effect windows are cut
into the tunnel-vaults and saucer domes of choir and nave.
Wren's style in churches and palaces is Palladian, no doubt,
but it is a Baroque version of Classicism. Such city churches
as the ingeniously multiform St Stephen's, Walbrook (1672–
87, pl. 58a and fig. 88), show this especially clearly.

To analyse its ground plan is almost as hard as to analyse
Vierzehnheiligen. Yet its expression is of cool clarity. Outside
it is a plain rectangle as silent about the interior surprises as

Vierzehnheiligen. Inside its centre is a spacious gently-rising saucer dome resting on eight arches supported by nothing but twelve slender columns. The technical achievement is as re-markable as the effortless lightness of appearance. The twelve columns form a square, and four arches connect the two

88. *Sir Christopher Wren: St Stephen's, Walbrook, London, 1672–87.*

central columns of each side of the square, while fragmentary vaults curve up from the three columns of each corner of the square to form four more arches in the corners. Now these three corner columns on each side are also tied together by straight entablatures, so that each of the four sides has a rhythm of straight and low – arched and tall – straight and low. Here is a first ingenious interlocking of effects. Looking up the dome we perceive eight arches of identical height, but looking straight in front of us towards any one side of the square there is differentiation of the bays. However, that is not all. The arched centres of the sides can also be regarded as the entrances to four arms of a cross, a Latin cross, since the tunnel-vaults of the south and north arms are very shallow, whereas the east arm with the altar has a somewhat longer cross-vault, and the west arm one double the length of the altar arm. To achieve that, the western arm consists of two bays separated by columns in the normal manner of longitudinal churches. As these columns are exactly identical with all the other columns, the first impression one receives on entering the church is one of a short nave with aisles leading towards a dome of unaccountable width. To finish the story, this seeming nave has narrow flat-ceilinged outer aisles as well, and these outer aisles run right through to the east wall. Only we cannot call them aisles all the way through, because at one point they rise into being the north and south arms of the cross and then sink again to become chancel aisles. The inner aisles of course, one discovers later, run into the wide crossing just as does the nave. The whole rectangle of the church is set out with sixteen columns altogether, noble columns of almost academic neutrality. Yet they are used to create a spatial polyphony which only the Baroque could appreciate – architecture of Purcell's age.

It is in connection with the spatial qualities of his ground plans that one should consider Wren's plan for the rebuilding of London after the fire of 1666. He suggested sweeping alterations in the pattern of the city, new long, wide, and straight streets meeting in star-shaped squares. Now this principle of the *rond-point* with radiating streets originated from the Italy of the Renaissance (see p. 117), was put into practice by the Mannerists – the most famous example is Scamozzi's nonagonal town and fortress of Palmanova in the Veneto (1593), a Baroque example of about 1660 is the Piazza del Popolo in Rome with the Corso and the two other straight streets (see p. 163) – and taken over late in the 16th century by the French under Louis XIV. France (where the radiating chapels of the church plan had been conceived six hundred years before) became the second home of the *rond-point*. From Louis's reign dates the Place de l'Étoile, although it was then in the country and became part of the city of Paris only after 1800. The grandest example of such planning on an enormous scale is, of course, Versailles (fig. 89). The garden front of the palace, 1800 feet long, faces Le Nôtre's magnificent park with its vast parterres of flowers, its cross-shaped sheet of water, fountains, seemingly endless parallel or radiating avenues, and walks between tall, trimmed hedges – Nature subdued by the hand of

89. *Versailles. Enlarged by Jules Hardouin-Mansart, 1676–88, from a core o f 1623 with wings of 1661–65; the gardens by André Le Nôtre, begun 1667*

Man to serve the greatness of the king, whose bedroom was placed right in the centre of the whole composition. On the town side the *cour d'honneur* receives three wide, converging roads coming from the direction of Paris. Town-planning was strongly influenced by these principles everywhere. Of the 18th century the most notable examples are perhaps Karlsruhe in South-West Germany, a whole town designed in 1715 as one huge star with the Ducal Palace as its centre, and L'Enfant's plan of 1791 for Washington, D.C.

As for Britain, Wren's plan fell through after having been considered by the king for only a few days. Was it too daring? Could it have been carried out only in an absolute monarchy, where expropriation for schemes of civic grandeur was easier than in the City of London? Or was this logical, uncompromising programme to organize the background for future London life simply too un-English ever to be taken seriously? The fact remains that the contribution of London to townplanning of the 17th and 18th centuries is the square – introduced, as has been said, by Inigo Jones – i.e. an isolated, privately-owned area with houses of, as a rule, similar but not identical design, examples of good manners and not of regimentation. It might be worth adding that the sensation in walking through the West End of London from square to square is clearly a modern and secular version of the typically English sensation of the visitor passing from isolated compartment to isolated compartment in a Saxon or Early English church.

Regarding the individual town house, there is the same contrast between London and Paris. In London, but for a few exceptions, the nobleman and the wealthy merchant lived in terrace houses, in Paris in detached *hôtels*. In London a ground plan had been evolved for these houses that was convenient enough to become standardized before the end of the 17th century. With its entrance on one side, leading straight to the staircase, one large front room and one large back room on each floor, and the service rooms in the basement, it remained practically unaltered for the largest and the smallest house until the end of the Victorian era. Of spatially effective elements it has little. In Paris, on the other hand, architects from about 1630 onwards developed house plans with great consistency and ingenuity towards ever subtler solutions of functional requirements and spatial desires. The standard elements were a *cour d'honneur*, screened off from the street, with offices and stables in wings on the right and the left, and the *corps de logis* at the back. The earliest plan of wholly symmetrical organization is the Hôtel de Bretonvillers of about 1625–30. The first high-water marks are Mansart's Hôtel de la Vrillière of about 1635 and Levau's Hôtel Lambert of shortly after 1642, the latter with a courtyard with two rounded corners and an oval vestibule (fig. 90). A little later Lepautre's Hôtel de Beauvais (1655–60) revels in curves. Then the same reaction took place which we had seen between Vaux and the Louvre. Colbert did not like curves, he called them in 1669 'not in good taste, particularly in exteriors', and the *appartements* of Louis XIV's later years are of less spatial interest.

90. *Louis Levau: Hôtel Lambert, Paris, about 1645*

The most important development between 1700 and 1715 is concerned with interior decoration. In the hands of one of Hardouin-Mansart's chief executives, Jean Lepautre, it became more and more delicate and sophisticated. Grandeur was replaced by *finesse*, high relief by an exquisite play on the surface, and a virile deportment by an almost effeminate grace. Thus during the last years or Louis XIV's reign the atmosphere of the Rococo consolidated itself.

The Rococo is indeed of French origin, although we have introduced it in this book first in its German, that is its extreme and most brilliant spatial forms. The term Rococo is a pun, it seems, from *barocco*, alluding to the passion for those strange rock-like or shell-like formations which are typical of its ornament and have been analysed apropos Bruchsal and Vierzehnheiligen. They appear there in the fifties, but are a French invention of 1715–30 – or rather an invention made in France. For the leaders of the generation responsible for the step from Lepautre's thin grace to full-blooded Rococo were without exception not properly French: Watteau the painter was a Fleming, Gilles-Marie Oppenord (1672–1742) was the son of a Dutch father, Juste-Aurèle Meissonier (1695–1750) of Provençal stock and born at Turin, Toro has an Italian name and lived in Provence, and Vassé was Provençal too. It is due to these architects and decorators that vigour re-entered French decoration, that curves of Italian Baroque derivation made their appearance once more, that ornament launched out into the third dimension again, and that the fantastic, completely original ornament of the *rocaille* was conceived.

In exterior architecture less can be observed of this development than in interiors. Oppenord's and Meissonier's designs for façades were not carried out. It is in the planning and decoration of houses that the Rococo celebrates its greatest triumphs. The Rococo is a style of the *salon*, the *petit appartement* and of sophisticated living. Decoration is far more graceful and as a rule considerably less vigorous than in Germany, and planning is of an unprecedented subtlety.

One difficulty in the standard Parisian *hôtel* plan which the architects liked to face and overcome was, for instance, the fact that the front towards the *cour d'honneur* and the back towards the garden should both be symmetrical in themselves and even when they did not lie on the same axis. Courtonne's Hôtel de Matignon (fig. 92) shows one very neat solution. Here and in any of the other contemporary *hôtels* the ingenious tricks of ante-chambers and cabinets and *garderobes* and little inner service courts should be studied, all devised to facilitate the running of a house and fill the many odd corners behind curved rooms and alcoves. The form and position of the staircase was another problem. As to its position, it had to communicate easily with vestibule and service rooms, without interfering with the smooth run of room into room and the representational splendour of vistas. The same desire for a smooth run was

extended to the interaction between floor and floor, and staircase forms were chosen accordingly. It has been shown that
Spain was the most enterpri-
sing country in the 16th
century regarding staircases.
Only here the Baroque possibilities of the staircase were
sensed as early as that. Her
three main new types, the
square newel stair with the
open wall, the staircase on
the T-plan, and the so-called
Imperial staircase (fig. 91; see
also p. 185), all reached the
North in the 17th century.
The square newel stair became
popular in Jacobean England,
where it was interpreted in
timber, characteristically reduced in size to a somewhat
cramped medieval narrow-
ness, but gorgeously decorated by Flemish or English
woodcarvers (Hatfield, Audley End, etc.). Only when
we come to Inigo Jones at
Ashburnham House, London
(perhaps by him), is the spaciousness of Spain emulated.
However, Ashburnham
House and a few other examples of Baroque breadth such
as Coleshill, Berks (by Roger
Pratt, one of Wren's early
competitors), are rare excep-

91. *Two of the chief types of Baroque
staircases*

tions in England. There were at that time exceptions in Italy too
(Longhena: S. Giorgio Maggiore, Venice, 1643–45 – the
example from which Coleshill seems to be derived). Only

Genoa took a real liking to staircases as wide, light, and airy as those of Spain. France must have got to know of these through several channels. The T-type was taken up by Levau in the Escalier des Ambassadeurs at Versailles, in 1671, the Imperial type by Levau at the Tuileries, the square open newel type earlier still by Mansart at Blois. Mansart took over from Palladio the elegant method of construction by which the flights of stairs, instead of resting on solid walls, are anchored only into the outer walls, and towards the well carried on shallow arches without any other support. This type occurs with countless minor variations, all aiming at yet suppler forms, in most Paris *hôtels* and French country houses (see, e.g., fig. 92).

Externally the Paris *hôtels* are just as elegantly varied, though never anything like as boldly Rococo, as the palaces and houses in Germany and Austria, whereas in London the exterior of the 17th- and 18th-century brick house was, except for ornamental details, almost standardized. It has no connection with the classic French style, that much is certain, although it may have had some originally with the less pretentious domestic architecture of Henri IV and later with Holland.

As for country houses, they are – at least after 1660 – of minor importance in France, where the life of the ruling class was centred in the court, while in England most of the noblemen and nearly all the squires still regarded their London houses only as *pieds-à-terre*, and looked on their seats in the country as their real homes. Consequently it is here that one can expect variety and, indeed, find it. All the more noteworthy, however, is it that about 1700, when the standardized town house had become an accepted fact, a type of smaller country house had also been introduced (clearly on the Mauritshuis pattern) that – with many and delightful minor variations – is to be found all over the countryside, in the villages round London, at Hampstead, Roehampton, Ham, Petersham, round the close at Salisbury – everywhere. They are usually built of brick with stone quoins, either completely rectangular or with two short wings on the sides, the entrance with a pediment, hood, or porch, and with a larger pediment

to crown the centre of the house (fig. 93). These lovable houses
of mellow and undated rightness are too well known to need
further description. Their origin and diffusion have however
not yet been fully elucidated. The earliest example seems to be
Eltham Lodge, near London, of 1663. It was designed by Hugh

92. *Jean Courtonne: Hôtel de Matignon, Paris, begun* 1722

May, with Pratt and Webb, Wren's most important com-
petitor in the 'sixties. By 1685 or 1690 the type was certainly
fully established. It has as a rule a generously-spaced three-
flight staircase with an open well and rich woodcarving and
rooms of simple and straightforward shapes; of that ingenious
commodité on which all the French 18th-century architects insisted in their writings, they have little.

Apparently, to the British, comfort was something quite different from what it was to the French. But while these houses of about 1700 are, whatever French critics might have said against them, as serviceable to-day as at the time when they were built, there are indeed certain English 18th-century

93. Fenton House, Hampstead, London, 1693

country houses on a larger scale which – from our point of view at least – seem to be designed for display and not for comfort. This is an argument heard frequently against Blenheim near Oxford (pl. 58b, 59a and fig. 94), the palace which the nation presented to Marlborough. It was designed by Sir John Vanbrugh (1664–1726) in 1705. His style derives from Wren at his grandest and most Baroque – the Wren of Greenwich Hospital – but is always of a distinctly personal character. Wren never seems to forget himself. He is never carried away by forces stronger than his reason. Vanbrugh's designs are of a violence and ruthless directness that could not but offend the rationalists of his age. His family came from Flanders; his expansive temperament seems more of Rubens's country than of Wren's and Reynolds's. He studied art in France, was arrested and imprisoned in the Bastille. After his release he returned to England and began to write plays. They were a huge success. Then suddenly one finds him engaged in architectural work at

94. *Sir John Vanbrugh: Blenheim Palace, begun 1705*

Castle Howard. In 1702 he was appointed Comptroller of Works – a curious career, very different from Wren's.

Blenheim is planned on a colossal scale. One does not know whether the Palladian villa with its wings or Versailles with its *cour d'honneur* stands behind its plan. The *corps de logis* has a massive portico with giant columns between giant pillars, and a heavy attic above. The same Baroque weight characterizes the side elevations, especially the square squat corner towers of the wings (pl. 59a). If in the case of Wren the term Baroque could be used only with careful qualifications, these towers would be called Baroque by anyone familiar with the work of

Bernini, Borromini, and the others in Italy. Here is a struggle, mighty forces opposing overwhelming weights; here are fiercely projecting mouldings and windows crushed by thick-set pilasters placed too close to them; here is the deliberate discordance of the semicircular window placed against a semicircular arch right above, and higher up again a segmental arch. Everything jars, and the top of the daring composition has nothing of a happy end either. Vanbrugh, in the forms which crown the tower, the obelisks, and the ball, does not accept any indebtedness to anybody. The pilasters and the windows are also highly original, but not to the same extreme degree. In some details they appear reminiscent of Michelangelo. However, the mentioning of Michelangelo makes Blenheim – the whole of the entrance front – at once appear coarse, even meaty, and certainly theatrical and ostentatious: that is, Flemish as well as Baroque. Yet in spite of that Vanbrugh, seen side by side with Michelangelo or Bernini, is also a classicist. It seems a contradiction but it is not. It simply is, just as in the case of Wren, the special English twist given to the Baroque. There is very little in Wren and Vanbrugh of that plastic treatment of walls which Michelangelo had first conceived and which produced the undulating façades and interiors of Baroque buildings in Italy and Southern Germany. Movement is never in England so insinuating, nor so frantic. Spatial parts never abandon their separate existence, to merge into each other, as they do at S. Carlo or Vierzehnheiligen. The individual members, especially the solid round detached columns, also try to keep themselves to themselves. Vanbrugh's drama lies in the visible forcing of this English aloofness into the service of an over-mighty plan. English Baroque is Baroque asserting itself against an inborn leaning towards the static and the sober.

The same conflict will be experienced in interiors of Wren's and Vanbrugh's time. There again spatial relations bind rooms together which are articulated and decorated according to the principles of Classicism – by panelling if they are small, by columns or pilastes, if they are larger. At Blenheim there is an enormous entrance hall leading into the saloon which forms the centre of two symmetrical groups of rooms along the whole garden front, with all the doors in one axis, or as it is called, one *enfilade*, as at Versailles. But – this is of the greatest significance – the staircase, the dynamic element *par excellence*, is nothing like as prominent as it would be in a contemporary palace in France or Germany. This lack of interest in spatial dynamics is by no means a sign of meanness in planning. On the contrary, Blenheim is just as vast as the largest new palaces of the minor rulers of Germany, and just as impractical – at least from our point of view.

However, it seems rather cheap to harp on the fact that kitchen and service rooms are far away from the dining-room – in one of the two wings in fact, opposite the other with the stables (an accepted Palladian tradition). Servants may have had to walk a long way, and hot dishes may have got cold long before they reached their destination. To us that may seem a functional error. Vanbrugh and his clients would have called such arguments extremely low. Of servants they had plenty. And what we call comfort mattered less than a self-imposed etiquette more rigid than we can imagine. The function of a building is not only utilitarian. There is also an ideal function, and that Blenheim did fulfil. However, not all Vanbrugh's contemporaries agreed that it did. There is, for example, Pope with his famous, often quoted ''tis very fine, But where d'ye sleep, or where d'ye dine?' What did he mean by that? Critics to-day interpret it as referring to a lack of material comfort. Pope was more philosophical than that. What, in the name of good sense, he asked for, is that a room and a building should look what they are. He disliked Vanbrugh's colossal scale and decorative splendour as unreasonable and unnatural. For 'splendour', he insists, should borrow 'all her rays from sense', and again :

> 'Something there is more needful than expense,
> And something previous ev'n to taste – 'tis sense.'

In this he gave expression to the feelings of his generation, the generation following Vanbrugh's. For Pope was born in 1688, whereas Vanbrugh was almost the same age as Swift and Defoe (and Wren as Dryden).

The architecture that corresponds to Pope's poetry is that of Lord Burlington and his circle. Richard Boyle, Earl of Burlington, was some years younger than Pope. He went to Italy at the age of twenty, and, when he came back, brought with him several artists and architects attached to him by a common admiration of Palladio. Already in 1716 a sumptuous English edition of Palladio had been published by the Italian architect Leoni; now Burlington paid for Colin Campbell's *Vitruvius Britannicus*, consisting of illustrations of the best modern buildings in Britain (1715–25), and for the publication of Inigo Jones's works by William Kent, painter, landscape gardener, and architect (1727). These publications set a Palladian fashion in British country houses that lasted almost unchallenged for fifty years, and with certain modifications for nearly a hundred.

The town house, however, was hardly affected. There are very few examples of Palladian influence beyond façade motifs. And where, as in a house designed by Lord Burlington himself, an attempt was made to interfere with the standardized London plan, the outcry against this imposition of the rationalist's new rules was just as pronounced as the rationalist's outcry had been against Vanbrugh's unruliness. Lord Chesterfield suggested to the owner that he should take a house opposite, so as to be able to admire his own at leisure without having to live in it.

It is the country house that became wholly Palladian by Lord Burlington's efforts. In Vanbrugh's work the variety of plan and exterior compositions had been unlimited. Now the *corps de logis* with a centre portico and isolated wings connected to the main body by low galleries became *de rigueur*. Prior Park near Bath (pl. 56b), is a typical example. It was designed for Ralph Allen in 1735 by the elder John Wood (*c.* 1700–54), local architect, but, by virtue of his talent and the opportunities which he had in the most fashionable spa of England, one of the leading architects of his generation. Compared with Palladio's villas, these British derivations are larger and heavier. They also often incorporate motifs freer than Palladio would have tolerated: more variation in the shapes of rooms, or a boldly curved outer staircase into the garden (the one at Prior

Park is of the 19th century). The sites, as a rule on a gentle slope, also add a quality that is absent in Palladio's work for a flat country. But more important still is the fact that Palladian country houses in Britain were designed to stand in English parks.

It seems at first contradictory that the same patrons should have wanted the formal Palladian house and the informal English garden, and that the same architect should have provided both. Yet it is a fact that William Kent, Lord Burlington's protégé, was celebrated as one of the creators of the English style in laying out grounds, and that Lord Burlington's own villa at Chiswick (about 1720), a free copy of Palladio's Villa Rotonda, was one of the earliest examples of what was called 'the modern taste' in gardening. How can this have come about? Was the landscape garden just a whim? It was not; it was a conscious part of an anti-French policy in the arts. Le Nôtre's parks express absolutism, the king's absolute rulership over the country, and also Man's rulership over Nature. The active, expansive Baroque force that shapes the house, flows over into nature. Progressive English thinkers recognized this and disliked it. Shaftesbury spoke of 'the mockery of princely gardens', and Pope satirized them in his neat couplet:

> 'Grove nods at grove, each alley has a brother,
> And half the platform just reflects the other.'

Now this enforcing of architectural rule on the garden is certainly something unnatural. And so Addison wrote in *The Spectator* in 1712: 'For my own part I would rather look upon a tree in all its luxuriance and diffusion of boughs and branches than when it is cut and trimmed into a mathematical figure.' That profession of faith in nature not tampered with is evidently a revolt of liberalism and tolerance against tyranny; it is a Whig revolt. But the curious thing about it is that although these attacks were made in the name of nature, nature was still understood by Addison and Pope in Newton's and indeed in Boileau's sense. Boileau's objections in his *Art of Poetry* of 1674 against the Baroque of the South were that it was unreasonable and therefore unnatural. Reason and nature are still synonyms with Addison and Pope, as we have seen in Pope's comments on Blenheim.

Add to this Shaftesbury's 'passion for things of a natural kind,' and his idea that 'the conceit or caprice of Man has spoiled their genuine order by breaking in upon (their) primitive state', and you will be near an answer to the puzzling parallelism between classicist architecture and natural gardening. The original state of the universe is harmony and order, as we see it in the ordered courses of the stars which were revealed by the new telescopes, and in the structures of organisms which were revealed by the new microscopes. 'Idea of Sense, Order, Proportion everywhere', to use Shaftesbury's words once more. Now to illustrate the superiority of harmony over chaos Shaftesbury explicitly refers to the superiority of the 'regular and uniform pile of some noble Architect' over 'a Heap of Sand or Stones'. But is not the heap of sand nature in her primitive state? That the early 18th century did not want to recognize. So we arrive at this curious ambiguity. Simple nature is order and harmony of proportion. So a natural architecture is an architecture according to Palladio. But simple nature is also, in the common speech of everybody, fields and hedgerows, and of these people were genuinely fond, at least in England. So the garden should be left as close to this simple nature as possible. Addison was the first to reach this conclusion. He exclaimed: 'Why may not a whole estate be thrown into a kind of garden?'; and 'A man might make a pretty landscape of his own possessions.' Pope followed Addison in a contribution to *The Guardian* in 1713 and, more important still, in his own miniature garden at Twickenham. However, when it came to 'improving' Twickenham (to use the 18th-century term) in 1719–25 another equally remarkable thing happened. These earliest anti-French gardens were by no means landscape gardens in the later sense. They were not Pope's 'Nature unadorned'. Their plans with elaborately meandering paths and rills are of as artificial an irregularity as Baroque regularity had been before. Or as Horace Walpole put it in 1750: 'There is not a citizen who doesn't take more pains to torture his acre and a half into irregularities than he formerly would have employed to make it as formal as his cravat.' Now all that, this 'twisting and twirling' (to use Walpole's word again), is evidently Rococo, and nearer in spirit to the Bruchsal Rocaille than to those gardens of the later 18th century which really tried to look like untouched nature. It is the English version of Rococo – as characteristically English as Wren's Baroque had been in comparison with Continental Baroque.

So while one remembers the grandeur and elegance of French 17th- and 18th-century architecture as urban all the way through – for the straight avenues in the park of Versailles are urban in spirit too – one should never forget in looking at the formality of English Palladian houses between 1660 and 1760 that their complement is the English garden. John Wood's Prior Park possesses such informal natural grounds. And even in the most urban developments of Georgian England such as New Edinburgh and above all Bath nature was close at hand and willingly admitted.

John Wood was the first after Inigo Jones to impose Palladian uniformity on an English square as a whole. All the squares in London and elsewhere laid out since 1660 had left it to each owner of a house to have it designed as he liked, and it was due only to the rule of taste in Georgian society that not one of these houses ever clashed violently with its neighbours. John Wood now made one palace front with central portico and secondary emphasis on the corner blocks out of his Queen Square in Bath. That was in 1728. Twenty-five years later he designed the Circus (1754–c. 1770), again as a uniform theme. His son, the younger John Wood (died 1781), in the Royal Crescent of 1767–c. 1775 (pl. 56c) broke open the compactness of earlier squares and ventured to provide as the only response to his vast semi-elliptical palace frontage of thirty houses with giant Ionic columns a spacious, gently-sloping lawn. Here the extreme opposite of Versailles had been reached. Nature is no longer the servant of architecture. The two are equals. The Romantic Movement is at hand.

In London the principle of the palace façade for a whole row of houses was introduced by Robert Adam in his Adelphi (that magnificent composition of streets with its Thames front known all over Europe, which was destroyed, not by bombs, but by mercenary Londoners just before the war) and then taken up at Fitzroy Square and Finsbury Square. But Adam's work, which won international fame in the sixties and seventies – at the same moment when the English garden also began to influence Europe – should not be discussed so close to the Palladianism of the Burlington group. It is of fundamentally another kind. As a rule this difference is expressed by placing Adam at the beginning of the so-called Classical Revival. But that is not the whole answer, for the Classical Revival is really only a part of a much wider process, the Romantic Movement. So from the renewed direct approach to Greek and Roman antiquities as well as from the English creation of landscape gardening we are led into a consideration of the central European problem of 1760–1830: the Romantic Movement.

CHAPTER EIGHT

Romantic Movement, Historicism and Modern Movement

FROM 1760 TO THE PRESENT DAY

THE Romantic Movement originated in England. In literature this fact is well enough known. For the arts and for architecture in particular it has yet to be established. In literature Romanticism is the reaction of sentiment against reason, of nature against artificiality, of simplicity against pompous display, of faith against scepticism. Romantic poetry expresses a new enthusiasm for nature and a self-abandoning veneration of the whole, elemental, undoubting life of early or distant civilizations. This veneration led to the discovery of the Noble Savage and the Noble Greek, the Virtuous Roman and the Pious Medieval Knight. Whatever its object, the Romantic attitude is one of longing, that is antagonism to the present, a present which some saw predominantly as Rococo flippancy, others as unimaginative rationalism, and others again as ugly industrialism and commercialism.

The opposition to the present and the immediate past goes through all utterances of the Romantic spirit, although certain tendencies within the new movement grew out of the 18th century's Rationalism and Rococo. It has been shown for instance how the conception of the landscape garden – a truly Romantic conception – dates back to Addison and Pope, but appears at first in Rococo dress. Similarly that most popular architectural expression of Romanticism, the revival of medieval forms, started long before the Romantic Movement proper and went through all the phases of 18th-century style, before it became wholly Romantic in character.

In fact the Gothic style had never quite died in England. There is college work in Oxford of the 17th century which is unselfconscious Perpendicular, notably the staircase up to the hall of Christ Church. Wren also used Gothic forms in some of the London City churches, and others followed him. But the beginnings of an original handling of medieval elements, a revival and not a survival, are connected with Vanbrugh and his school. His own house at Blackheath of 1717–18 is castellated and has a fortified-looking round tower. He also introduced castellated structures into some of the grounds which he furnished or laid out. His reason for doing so was that medieval forms suggested strength, and he always wanted to be *masculine* in his designs. Hence thick round towers and battlements occur even in his country houses which are otherwise in the current style. However, it was not only their aesthetic qualities which tempted him in medieval castles. He saw more in them. Not that he actually built sham ruins as the later 18th century did, but he defended the preservation of genuine ruins when he found them, because they 'move lively and pleasing reflections . . . on the persons who have inhabited them (and) on the remarkable things which have been transacted in them', and because 'with yews and hollies in a wild thicket' they make 'one of the most agreeable objects that the best of landscape painters can invent'.

Vanbrugh's austere version of medievalism found no successors, but the two passages quoted from his memorandum of 1709 on Blenheim form the foundation of Romantic Revivalism. As will have been noticed Vanbrugh uses two arguments: the associational and the picturesque. Both were developed by theorists of the 18th century. A building is clothed in the garb of a special style, because of the meditations which that style will rouse. And a building is conceived in conjunction with the surrounding nature, because the virtuosi had discovered on the Grand Tour amid the ruins of Roman architecture in and around Rome the truth and the picturesqueness of the heroic and idyllic landscapes of Claude Lorraine, Poussin, Dughet, and Salvator Rosa. These were bought freely by English collectors and helped to form the taste of artists and gardeners, amateur and professional.

Lorraine may have been admired by Pope and Kent (who

after all was a painter before he became an architect), but the gardens of Twickenham and Chiswick had nothing of the serene calm of a Lorraine landscape. The Rococo had to die before this kind of beauty could be reproduced. The Leasowes, the garden which William Shenstone the poet had laid out for himself about 1745, was apparently amongst the first to replace the 'twisting and twirling' of the earlier style by a gentler flow of curves which, together with the many memorial seats and temples which he erected, helped to rouse feelings of pleasant meditation. The great name in the history of mid-18th-century gardening is Lancelot Brown (Capability Brown, 1715–83). His are the wide, softly sweeping lawns, the artfully scattered clumps of trees, and the serpentine lakes which revolutionized garden art all over Europe and America (pl. 60a). This is no longer Rococo, it has the gentle simplicity of Goldsmith's *Vicar of Wakefield* and the chaste elegance of Robert Adam's architecture.

But Adam's is a more complex case than Brown's. Robert Adam (1728–92) is internationally known as the father of the Classical Revival in Britain. His revival of Roman stucco decoration and his delicate adaptation of classical motifs have influenced the Continent just as widely as the new English style in gardening. Yet delicacy is hardly what our present knowledge of Greece and Rome would lead us to expect from a true classical revivalist. Where in Adam's work is the severe nobility of Athens or the sturdy virility of Rome? There is in fact more severity in Lord Burlington's Palladianism and more virility in Vanbrugh than can anywhere be found in Adam. Compare, for example, the walls of Adam's Long Gallery at Syon House (pl. 60b) with those of any Palladian mansion. Adam covers his walls with dainty and exquisitely executed stucco work in a light and quick rhythm. And he loves to run out a room into a gently rounded niche screened off by two free-standing columns with an entablature above. This veiling of spatial relations, this transparency – air floating from room to apse between the columns and above the entablature – is decidedly anti-Palladian, original, and spirited. It occurs again in exterior architecture in the entrance screen to the grounds of

Syon House (pl. 59b). Here too Lord Burlington would have spoken of flippancy and frippery. And Vanbrugh's centre pavilions in the wings of Blenheim Palace (pl. 59a) look, compared with Adam's screen, like boulders piled up by a giant. Adam's gracefully ornamented pilasters and the lion in profile silhouetted against the sky make Vanbrugh appear a tartar, Burlington a pedant. What Adam admired in a building is, in his own words: 'the rise and fall, the advance and recess, and other diversity of forms', and 'a variety of light mouldings'.

Now this is eminently revealing. It is neither Baroque nor Palladian – although in the exteriors of his country houses Adam did not often depart from Palladian standards – nor is it classical. It is Rococo if anything – yet another passing and concealed appearance in England of the general European style of the mid 18th century. All the same, it is not wrong either to see in Robert Adam a representative of the Classical Revival. He did go to Rome as a young man, from there crossed over to Spalato to study and measure the remains of Diocletian's Palace, and after his return home published the results of his research as a sumptuous volume in 1763. Now these engraved folios of the monument of antiquity are quite rightly regarded as a hall-mark of the Classical Revival. Adam's was preceded by the most important of all, James Stuart and Nicholas Revett's *Antiquities of Athens*, of which the first volume came out in 1762. The two architects had worked at the expense of the recently founded Society of Dilettanti, the London club of archeologically interested gentlemen. Six years later the temples of Paestum were illustrated by Thomas Major. In these books the architect and the virtuoso in England could see for the first time the strength and simplicity of the Greek Doric order. For what until then, and ever since the Books of Orders of the 16th century, had been known and used as Doric, was the much slenderer variety now known as Roman, if fluted, and Tuscan, if not fluted. The short and thick proportions of the Greek Doric order, and the complete absence of a base, shocked the Palladians. Sir William Chambers, champion of Palladian traditions in the generation after Burlington and one of the founders of the Royal Academy in 1768, called it downright barbaric. Adam did not like it either. Its reappearance in the books of the 'sixties is memorable. It became the *leitmotif* of the severest phase or variety of the Classical Revival, that known in England as the Greek Revival. Stuart and Revett's work was paralleled in French by Le Roi's skimpier *Ruines de Grèce* of 1758 and in German by Winckelmann's classic *History of Ancient Art* of 1763 – the first book to recognize and analyse the true qualities of Greek art, its 'noble simplicity and tranquil greatness'.

However, Winckelmann's recognition of these qualities was still more literary than visual; for he placed the Apollo Belvedere and the Laocoon, that is, examples of Late Greek Baroque and Rococo, higher than any other antique statuary. Would the figures of Olympia and Aegina and perhaps even those of the Parthenon have shocked him? It is not at all unlikely. His Grecian tastes probably did not go further than, say, Josiah Wedgwood's. Wedgwood copied vases from those Greek examples of the 5th century which were then believed to be Etruscan, and even called his new factory up by Stoke-on-Trent Etruria. But the style of Wedgwood ware is gentle and elegant – an Adam not a Greek style. Still, there is the undeniable desire to be Greek, the marked tendency in archeological publications to prefer the Greek to the Roman, and there is, if not in Adam, in his contemporary James Stuart, 'Athenian' Stuart (1713–88), the actual copying in earnest of complete Greek structures on Northern soil and the putting up of Doric temples for Northern patrons. If this is not a genuine Greek Revival, what is? But once again, if we forget about associations and intentions and simply use our eyes, we see miniature pavilions in Doric forms placed into landscape gardens – picturesque pieces of garden furnishing. Such a Doric temple of Stuart's, for example, graces the grounds at Hagley, near Birmingham, and close to it the same owner put up at the same time a Gothic ruin as a keeper's lodge and a rustic seat to the memory of Thomson of the *Seasons*.

The only difference between the Doric and the Gothic of Hagley is that the one is tolerably correct and the other is not. The owner, owing to his classical education, watched the one, but could not watch the other. Architects too and even country builders knew by 1760 enough of the orders and the details of antiquity to be able to reproduce a Pantheon *en miniature* or a half-broken Roman aqueduct without too many blunders. But in the case of the earliest Gothic Revival antiquarian knowledge was still scanty. Thus while the result in the Greek and Roman copies tends to be somewhat dry, the innumerable

Terminary Seat.

95. *Garden seat from P. Decker's 'Gothic Architecture Decorated', 1759*

Gothic seats, hermits' cells, 'umbrellos', and sham ruins (fig. 95) are charmingly naïve and lighthearted – a Gothic Rococo, as Adam's was a classical Rococo.

To Horace Walpole belongs the credit of having established the Gothic as a style for the English country house. His Strawberry Hill, near London, became famous among connoisseurs and architects of the younger school all over Europe. He gothicized and enlarged the original cottage in 1750. In one respect he was in his Gothic work ahead of others with similar tastes, notably William Kent, whom we have met as a Palladian and a pioneer of picturesque gardening. Walpole insisted that his interiors should have correct details. Fireplaces or wall panelling were copied from engravings after medieval tombs and screens. Yet he evidently admired other qualities in the Gothic style than we do. In letters of 1748 and 1750 he talks of 'the charming venerable Gothic' and the 'whimsical air of novelty' which Gothic motifs give to contemporary buildings. And charming and whimsical Strawberry Hill is indeed with its thin, papery exterior work and the pretty gallery inside whose gilt fan-vaults and tracery have mirrors set in as panels. This playful use of Gothic forms is closer in spirit to Chippendale's Chinese furniture than to Wordsworth's feelings at Tintern Abbey or to Victorian Neo-Gothic churches. Walpole himself was against the fashion of the *Chinoiserie*; but for a generalizing view of the style of 1750 a Chinese bridge, a miniature Pantheon, and a Gothic ruin all belong together. In fact we find that even Robert Adam enjoyed drawing ruins with all the Rococo sparkle of Piranesi, and occasionally designed domestic work in a mildly medieval taste. And we also find Sir William Chambers, in spite of his staunch adherence to Palladianism, designing the Pagoda at Kew Gardens.

Kew had originally the most varied set of such Rococo garden extravaganzas: besides the Pagoda (which alone survives) a temple of Pan, a temple of Aeolus, a temple of Solitude, a temple of the Sun, a temple of Bellona, a temple of Victory, a house of Confucius, a Corinthian colonnade, an Alhambra, a mosque, a Gothic cathedral, a ruin, various stone seats, etc. The fun of Turkish, Moorish, Gothic, and Chinese in this *omnium gatherum* of exotic styles is that of Voltaire's *Zadig* and *Babouc* and of Montesquieu's *Lettres Persanes*, that is one of a sophisticated Rococo double-meaning. Not much of the solemn meditation of the Romantics could in fact be evoked by a Pagoda. When the Romantic Movement somewhat later instilled these sentiments into gardening, a good many of the current garden adornments were eliminated as unsuitable. Yet to Walpole too Strawberry Hill had associational qualities. It was, in some ways, his *Castle of Otranto*. It seems difficult to believe that; but that Beckford's mansion, Fonthill Abbey, with its vast galleries and enormous tower had to him some of the awe-inspiring qualities of the dark Middle Ages can be appreciated from surviving illustrations. Here the eccentricity of a millionaire seems to have created something truly romantic. Fonthill was built by James Wyatt (1746–1813) from 1796 onwards. But already as early as 1772 Goethe in front of Strasbourg Cathedral had found words of passionate admiration for the Gothic spirit in architecture. 'It rises like a most sublime, wide-arching Tree of God, who with a thousand boughs, a million of twigs, and leafage like the sands of the sea, tells forth to the neighbourhood the glory of the Lord, his master. . . . All is shape, down to the minutest fibril, all purposes to the whole. How the firm-grounded gigantic building lightly rears itself into the air! How filagreed all of it, yet for eternity. . . . Stop brother, and discern the deepest sense of truth . . . quickening out of strong, rough, German soul. . . . Be not girled, dear youth, for rough greatness by the soft doctrine of modern beauty-lisping.'[1]

Now here the Gothic style is no longer something in the same category as Rococo, Chinese, and Hindu; it stands for all that is genuine, sincere, elemental – in fact very much for what Winckelmann, and only a little later Goethe himself, saw in the art of Greece. The Greek and the Gothic were both, in the minds of serious aestheticians and artists, the salvation from 18th-century flippancy. But they could not be an effective remedy. For no healthy style can stop at the mere imitation of another. The Renaissance had not done it. The Grecian of the early 19th century did it too often. Goethe in the most classical mood of his *Iphigenia* remained essentially original. But in fact what he had praised more than anything at Strasbourg was originality in the sense of Young. And so the few architects of Goethe's era who possessed true genius used the forms of Greece and Rome with the greatest freedom. Of Greece and Rome; for an equally free and masterly style based on Gothic

1. Geoffrey Grigson's translation, published in *The Architectural Review*, vol. 98, 1945.

principles time was not yet ripe. The sense of medieval building had not yet been sufficiently digested to allow for a revival
in another than an imitative sense.

Three architects above all others must be mentioned as the
creators of an original idiom of the late 18th century: Claude-
Nicolas Ledoux in France, Sir John Soane in England, and
Friedrich Gilly in Prussia. Ledoux (1736–1806) has only within
the last twenty years been rediscovered. He was an eccentric,
cantankerous and quarrelsome. But his designs since 1776 are
amongst the most original ever conceived by any architect,
original sometimes to the verge of mania: a completely
spherical house, a pyramidal house, fantastic projects for vast
community buildings. His planning is boldly Baroque, but his
predilection for squat Tuscan and Greek Doric columns shows
him up as an innovator. The *terribilità* of archaic and indeed
5th-century Greek architecture had not yet been fully understood, certainly not by Athenian Stuart. Yet Ledoux was no
doubt influenced by Stuart and even by Adam, and the publication of his *L'Architecture considérée sous le rapport de l'art, des
mœurs et de la législation* in 1806 may have influenced England
in turn.

How far it can have influenced Soane (1753–1837) has
never yet been considered. It may well be doubted considering the amazing personal blend of Baroque grandeur of composition with Grecian severity of detail which appear even
in Soane's earliest designs, designs made before he went to
Rome in 1776. Even Greek Doric columns occur in his work
in 1776–78. Then during the nineties Soane discovered that
the severity which was his aim could be achieved by sheer unadorned surfaces.

He was appointed architect to the Bank of England in 1788.
The exterior, before it was converted by recent governors
and directors into a podium for a piece of 20th-century commercial showiness, indicates this new and, to the majority,
shocking austerity. The interiors, preserved though atrociously
ill-treated, give an even clearer idea of his sense of surface integrity. Walls flow smoothly into vaults. Mouldings are reduced to a minimum. Arches sit on piers which they seem to

touch only in points. No precedent is allowed to cramp the master's style. The Dulwich Gallery of 1811–14 (damaged by bombs but not irreparably) and Soane's own house in Lincoln's Inn Fields (pl. 61b), built in 1812–13 and intended to be carried on to more than double its width, are his most independent designs. The ground floor of the house has severely plain arcading in front of the actual wall; the first floor repeats this unusual motif with the variation of a centre with Ionic columns supporting the thinnest of architraves, and wings where the

96. *Claude-Nicolas Ledoux: one of the city gates of Paris, designed between 1784 and 1789*

weight of the piers is lightened by typically Soanian incised ornament. The top pavilions on the left and the right are equally original. Except for the Ionic columns there is not one motif in the whole façade that has a Greek or Roman ancestry. Here more than anywhere in architecture England approached a new style unhampered by the past, and a style moreover that possesses the crispness and precision of the dawning machine age. Soane for all we know was not in special sympathy with that age, which in most of its social and visual aspects was still sordid enough. Soane was a wilful, obstinate, and irritable character, and wilful is his almost *Art-Nouveau*-looking ornament. But its meaning is clear. These delicate lines emphasize the planes into which they are cut, just as the lack of pediments on the flat roofs emphasizes the cubic relations of such planes.

Soane had from the beginning of his career been fascinated by the problem of cubic relations.

While in his case connections with Ledoux are doubtful, they are in the case of Friedrich Gilly (1772–1800) quite certain. Gilly had his training in Berlin, one of a small group of young architects who about 1790 discovered the force of the true Doric order in Italy. Gilly himself, however, never saw Italy, and went to Paris and London only after he had designed one of the two masterpieces which are left us to bear witness of his genius – left, however, only in drawings. Neither was ever carried out. The first is the National Monument to Frederick the Great (1797), the second a National Theatre for Berlin – clearly a conception of the Goethe age (pl. 61a). The Doric portico without a pediment is a strong and grave opening. The semicircular windows, a favourite motif of the revolutionary architects of Paris, though imported from England, add strength to strength, and the contrast between the semicylinder of the auditorium walls and the cube of the stage is functionally eloquent and aesthetically superb. Here again we are close to a new style of the new century.

Why is it then that a hundred years had to pass before an original 'modern' style was really accepted? How can it be that the 19th century forgot about Soane and Gilly and remained smugly satisfied with the imitation of the past? Such a lack of self-confidence is the last thing one would expect from an epoch so independent in commerce, industry, and engineering. It is the things of the spirit in which the Victorian age lacked vigour and courage. Standards in architecture were the first to go; for while a poet and a painter can forget about their age and be great in the solitude of their study and studio, an architect cannot exist in opposition to society. Now those to whom visual sensibility was given saw so much beauty destroyed all around by the sudden immense and uncontrolled growth of cities and factories that they despaired of their century and turned to a more inspiring past. Moreover the iron-master and mill-owner, as a rule self-made men of no education, felt no longer bound by one particular accepted taste as the gentleman had been who was brought up to believe in the rule of taste. It would have been bad manners to build against it. Hence the only slightly varied uniformity of the English 18th-century house. The new manufacturer had no manners, and he was a convinced individualist. If, for whatever reasons, he liked a style in architecture, then there was nothing to prevent him from having his way and getting a house or a factory or an office building or a club built in that style. And unfortunately for the immediate future of architecture he knew of a good many possible styles, because – as we have seen – some sophisticated and leisurely *cognoscenti* of the 18th century had explored for fun certain out-of-the-way architectural idioms, and a set of Romantic poets was revelling in nostalgic fantasies of the distant in time and space. The Rococo had reintroduced alien styles, the Romantic Movement had endowed them with sentimental associations. The 19th century lost the Rococo's lightness of touch and the Romantics' emotional fervour. But it stuck to variety of style, because associational values were the only values in architecture accessible to the new ruling class.

We have seen Vanbrugh's defence of ruins for associational reasons. Sir Joshua Reynolds in his thirteenth *Discourse* of 1786 made the same point more neatly. He explicitly counts amongst the principles of architecture 'that of affecting the imagination by means of association of ideas. Thus,' he continues, 'we have naturally a veneration for antiquity; whatever building brings to our remembrance ancient customs and manners, such as the castles of the Barons of ancient Chivalry, is sure to give this delight.'

Hence on the authority of the late President of the Royal Academy the manufacturer and merchant could feel justified in placing associational criteria foremost. Visual criteria his eyes were not trained to appreciate. But the eyes of architects were; and it was a grave symptom of a diseased century that architects were satisfied to be story-tellers instead of artists. But then painters were no better. They too, to be successful, had to tell stories or render objects from nature with scientific accuracy.

Thus by 1830 we find a most alarming social and aesthetic situation in architecture. Architects believed that anything created by the pre-industrial centuries must of necessity be better than anything made to express the character of their own era. Architects' clients had lost all aesthetic susceptibilities, and wanted other than aesthetic qualities to approve of a building. Associations they could understand. And one other quality they could also understand and even check: correctness of imitation. The free and fanciful treatment of styles developed into one of archeological exactitude. That this could happen was due to that general sharpening of the tools of historical knowledge which characterizes the 19th century. It is in truth the century of Historicism. After the system-building 18th century, the 19th appears to an amazing extent satisfied with, say, a historical and comparative study of existing philosophies instead of the study of ethics, aesthetics, etc., themselves. And so it was in theology and philology too. Similarly architectural scholarship abandoned aesthetic theory and concentrated on historical research. Thanks to a subdivision of labour which architecture, like all other fields of art, letters, and science, took over from industry, architects were always able to draw from a well-assorted stock of historical detail. No wonder that little time and desire were left for the development of an original style of the 19th century. Even with regard to Soane and Gilly we have to be careful not to overestimate their originality and 'modernity'. Soane did a great deal that is more conventional than his own house. There are even some Gothic designs by him. And Gilly drew and published in detail the grandest of the medieval castles of the German knights in East Prussia. Exquisite as these drawings are, the attitude that made Gilly spend so much time on them is only partially romantic and patriotic. Antiquarian ambition is at least as conspicuous in these careful renderings. The case of Girtin's and Turner's early water colours is very similar. They are the transition (though still a romantic transition full of creative power) between the polite 18th-century engravings of Athens and Paestum and the voluminous 19th-century books on cathedral antiquities and medieval details.

Amongst such books the transition can also be noted: the earliest are still rather sketchy, while later they became more and more thorough and as a rule rather dull. In actual buildings we find exactly the same development from the elegant and whimsical but sometimes inspired to the learned but sometimes deplorably pedestrian. Strawberry Hill stands for Rococo-Gothic, Robert Adam for a Rococo-Classical Revival. The next generation is characterized by John Nash (1752–1835). Nash had nothing of the intransigent creative fury of Soane. He was light-handed, careless, socially successful, and artistically conservative. His frontages of old Regent Street and most of his palace-like façades round Regent's Park, planned and carried out between 1811 and about 1825, are still of an 18th-century suppleness. What makes them memorable is the way in which they form part of a brilliant town-planning scheme, a scheme linking up the Picturesque of the 18th century with the Garden City ideas of the 20th. For these vast terraces face a landscape park, and a number of elegant villas are placed right in the park – the fulfilment of what had been foreshadowed in the juxtaposition of houses and lawn in the Royal Crescent at Bath. While the Regent Street-Regent's Park frontages are almost entirely classical, Nash built with the same gusto Gothic if required. He had a nice sense of associational propriety; as shown in his choice of the Neo-Classical for his town house and of the Gothic for his country mansion (complete with Gothic conservatory). Moreover he built Cronkhill, in Shropshire (1802), as an Italianate villa with a round-arched loggia on slender columns and with the widely projecting eaves of the Southern farmhouse (Roscoe's *Lorenzo Medici* had come out in 1796); he built Blaise Castle, near Bristol (1809), in a rustic Old-English cottage style with barge-boarded gables and thatched roofs (one is reminded of the *Vicar of Wakefield*, Marie Antoinette's dairy in the Park of Versailles, and Gainsborough's and Greuze's sweet peasant children), and he continued the Brighton Pavilion in a Hindu fashion, first introduced just after 1800 at Sezincote, in the Cotswolds, where the owner, because of personal reminiscences, insisted on the style. 'Indian Gothic' was the eminently characteristic contemporary name of the style.

So here, in the early years of the 19th century, the fancy-dress ball of architecture is in full swing: Classical, Gothic, Italianate, Old-English. By 1840 pattern-books for builders and clients include many more styles: Tudor, French Renaissance, Venetian Renaissance and others. That does not however mean that at all moments during the 19th century all these styles were really used. Favourites changed with fashion. Certain styles became associationally branded. A familiar example is the Moorish synagogue. Another is the perseverance of the battlemented castle for prisons. An account of architecture from 1820 to 1890 is bound to be one of the coming and going of period styles.

On the Classical side 1820–40 is characterized by the most correct Neo-Greek. Fancy had left the treatment of antiquity even earlier than that of the Middle Ages. The results are competent and, in the hands of the best architects, of a noble dignity. The British Museum, begun in 1823 by Sir Robert Smirke (1780–1867), is amongst the best examples in Britain (pl. 62b), or would be if its front with its grand Ionic order of the Erechtheum in Athens could be seen from a distance; Carl Friedrich Schinkel (1781–1841), Gilly's pupil, is the greatest, most sensitive, and most original representative on the Continent (fig. 97), William Strickland (1787–1854) probably the most vigorous in the United States.

For now, with the Greek Revival, America can no longer be left out of the picture of Western architecture. American building had been colonial to the end of the 18th century; colonial as the latest Gothic, Renaissance, and Baroque buildings of the Spanish and the Portuguese in North, Central, and South America. The Greek Revival in the United States is also still closely dependent on European, especially English, examples, but national qualities, such as a remarkable stress on engineering technique, sanitary installation, and equipment in general, now come to the fore. The ideological background of the strict Neo-Greek is the liberal humanism of the educated classes in the early 19th century, the spirit of Goethe, i.e. the spirit which created our first public museums and art galleries, and our first national theatres, and which is responsible for the reorganization and the broadening of education.

97. *Carl Friedrich Schinkel: the Old Museum (Altes Museum), Berlin, 1822–30*

On the Gothic side the corresponding development leads back to the Romantic Movement. Young Goethe's enthusiasm for Strasbourg had been a revolutionary genius's worship of genius. To the generation after his, the Middle Ages became the ideal of Christian civilization. Friedrich Schlegel, one of the most brilliant of Romantic writers and one of the most inspired Gothicists, became a convert to the Roman Catholic church. That was in 1808. Châteaubriand had written his *Génie du Christianisme* in 1802. Then, about 1835 in England, Augustus Welby Pugin (1812–52) transferred the equation of Christianity and Gothic into architectural theory and practice. With him, to build in the forms of the Middle Ages was a moral duty. And he went further. He contended that, as the medieval architect was an honest workman and a faithful Christian, and as medieval architecture is good architecture, you must be an honest workman and a good Christian to be a good architect. In this the associational attitude appears fatefully extended. Similarly contemporary Classicists began to brand the architect who favoured Gothic as an obscurantist and, worse still, his work as popery. On the whole the arguments of the Gothicists proved stronger and had, in an unexpected way, a more beneficial effect on art and architecture, but the aesthetic value of the buildings designed by the Classicists was higher. The Houses of Parliament, begun in 1836, are aesthetically more successful than any later large-scale public building in the Gothic style (pl. 62a). The competition – a significant symptom – had demanded designs in the Gothic or Tudor style. A monument of national tradition had to be in a national style. The architect, Sir Charles Barry (1795–1860), preferred the Classical and the Italian. But Pugin worked with him and was responsible for nearly all the detail inside and outside. Hence the building possesses an intensity of life not to be found in other architects' endeavours in the Perpendicular style.

Yet even Pugin's Gothic turns out to be only a veneer, as soon as the Houses of Parliament are examined as a whole. They have, it is true, a picturesque asymmetry in their towers and spires, but the river front is, in spite of that, with its emphasized centre and corner pavilions, a composition of

Palladian formality. You can without much effort visualize it with porticoes of a William Kent or John Wood type. And strangely enough the British Museum, perfectly Greek as it appears, reveals to the deeper-searching an equally Palladian structure. Centre portico and projecting wings are familiar features. The Athens of Pericles never conceived anything so loosely spread-out.

So while the battles raged between Goth and Pagan, neither realized how all this application of period detail remained on the surface. Moral arguments and associational tags were freely used, but architecture as a job of designing to fulfil functions remained unheeded – or at least undiscussed. Even to-day in such cases as the British Museum and the Houses of Parliament people think much too much of aesthetics and too little of function. Yet it should not be forgotten that to build a palace for democratic government and a palace for the instruction of the people was equally new. In fact to erect public buildings, specially designed as such, had been extremely rare before 1800. There were town halls of course, the most splendid of them all that of Amsterdam (now Royal Palace) built in 1648–55, and there were the Exchanges of Antwerp, London, and Amsterdam. Somerset House in London also had been intended from the beginning for Government offices and learned societies. But these were exceptions. If one takes the 19th century on the other hand, and tries to pick out the best examples of town architecture of all dates and all countries, a number of churches will have to be included, palaces rarely, private houses of course; but the vast majority of what one would collect are Governmental, municipal, and later private office buildings, museums, galleries, libraries, universities and schools, theatres and concert halls, banks and exchanges, railway stations, department stores, hotels and hospitals, i.e. all buildings erected not for worship nor for luxury, but for the benefit and the daily use of the people, as represented by various groups of citizens. In this a new social function of architecture appears, representative of a new stratification of society. But the work in evolving plan forms for these new uses was more often than not anonymous, or at least appears so to us.

The Renaissance library had been a hall of two or three aisles. The Renaissance hospital had been almost exactly identical in plan. Both came without essential modifications from the monastic buildings of the Middle Ages. Now schemes were worked out for special library stores with stacking apparatus. For hospitals, systems were tried of groups of separate wards and separate buildings for each kind of disease. For prisons the star-plan was invented (Pentonville) and accepted. For banks and exchanges the glass-covered centre hall or court proved the most serviceable solution. For museums and galleries a specially good system of lighting was essential, for office buildings the most flexible ground plan. And so every new type of building required its own treatment.

But the academician architects were too busy with new trimmings for façades to notice much of all that. When the struggle between Classicists and Gothicists began to subside, other styles took their place. In the medieval field the generations before Pugin had been all for Perpendicular. To Pugin and those who followed him, notably Sir George Gilbert Scott, Perpendicular was anathema. Gothic had now to be of the 13th and early 14th century to be right, and Scott and his colleagues never minded replacing a genuine Perpendicular window by an imitation earlier one when they had to restore a church. Their archeological knowledge sharpened and on the whole their imitations grew in sensitivity as the century progressed. The change from Perpendicular to Early English belongs to the 'thirties. In the last quarter of the century Bodley's and especially Pearson's work (St Augustine's, Kilburn, London; St John's, Red Lion Square, London; Cathedral, Truro) are the most refined. When it comes to originality, however, these accomplished revivalists were far surpassed by such characters as William Butterfield and James Brooks. Butterfield's detail is original to the extreme of harshness and demonstrative ugliness (All Saints, Margaret Street, London; St Alban's, Holborn, London), and Brooks's plans occasionally abandon all dependence on English Gothic precedent (Ascension, Lavender Hill, London).

No other country took so whole-heartedly to the Gothic

Revival in all its tendencies and shades as England. France kept away from it for a long time and has only a few Neo-Gothic churches of the first order (and Gau, the architect of Ste Clotilde, was born at Cologne). In Germany the change from Schinkel's sometimes romantic and sometimes free functional treatment of Gothic form to the archeological phase is connected with the effort to complete Cologne Cathedral, after the original plan had been found in 1841. Since then good Gothic churches and later on public buildings appeared from Hamburg to Vienna.

In the opposite camp of the Southerners the grand style of the Italian High Renaissance *palazzi* replaced the chastity of the Neo-Greek. The first European Neo-Renaissance palace is Klenze's Beauharnais Palace, in Munich, of 1816. Munich after that produced a number of excellent examples in the 'thirties (National Library by Gärtner, 1831). So did Dresden, thanks to Gottfried Semper (Opera, 1837). In London the style makes its appearance with Sir Charles Barry's Travellers' and Reform Clubs (1829 and 1837). What helped to popularize the Renaissance style must have been its plasticity as against the flatness of Neo-Classical and the thinness of Neo-Perpendicular form. Also it represented a more substantial prosperity, and this, as is well known, was the ideal of the leading classes during the Victorian age (pl. 63a).

Then, already shortly after 1831, France rediscovered her native Early Renaissance, and Paris added vast extensions to its 16th-century town hall, with picturesque gables and playful pilasters. To this corresponded in England a revival of Elizabethan and Jacobean forms, especially for country houses. Their associational value was of course national; their aesthetic appeal lay in a still livelier play of ornaments on surfaces. Apparently the underground tendency, covered up by changing period costumes, was towards the *mouvementé* and spectacular, the flamboyant style of Disraeli and the pompousness of Gladstone. Thus about 1850–60 Italianate forms became also more and more exuberant, until a Neo-Baroque was reached. Charles Garnier's Opera in Paris of 1861–74 is one of the earliest and best examples (pl. 63b). Another is Poelaert's enormous Law

Courts at Brussels (1866–83). In England there is little of this *Second Empire* style. A revival of Palladianism in its most Baroque form took its place, and a strong inspiration from the Wren of Greenwich Hospital. Then with a slight sobering of form and a marked influence from a Classical Re-revival in America (McKim, Mead, and White) a characteristically prosperous Edwardian Imperial style was arrived at (Selfridge's). In Germany the late 19th- and early 20th-century Neo-Baroque goes under the name of Wilhelmian; in Italy it has disgraced Rome with the national monument to King Victor Emmanuel II.

However, by the time these buildings were designed, a reaction had come and spread against so superficial – truly superficial – a conception of architecture. It did not originate with the architect. It could not; because it concerned problems of social reform and of engineering, and architects were not interested in these. Most of them loathed the industrial development of the age just as heartily as the painters. They did not see that the Industrial Revolution, while destroying an accepted order and an accepted standard of beauty, created opportunities for a new kind of beauty and order. It offered to the imaginative new materials and new manufacturing processes, and opened up a vista towards architectural planning on an undreamt-of scale.

As for new materials, iron, and after 1860 steel, made it possible to achieve spans wider than ever before, to build higher than ever before, and develop ground plans more flexible than ever before. Glass, in conjunction with iron and steel, enabled the engineer to make whole roofs and whole walls transparent. Reinforced concrete, introduced at the end of the century, combines the tensile strength of steel with the crushing strength of stone. Architects knew little of these things. They left them to the engineers. For about 1800, in connection with the growing subdivision of competencies, the architect's and the engineer's had become separate jobs for which a separate training was provided. Architects learnt in the offices of older architects and in schools of architecture, until they set up in practice themselves doing what the civil-servant-architect had done in the 17th century, but now chiefly for private clients instead of the State. Engineers were trained in special university faculties or (in France and Central Europe) special technical universities. The most perfect examples of early iron architecture, the suspension bridges, such as Brunel's Clifton Bridge, designed in 1829–31 and begun in 1836, are the work of engineers, not of architects. Paxton, who conceived the Crystal Palace of 1851, was a landscape gardener used to the iron and glasswork of conservatories. The men who introduced iron stanchions into the construction of American warehouses and occasionally, in the 'forties and 'fifties, opened whole fronts by glazing the whole interstices between the stanchions, are mostly unknown or undistinguished as architects. And in France, where a few trained and recognized architects (Labrouste: Geneviève Library, 1845–50) used iron conspicuously – even occasionally for a whole church interior (St Eugène, Paris, begun 1854)–they were attacked and ridiculed by the majority.

In all this a fundamentally unsound conception of architecture as a social service is apparent. This was first recognized by Pugin, who saw only one remedy: the return to the old faith of Rome. Then shortly after him, John Ruskin preached in *The Seven Lamps of Architecture* (1849) that a building must be truthful first of all. And a little later he began to realize that to achieve this thought had to be given to social as well as aesthetic problems. The step from theory to practice was taken by William Morris (1834–96). He had undergone the influence of Ruskin and the Pre-Raphaelites, had actually been for a time a pupil of Rossetti, and also of one of the most conscientious Neo-Gothic architects. But he was not satisfied with either painting or architecture as he saw them practised, i.e. painting as the art of making easel pictures for exhibitions, and architecture as writing-desk and drawing-board work.

And whereas Ruskin kept his social activities apart from his aesthetic theory, Morris was the first to link up the two in the only way they could be successfully linked up. Instead of becoming a painter or an architect, he founded a firm for designing and making furniture, fabrics, wallpaper, carpets, stained glass, etc., and got his Pre-Raphaelite friends to join him. Not until the artist becomes a craftsman again – this was his belief – and the craftsman an artist, can art be saved from annihilation by the machine. Morris was a violent machine-hater. He attributed to mechanization and subdivision of labour all the evils of the age. And from his point of view he was right. The solution he found was aesthetically sound, though socially not in the long run adequate. To build up a new style on design was sound; to try to build it up in opposition to the technical potentialities of the century was just as much escapism as the Classicist's disguising of a town hall as a Greek temple. The forms which Morris & Co. chose for their products were inspired by the late Middle Ages, as was Morris's poetry. But Morris did not imitate. He recognized Historicism as the danger it was. What he did was to steep himself in the atmosphere and the aesthetic principles of the Middle Ages, and then create something new with a similar flavour and on similar principles. This is why Morris fabrics and wallpapers will live long after all applied art of the generation before his will have lost its significance.

Morris's social-aesthetic theory as it was embodied in the many lectures and addresses he delivered from 1877 onwards will keep its life in history too. By trying to revive the old faith in service, by indicting the contemporary architect's and artist's arrogant indifference to design for everyday needs, by discrediting any art created by individual genius for a small group of connoisseurs, and by forcing home with untiring zest the principle that art matters only 'if all can share it', he laid the foundation of the Modern Movement.

What Morris did for the philosophy of art and for design, Richardson in the United States and Webb and Norman Shaw in Britain did concurrently for the aesthetics of architecture. Henry Hobson Richardson (1838–86) unquestionably still belongs to the era of period revivals. He studied in Paris and returned to New England deeply impressed by the power of the French Romanesque style. He continued to make use of it for churches, public and office buildings (Auditorium, Chicago), but no longer just for imitative or associational reasons. He saw that these plain massive stone surfaces and mighty round arches

could convey emotional contents more suited to our own age
than any other familiar to him. And he and his followers designed country houses in the 'eighties freer and bolder than any
Europe did at the same time – or should one say Europe with
the exception of Philip Webb in England? Webb (1830–1915)
liked plain brick walls and introduced into them the plain
slender windows of the William and Mary and Queen Anne
period, remaining nevertheless in sympathy with the sturdy
honest building traditions of the Gothic and Tudor styles. The
Red House at Bexley Heath, near London, his first work,

98. *Robert Norman Shaw: stores and inn at the Bedford Park Garden Suburb,
Chiswick, 1878.*

designed for (and with) Morris in 1859 shows already a combination of pointed arches and long segment-headed sash
windows.

The picturesque possibilities of a mixture of motifs derived
from widely different styles were more readily taken up by
Richard Norman Shaw (1831–1912). He had a much lighter
touch, a quicker imagination, but a less discriminating taste. In
a professional career extending over more than forty years he
never ceased to try the contemporary appeal of new period
styles. Thus he went in for half-timbered Tudor country
houses, then for the many-gabled brick architecture of the
Dutch Renaissance, then for a very restrained Neo-Queen
Anne, or rather Neo-William and Mary, and finally joined in
the pompous Edwardian Imperial. He enjoyed, however,
nothing more than playing with motifs of different centuries
(fig. 98). By combining a few Tudor and a few 17th-century

motifs with others of his own invention, he achieved a lightness and animation that make Morris designs appear gloomy.

Norman Shaw's influence on the architectural profession was immediate and very widespread. A generation of architects came from his studio to whom he left the freedom of following Morris's ideas, while following his own forms. They and some closer disciples of Morris founded the Arts and Crafts Movement. Once one knows what Morris taught, the name becomes self-explanatory. More and more original interpretations of architectural traditions were worked out by the members of this group, almost exclusively in designs for town and

99. *Charles F. Annesley Voysey: house at Colwall, Malvern,* 1893

country houses. Lethaby, Prior, Stokes, Ricardo, Halsey are amongst the most noteworthy names. They are little known nowadays, but the freshness and independence of their approach was unique in Europe at the date of their early activity, say between 1885 and 1895. The most brilliant of them all was connected personally with neither Shaw nor Morris – Charles F. Annesley Voysey (1857–1941). His designs for fabrics, wallpapers, furniture, and metalwork especially, so novel and so graceful, had an effect no less revolutionizing than Morris's. In his buildings he appears just as dainty and lovable (fig. 99). Of period detail little is kept, but no effort is made to eliminate a general period flavour. In fact it is just the effortless, unaffected nature of Voysey's architecture that gives it its charm. Moreover, going more closely into it, one will be struck by the boldness of bare walls and long horizontal bands of windows. In such buildings of the 'nineties England came nearest to the idiom of the Modern Movement.

For the next forty years, the first forty of our century, no British name need here be mentioned. Britain had led Europe and America in architecture and design for a long time; now her ascendancy had come to an end. From Britain the art of landscape gardening had spread, and Adam's and Wedgwood's style, in Britain the Gothic Revival had been conceived, to Britain the degradation of machine-produced applied art was due, to Britain the constructive reaction against it. The domestic revival of Morris, Norman Shaw, and Voysey was British; British was the new social conception of a unified art under architectural guidance, and British the first achievements of design completely independent of the past. They are to be found in the work of Arthur H. Mackmurdo's Century Guild about 1885 and then in that of Voysey and some architects influenced by him, Baillie Scott, C. R. Ashbee, and above all Charles Rennie Mackintosh (1869–1928).

Art Nouveau, the first novel style on the Continent, and in fact a style, it seems now, desperately set on being novel, drew its inspiration from English design. It started in Brussels in 1893 and had by 1895 become the *dernier cri* amongst the young artists and architects of Germany, Austria, and France. Of Continental buildings designed between 1760 and the years of Art Nouveau not many have so far been mentioned in this chapter. All that was of importance either happened in Britain or could at least be followed just as easily in Britain as abroad.

The position changed a few years before 1900. The stage reached by Britain at that moment was one of truly contemporary design, but of a free traditionalism (as against the earlier more pedantic Historicism) in architecture. The step that had to be taken to recover a genuine, original design was that from Voysey's designs to a style in building equally bold. And the British character was (and is) all against such drastic steps, so uncompromising an attitude, so logical a procedure. Thus progress in Britain stopped for thirty years. Voysey's Tudor traditionalism was followed by a Wren and Georgian traditionalism, equally pleasant in domestic architecture, but feeble if not painfully inflated-looking in representational buildings.

The first private houses in which the new, original style of the 20th century can be recognized are Frank Lloyd Wright's (born 1869), built in the 'nineties in the neighbourhood of Chicago. They have the freely spreading ground plans, the interweaving of exteriors and interiors by means of terraces and cantilevered roofs, the opening up of one room into another, the predominant horizontals, the long window bands that are familiar in to-day's houses. Also at Chicago, and as early as the 'eighties and 'nineties, the first buildings were erected with steel skeletons (William Le Baron Jenney: Home Insurance Company, 1884–85) and façades not disguising them (Holabird and Roche: Marquette Building, 1894). If a period style was still used for external detail it was usually Richardson's severely plain American Romanesque. As against this American priority in the appreciative use of steel, France was the first country to design houses of a genuine concrete character. They are of the first years of our century (Tony Garnier, born 1869; Auguste Perret, born 1873).

Then, between 1905 and 1914, Germany became the most important country. Here the liaison of design and architecture was most successful. Peter Behrens (1868–1938) designed factories and their products. The *Werkbund* was founded to be a meeting-place of progressive manufacturers, architects, and designers. And while in the United States and France the pioneers remained solitary, in Germany, twenty years ago, a style independent of the past had been accepted by quite a large public. In 1914, Walter Gropius (born 1883) showed the world, at an exhibition in Cologne, a factory so completely of to-day in every detail that it might be mis-dated by anybody (pl. 64). It had a flat roof, again the general stress on horizontals, and two staircases entirely encased in curved glass so that the skeleton and the interior workings were proudly exposed. It will at once be recognized that in this motif, as in the floating ground plan of Wright (and later on of Le Corbusier), and as, incidentally, also in the fantastic American highways intersections with wide areas given up to nothing but traffic bands on various levels, the eternal passion of the West for spatial movement once more expresses itself.

So by 1914 the leading architects of the younger generation had courageously broken with the past and accepted the machine-age in all its implications: new materials, new processes, new forms, new problems. Of these the most important is symbolized to an extent that probably future civilizations will find as obscure as we find Avebury Circle and the Kennet Avenue, by the American traffic crossings just mentioned: namely the problem of modern town-planning. It has been said before that one of the greatest changes brought about by the Industrial Revolution was the sudden growth of cities. To cope with this, architects should have concentrated on the adequate housing of the vast new working-class populations of these cities and on the planning of adequate routes of traffic for the worker to get to his job and back every day. But they were interested in façades and nothing else; and so in a way were municipalities of the 19th century. New public buildings cropped up everywhere. They were as splendid as money could buy. Take Manchester Town Hall, Glasgow University, the Law Courts in Birmingham, London County Hall, or take the series of magnificent but characteristically unrelated monuments along the Ringstrasse in Vienna: the Gothic Town Hall, the Classical Houses of Parliament, the Renaissance museums, etc.; one cannot say that Governments and city councils failed in their undeniable duty to give representational architecture a chance.

Where they failed was in their infinitely greater duty to provide decent living conditions for their citizens. One may say that this was an outcome of the philosophy of liberalism, which had taught them that everybody is happiest if left to look after himself, and that interference with private life is unnatural and always damaging; but while this explanation will satisfy the historian, it could not satisfy the social reformer. He saw that 95 per cent of the new houses in industrial towns were put up by speculative builders as cheaply as the scanty regulations would allow, and acted as best he could. If he was a man like William Morris, he preached a medievalizing socialism and escaped into the happier world of handicraft. If he was like Prince Albert and Lord Shaftesbury, he founded associations for improving by private generosity the dwellings of the artisan and labourer. If, however, he was an enlightened employer himself, he went one step further and commissioned an estate to be designed and built to a more satisfactory standard for his own workers. Thus Sir Titus Salt founded Saltaire, near Leeds, in 1853. It looks very drab now, but it was pioneer work. Lever Brothers began Port Sunlight in 1888 and Cadbury's Bournville in 1895. These two were the first factory estates planned as garden suburbs. From them – and Bedford Park, near London, which had been designed as early as 1875 by Norman Shaw on the same principle, though for private tenants of a wealthier class – the garden suburb and the garden city movement spread, another British contribution to the pre-history of modern European architecture.

Now, in connection with this movement, architects re-entered the domain of town-planning. The greatest town-planning scheme between 1830 and 1880 had been the work of an administrative genius, Baron Haussmann, Napoleon III's prefect of the Seine department. His long, wide, and straight roads all through the centre of Paris were drawn for the sake of civic magnificence and military security, but also for easier traffic to such focal points as railway stations. Haussmann was, however, not interested in housing, in the slums that developed behind his tall new façades, nor did he extend his appreciation of transport needs to the railways themselves.

But this problem, too, could not in the long run be neglected by the architect, once he accepted it as his job to design whole estates and suburbs. These new estates of small houses in their own gardens took a great deal of space. They were possible only right outside the built-over areas of towns. So the question of well-organized road and rail traffic became imperative. This question until then had been in the hands of the business man and again the engineer. Both had shown themselves staggeringly obtuse to architectural values. Some of the best vistas of London were cut into by railway bridges: the approach to St Paul's, for example, and the views down the Thames.

Station buildings themselves, except for a few early ones such as old Euston and King's Cross, and except for the bewildering splendour of Gilbert Scott's Early English St Pancras Station, were mean and untidy – at least in Britain. This unwillingness to accept the care for decent design as a public duty still applied quite universally to British big business and public services thirty years ago. The first to set an example of what immense improvements personal initiative can achieve was Frank Pick, to whom London owes a transport system beautifully designed from the station building down to the lighting standards and the litter baskets.

Frank Pick must be mentioned in a history of architecture as the prototype of the 20th-century patron. A Medici, a Louis XIV, are impossible in an age such as ours. The new Maecenas is an administrator, a worker himself, with a house not much bigger than yours and mine, a cottage in the country, and a car far from spectacular. But as Managing Director of the London General Omnibus and the London Underground Companies, Pick saw that to assemble artists and architects round such a vast business enterprise would be to bring Morris's ideals up to date. So before the First World War he began to reform the lettering used, had one of the best modern type-faces designed especially for his purpose and impressed it so deeply on the minds of millions that a revolution in British lettering ensued. Concurrently he started a campaign for better posters, and again succeeded in establishing Britain in the front rank of modern poster art. And when in the 'twenties and 'thirties many new stations had to be built, he realized that the Continent had evolved a style more suited than contemporary English Neo-Georgian to express the synthesis of function and civic dignity that was his ideal. So he found the right architect in Mr Charles Holden, and the London Underground stations (fig. 100) became the most perfect examples in London of the style of today, serviceable, uncompromisingly modern, and yet in keeping with the quiet distinction of the Georgian brick house.

Those who are doubtful about the blessings of the Modern Movement in architecture often say that the strongest argument against it is the very fact that its most representative examples are stations, factories, office buildings, and the like. Now this is certainly not an accident. It would not be possible to find anything like the same number of good contemporary buildings for private luxury as for workaday use. But then, does not the architect to-day build for a population with nothing like the leisure for luxuries which patrons of the Baroque enjoyed? Must that not change the style, if it is a genuine style? Moreover, as has already been said, nearly every building that is designed nowadays serves masses and not individuals. Must not therefore our style be one adapted to mass

100. *Charles Holden: Arnos Grove Station, of the London Underground, 1932*

production, in the sense of production not only in masses but also for masses?

Thus, if the new style is bare, if it goes straight to the point, there are good reasons for it. The ground had first of all to be cleared of the weeds of 19th-century sham ornamentation. Once that had been done, all available energy had to be devoted to research into function. What during the 19th century had been done slowly and anonymously now became the central task of the architect. If you have to build a soap factory, you must know how soap is being made. If your job is to design a nursery-school, you must find out all about nursery-school work. You cannot accept any plan on authority; it must be evolved anew every time from fundamentals. This Back-to-Fundamentals attitude with regard to function encouraged the same attitude to form. Again no authority was accepted, and again – after the first Art Nouveau flourish of unshackled imagination – the basic principles were rediscovered. This happened – a very hopeful sign – not only in architecture, but also in painting and sculpture. Cubism and then abstract art were the outcome, the most architectural art that had existed since the Middle Ages. In architecture, sheer proportion at last took its legitimate place again. No mouldings, no frills were permitted to distract one's attention from true architectural values: the relation of wall to window, solid to void, volume to space, block to block. I need not here go into more detail about things which belong to our own day and not to history yet.

The one fact that matters to the historian already, and the one that he can state without falling into the rôle of counsel for the defence or for prosecution, is that the Modern Movement is a genuine and independent style. This fact is full of promise. For over a hundred years no style in that sense had existed. As Western civilization had become more and more subdivided, it had lost its faculty to create a language of its own. An atomized society cannot have an architectural style. Can we not take it then that the recovery of a true style in the visual arts, one in which once again building rules, and painting and sculpture serve, and one in which form is obviously representative of character, indicates the return of unity in society too? Granted that this new style often looks rather forbidding and seems to lack human warmth, is not the same true of contemporary life? Here, too, amenities to which we have been used are being replaced by something more exacting and more elementary.

Beyond stating this the historian should not go. Whether the new social and architectural attitude heralds a last phase of Western civilization or the dawn of a new, whether the style of the future will be at all similar to our own, and whether we shall like it – all this it is not for the historian to foretell. His job is done when he has applied the principles of historical analysis as far into the problems of the present day as they can safely be applied.

American Postscript

THE most obvious difference between the history of architecture in the United States and in Western Europe is that American architecture, as part of Western architecture, is only less than five hundred years old, whereas in England, in France, in Italy, in Germany, in the Netherlands, in Spain, one coherent and unbroken development runs through the last thousand years and more. During these ten or eleven centuries every new step of importance was taken within the compass of no more than fifteen hundred miles across from the German Sea to Sicily and from Ireland and Galicia to West Prussia and Bohemia. In this territory, less in extent than the United States, Charlemagne restored a Roman Empire and, against his will, helped to raise the first monuments of a youthful Western spirit, the Cluniacs in France and the Saxon Emperors in Germany evolved the Romanesque style, in the Île de France ingenious masons devised the Gothic system, English, Spanish, German, Italian masons somewhat later modified it to suit their growing national consciousness, Italy revolted against it for a new purity, scientific order, and grace, then for a newer gravity and solemnity and then for a forced, self-tormenting artificiality, in her Early Renaissance, High Renaissance, and Mannerism.

All this – this mighty drama of the birth, adolescence, virile maturity, and first symptoms of ageing of the West – had taken place before any buildings of Western character existed in the United States. And even if we take the whole of the Americas there is only a faint echo here and there – say in the related rib-vaults of some Friars' churches in Mexico – of posthumous Western Gothic. Otherwise Mannerism is the first European style reflected on American soil.

Prehistory, on the other hand – in the sense in which we use
the term in Europe for the Mediterranean before the advent of
historic styles first in Egypt and Asia Minor, then in Greece
and the Hellenistic States, and then in Rome and the Roman
Empire, and for the North roughly up to the coming of
Roman and in some parts Carolingian civilization – applies in
the Americas to everything before Columbus, before Cortez,
before Pizarro, before Raleigh, the Pilgrim Fathers, and
Penn.

Thus not even the shortest outline of prehistoric art and
architecture could afford to omit Mexican, Maya, and Inca
temples and the artefacts of North American Indians, but an
outline of Western architecture can, it is my contention, do
without any mention of buildings in America prior to the 18th
or indeed the 19th, century. In a book in which the sever
Mannerism of Herrera and his followers in Spain appears only
in a few lines, it would be as perverse to devote space to th
ruin of Tecali – the 'purist' Franciscan church in Mexico
dated 1569 – as it would be to choose Dalmatian examples t
discuss Venetian architecture or Nicosia on Cyprus to discu
French Gothic church buildings.

Again, the *incunabula* of New England's domestic architecture, while they are rightly treasured by New Englanders an
treated with all the affectionate respect and care with which t
English should treat (and often don't) their heritage of farn
and manor-house all up and down a country altogether not
much bigger than New England, can have no place in a bri
textbook. What America did during the 17th century in th
way of house-building has all 'the charm of sincere effor
naïve ignorance, and unskilful execution', as Talbot Haml
says, but it is not one of the essential tributary forces to t
main stream of architectural development.

However, with the 18th century emphasis changes. Amer
can architecture is still Colonial, that is primarily depende
on colonizing countries – England, Spain, and Portugal, a
up to a point France – but dependence is no longer compl
and aesthetic quality certainly no longer necessarily provinci
The Sanctuary of Ocotlan at Tlaxcala, in Mexico, or the chur

of the Third Order of St Francis at Bahia, in Brazil, may be somewhat barbaric and sensational, but so is much of the Churrigueresque in Spain. And as this riotous superabundance, this overcrowding with clamorous detail, is part and parcel of Pyrenean Baroque, it would have been no less legitimate to illustrate it from Mexican or Brazilian examples than from the Caruja of Granada, as I have done. It is true that certain features in America may be due less to Spanish and Portuguese precedent than to Indian workmen, for whom the wildly distorted and elaborately intertwined decoration of Aztec and Inca temples was still alive and valid. Indian influence as early as about 1500 has been assumed (page 104) to explain Portuguese Manueline ornament. But there it was European artists impressed by the achievements of the natives; now it is the natives themselves transforming European patterns.

In North America during the same decades a similar change of balance can be observed, but with eminently significant modifications. Prosperity was just as firmly established in North as in Central and South America, but instead of the Roman Catholic social pattern of mission and skilled native labour, there grew in the North a system of secular land ownership and Protestant town civilization. The style of architecture was as English as it was Pyrenean in the South. Local variation in the home themes was as conspicuous. But as in the future United States both patrons and builders were Western by origin and traditions, and often even by birth, these variations were the outcome of climatic rather than racial conditions. Red Indian ingenuity was, alas, expelled and by degrees eradicated. Thus the colonial style of North America, the Colonial Style *par excellence*, is wholly English Georgian. The most notable American modifications are due to the prevalent use of timber as a building material. Wood accounts for the slimness of the columns, and wood also for the cheerful colour schemes. A warmer climate permitted terraces, porches, and loggias, and the wide spaces, only gradually to be populated, a more generous siting, the preservation of many trees and, in the little towns, the planting of those venerable avenues and greens which now give to Salem, Nantucket, Charleston,

and so on, and even to what is left of the oldest manufacturing towns of New England, their delightful garden-city
character.

Still, while a short general history of architecture could illustrate Christ Church, Philadelphia, or one of the churches of
Charleston instead of an English church, or Salem or Nantucket
as particularly carefully preserved specimens of the Georgian
country town, there is certainly no necessity that it should.
What there is of differences between American and English
Georgian does not go beyond the differences, say, between
Bavarian and Dresden Rococo. And as far as quality goes,
while the Mexican Baroque may be regarded in some ways as
the climax of Spanish Baroque, even the best examples of
American Colonial can hardly be placed upon the same level
as Vanbrugh's or Adam's works.

This last remark and all else I have so far ventured to say
about America is, I think, borne out by the published views of
American scholars. When it comes to the early 19th century,
however, I am a little at variance with at least some of the most
distinguished architectural historians in the United States. Mr
Hamlin, the author of the best general history of architecture
that I know, has as Chapters 2 and 3 of his immensely know-
ledgeable *Greek Revival Architecture in America* (Oxford University Press, 1944), 'The Birth of American Architecture'
dealing chiefly with Latrobe, and 'American Architecture
comes of Age', dealing with Mills, Strickland, and the other
Greek Revivalists. So the contention is that the Greek Revival
is the first national American style. I fail to see that. There i
to my mind no more that separates Latrobe from Soane, o:
Mills and Strickland from Smirke and Hamilton than ther
is between the 18th-century country houses of Virginia an
Louisiana and those by Robert Adam or Henry Holland
So the relation between Europe and America cannot, I think
be regarded as changed between 1770 and 1820. America de
veloped away from delicacy towards a new grandeur an
severity during these fifty years; but so did England, France
and Germany.

Thomas Jefferson was enthusiastic about Nîmes, when h

saw it in the 1780's, and the result was an architectural style ranging from the imitation of that sober Palladianism which Paris at that very moment was evolving from English precedent (Monticello, Capitol Richmond – cf. Clérisseau, and especially Ledoux and his group of French architects) to a much more naïve imitation of Roman detail (University of Virginia). Latrobe, Ramée, Mangin were themselves of French origin. Latrobe had passed through English training, Ramée had worked in Germany (and his son edited the second volume of Ledoux's *Architecture*). When Latrobe left England to settle in America in 1796, he could just have seen designs and perhaps more of Soane's revolutionary work at the Bank of England and at Tyringham. They would account for the most striking innovations in Latrobe – for instance, his determined change from Tuscan to Greek Doric, and also for some of the details inside North America's most beautiful church, Latrobe's Baltimore Cathedral of 1805–18. Here for once is true spatial composition, bold and imaginative, if dependent on Wren's St Paul's as much as on Soane.

England also is the background of Latrobe's Gothic Revival. He seems to have introduced the fashion to America ('Sedgeley'; Gothic designs for Baltimore Cathedral) in its romantic, not in its Rococo, form. The Gothic Rococo of Strawberry Hill is missing in the United States. The development of Neo-Gothic forms into antiquarian correctness, however, is again exactly parallel in England and the United States (Upjohn, Renwick), with English inspiration maintained by journeys as well as pattern-books and archeological publications.

So by 1850, while American architecture was throughout no longer colonial and in the work of the leading architects no longer provincial, it was not yet essentially original. It possessed a full share of Greek Revival on the largest and the smallest scale, and a fair dose of Gothic, Egyptian, and Old English Cottage Revival (complete with Downing's picturesque gardens – see Llewelyn Park), but all this had been introduced on the strength of European and chiefly English precedent.

When original features and original points of view are
looked for, they will be found, I think, in such things as the
adolescent vigour and crudity with which State Capitols and
other public buildings went on trying to combine the Greek
temple shape with a central dome (Davis and others). The
Madeleine in Paris had domes behind its colonnades, but wisely
refrained from showing them outside. Americans were not so
squeamish. But more important for the future rôle of America
in Western architecture than such lusty monstrosities is a
marked interest amongst architects in engineering and in up-
to-date equipment. Latrobe, we are told, studied under
Smeaton, the great engineer, as well as under Cockerell Senior;
Strickland 'was almost better known as an engineer than as an
architect' (Hamlin). Town, of Town and Davis, was the inventor of a successful type of truss for wooden bridges,
McComb designed lighthouses and fortifications besides the
old New York City Hall, Willard invented quarrying
machinery, and so on. As for the American advance over
Europe in matters of mechanical equipment, domestic comforts, sanitation, etc., it is enough to follow the reactions of
older nations to the American exhibits at Philadelphia in 1876,
or to compare the history of the hotel between 1825 and 1875
in America and in England and France.

Special emphasis has lately been laid (Giedion) on the
American introduction of the balloon frame about 1825 or so
– a primitive system of timber building with prefabricated
parts and exclusively unskilled labour on the site – and on the
American development of iron construction for office buildings, warehouses, and the like. How far the United States in
either of these fields were really inventors, and how far only
eager and intelligent promoters, is not yet clear. Regarding
iron, England had certainly done more on the engineering side
between 1800 and 1850 than has yet been acknowledged, while
Labrouste's outstandingly sympathetic handling of the new
material (Ste Geneviève Library, 1845–50) is known. In France
also the idea of a complete iron frame for buildings seems to
have been conceived (Viollet-le-Duc's lectures of 1863–64)
and the iron skeleton with outer walls bearing no weight and

serving only as screens carried out (Meunier's Chocolate Factory 1871–72, according to Giedion).[1]

While in America as in Europe iron developments took place essentially behind the architectural scene, and the new material was as a rule allowed to show only in utilitarian and temporary structures, architecture as a profession stopped within the framework of historicism as firmly on the west as on the east of the Atlantic.

However, one new development must now be listed. The United States freed themselves at last from English tutelage – a war of independence some eighty years late. And as after the political struggle the young nation first looked to France for inspiration (and Thomas Jefferson did in architecture too, although to a France under English influence), so now the young profession did the same. Richard M. Hunt (1828–95) studied under Lefuel in Paris, while the Louvre was finally completed in the revived florid style of Lescot and Delorme, and brought back the glamour of the Third Empire, ready for millionaires and proud municipal bodies to imitate.

But more significant than the Neo-French Renaissance (which after all captured London as well and may often have impressed Americans more in English than in French examples) is the other slightly later Franco-American relation, that between Henry Hobson Richardson (1838–86) and the Romanesque style of southern France. For here for the first time do we find an American architect acting independently. A Romanesque Revival was not a completely new idea. There existed already in various countries round-arched buildings called early Christian, or Byzantine, or Norman, as the case might be. But at that moment – Richardson returned to America from France in 1865 and started on his consistent Neo-Romanesque campaign about 1870 – neither England nor France nor Germany specialized in the Romanesque. Richardson's determination to build Romanesque and Romanesque only was a personal decision dictated by a strong feeling for the modern

1. From *The Builder*, vol. 23, 1865, pp. 296–97, it sounds as if Préfontaine and Fontaine's St Ouen Docks were constructed already on the same principle.

qualities which could be brought out by the use of such plain, elementary forms. Into his historic detail he instilled an uncouth, primeval directness, all American of his age. His sense of texture and rich surface pattern underlining the massive compactness of his buildings, on the other hand, was entirely his own.

Richardson's position in the history of American architecture corresponds in more than one way with William Morris's in England. Both kept within historicism, but both chose period precedent with an eye on modern needs and thus appear to us, in spite of their medievalisms of idiom, as the torchbearers of the approaching Modern Movement.

Richardson's influence was great. Somehow he must have been felt, if subconsciously, to be more American, that is more direct, than any of the other architects of his generation. Louis Sullivan (1856–1924) cannot be understood without Richardson, nor can the forms in which skyscrapers first presented themselves to an amazed Europe. For now, in the eighties, the United States reached the front of architectural creativeness. Up to the end of the 18th century America had been Colonial; between 1800 and 1880 it was one of the many provinces of the West. Now it had become one of the few centres of progress – unnoticed, it must be said, by the most successful American or European architects and critics of the day. Official, generally accepted architecture in America was, it must not be forgotten, still as imitative in 1890 and 1920 as it was in England. Sullivan was no more widely acknowledged than Voysey or Mackintosh. Growing American importance was, however, reflected in the fact that academic architecture of the United States now influenced England, and no longer English academic architecture America. The Edwardian Imperial style of Britain and the Dominions (page 258) derived a considerable amount of encouragement, if not more, from the Classical Re-Revival which in the United States had followed the Chicago Exhibition of 1893, and indeed had sometimes taken forms grander, vaster, and simpler than in England.

Of the Chicago Exhibition Sullivan said that the damage wrought by it would last for half a century. The prognostication has proved accurate, if we accept the Modern Movement as the only truthful expression of the spirit of our age. It had won a great victory in the Middle West just before 1893, and Chicago might have become the international centre of early modern architecture, if it had not been for the 'World's Fair'. For Chicago was the birthplace of the steel-skeleton skyscraper. and the peculiar, wholly original idiom worked out by Sullivan and his pupil Frank Lloyd Wright (born 1869).

The skyscraper had been conceived for reasons of commercial pride and lack of space, independent of the skeleton technique, but could be developed only if a method of building was found obviating the immense thickness of load-bearing masonry walls which a building of twelve or twenty stories otherwise demands. Who exactly invented the skyscraper has proved a question most tempting to American research, but one which *per se* can never be wholly answered. There were on the one hand Viollet-le-Duc's prophetic remarks, and on the other the iron framework inside factories in England and France. Buffington may well have been stimulated by them as early as 1882 into some vague and tentative thought of the possibility of steel skyscrapers, but it is certain now that he did not get to grips with the contructional problems involved until Le Baron Jenney had completed his Home Assurance Building at Chicago in 1886 (page 261). Buffington's patent dates from 1888, and was by then already obsolete. The first complete steel-frame skyscraper is Holabird and Roche's Tacoma Building of 1887–88. The most popular period style to express the boldness of these wholly American structures was Richardson's Neo-Romanesque. With its squareness and bareness and with what little it had of completely flat decoration it was indeed a suitable disguise, if disguise was felt to be needed. But some of the buildings about 1890 to 1900 – in steel-frame as well as masonry – already exhibit quite an independent aesthetic attitude, for instance Root's Monadnock Block, Holabird and Roche's Marquette Building, Sullivan's Guarantee Building at Buffalo, and – more amazingly up-to-date than any of the others – Sullivan's Carson, Pirie Scott and Company Building at Chicago. In this building there is already the long horizontal window band as the one and only dominant motif of the façade, and there is an almost complete absence of ornament. No European country had at that moment gone as far in the preparation of the style of to-day as the Middle West.

And no European country had at the same date private houses to compare with those of the United States. There again the initiative goes back to Richardson and such amazingly free, comfortable, rustic compositions of his as the F. L. Ames Gate Lodge at North Easton, Mass., of 1880, and the Stoughton House at Cambridge, Mass., of 1882. Early Sullivan houses followed, and some of them were designed by Frank Lloyd Wright while he worked in Sullivan's office. The Winslow House at River Forest (1893) shows his personal style in the making, the houses since *c.* 1900 show it complete, with their cantilevered-out slab roofs, spacious terraces, and rooms floating into each other. Their first publication in Germany in 1910 and 1911 helped towards the elaboration of the Continental modern style quite as much as the more familiar houses of Voysey, Baillie Scott, and Mackintosh. France and Austria, on the other hand, in their contribution of 1900–05 (Garnier, Perret, Loos, Hoffmann) seem to have been independent of America.

I have found it necessary in the foregoing pages to mention European architects left out of the chapters dealing with European architecture. This applies, for instance, to Loos and Hoffmann, and to Labrouste and Lefuel. My reason is that with the known history of architecture in the United States being virtually compressed into two hundred years, each trend assumes a greater importance than a corresponding trend in the longer history of building in Europe. All the interest we spend over here on Greek and Roman, Romanesque and Gothic, Renaissance and Baroque goes in the United States into the achievement of these two centuries.

This has another consequence, and one I want to point out in conclusion. With intensity of interest goes intensity of research. In Britain architectural research has not been very intensive during the last thirty years or so. Since Prior and Lethaby medieval research of an international outlook has all but stopped. Renaissance research is as scarce as everywhere. So it is in the English 17th and 18th centuries chiefly that consistent intelligent work is done. In the United States, thanks to a much more firmly and widely established system of teaching the history of art and architecture in the universities and colleges, and thanks to a national penchant towards doing things thoroughly and with international documentation, once they are being done at all, architectural research is infinitely more active and successful.

This is especially noticeable, if we compare books brought out between the two wars on matters referring to American architecture of the 18th and 19th centuries in America, with books on English architecture of the same period in England. I can enumerate only a few. First of all the State guides of the Federal Writers' Project (1937, etc.), uneven in quality, but on the whole far more alive and architecturally comprehensive than English guidebooks. Then there is the work of such scholars as Mr Fiske Kimball and Mr Talbot Hamlin. On British Georgian and Greek Revival architecture no such detailed handbooks and papers as theirs are yet in existence. Again regional surveys comparable with Mr Henry-Russell Hitchcock's of Rhode Island, to mention only one of several, are absent in England. So are books dealing with the interaction of social and architectural matters as soundly and attractively as Mr John Coolidge's *Mill and Mansion*. Finally there are monographs on the architects of 1760 to 1900. We have books (of varying standard) on Adam, Soane, Wyatt, Nash, and Pugin, and on Webb and Norman Shaw. But where are modern biographies of Vanbrugh and Hawksmoor, of Gibbs and Chambers, and then of Barry, Scott, Burges, Street, Brooks, Pearson, Sedding, Voysey, Mackintosh, and so forth? In America not everyone of the leaders has his book yet either – a Life of Latrobe for instance, a Life of Strickland, a Life of Downing are still sorely needed – but between the wars, and particularly in the last ten years, monographs have come out on McIntire, Jefferson, Bulfinch, Mills, Town and Davis,

Upjohn, Richardson, Burnham, McKim, Goodhue, to say nothing of additional papers in the magazines.

Why should an American Postscript to a small and unpretentious book end with a list of publications referring to architects and works hardly appearing in the text? The answer is that there is a lesson in it for the British as well as the Americans. One reason not yet sufficiently stressed for the more coherent progress of architectural research in the United States is that America is prouder of her achievements than Britain, or at least more attached to them. This leads to a most laudable seriousness in research even on such initially unpromising-looking topics as the development of architecture in Victorian Detroit (B. Pickens), whereas in England what attention is paid to Victorian buildings and design is still, with a very few exceptions, of the whimsical variety.

On the other hand, there is in the American concentration on local, regional, and national architecture the danger of parochialism. Things are regarded as peculiarly American, because all their antecedents, phases, and particulars are by now far better known in America than in Europe. Thus English or Continental precedent is disregarded because not familiar. Even Mr Hamlin's exemplary integrity and thoroughness have not always protected him from this unevenness of judgment.

If that is so with the scholars, may there not be quite an acceptable reason for offering to the layman in America a brief outline of architectural events on our side of the Atlantic?

Bibliography

GENERAL

A. Michel: Histoire de l'Art, 18 vols., Paris, 1905–29.

Sir Banister Fletcher: A History of Architecture, 14th ed., London, 1948.

R. Sturgis: Dictionary of Architecture and Building, 3 vols., New York, 1901–2.

Talbot F. Hamlin: Architecture through the Ages, New York, 1941.

Fiske Kimball and G. H. Edgell: A History of Architecture, New York, 1918.

Wasmuths Lexikon der Baukunst, 5 vols., Berlin, 1929–37.

U. Thieme and F. Becker: Allgemeines Lexikon der bildenden Künstler, 37 vols., Leipzig, 1907–50.

M. S. Briggs: The Architect in History, Oxford, 1927.

G. Dehio and F. von Bezold: Die kirchliche Baukunst des Abendlandes, 10 vols., Stuttgart, 1884–1901.

BRITAIN

W. Godfrey: The Story of Architecture in England, 2 vols., London, 1928.

F. Gibberd: The Architecture of England from Norman Times to the Present Day, 5th ed., London, 1944.

N. Lloyd: A History of the English House, London, 1931.

H. Avray Tipping: English Homes, 9 vols., London, 1920–37.

FRANCE

C. Enlart: Manuel d'archéologie française, 2nd ed., 4 vols., Paris, 1919–32.

P. Lavedan: L'Architecture française, Paris, 1944.

GERMANY

G. Dehio: Geschichte der deutschen Kunst, 2nd ed., 6 vols.,
   Berlin, 1921–31.

HOLLAND

F. Vermeulen: Handboek tot de Geschiedenis der Nederlandsche Bouwkunst, 3 vols., The Hague, 1928 *seqq*.
A. W. Weiszman: Geschiedenis der Nederlandsche Bouwkunst, Amsterdam, 1912.

ITALY

A. Venturi: Storia dell' Arte Italiana, 21 vols., Milan, 1901 *seqq*.
M. Salmi: L'Arte Italiana, 3 vols., Florence, 1943–44.
C. A. Cummings: A History of Italian Architecture, 2 vols.,
   New York, 1901.

SPAIN

B. Bevan: A History of Spanish Architecture, London, 1938.
Marqués de Lozoya: Historia del Arte hispánico, 4 vols.,
   1931–45.

MIDDLE AGES

EARLY CHRISTIAN AND BYZANTINE

O. M. Dalton: East Christian Art, Oxford, 1925.
O. Wulff: Altchristliche und Byzantinische Kunst (Handbuch
   der Kunstwissenschaft), 2 vols., Neubabelsberg, 1914–18.
D. Talbot Rice: Byzantine Art, Oxford, 1935.
C. Diehl: Manuel d'Art Byzantin, 2nd ed., Paris, 1925–26.
L. Bréhier: L'Art Byzantin, Paris, 1924.

MEDIEVAL: GENERAL

W. R. Lethaby: Medieval Art from the Peace of the Church
   to the Eve of the Renaissance, Revised edition, London,
   1949 (originally published 1904).
A. Kingsley Porter: Medieval Architecture, its origins and development, 2 vols., New York, 1909.

P. Frankl: Die Frühmittelalterliche und Romanische Baukunst (Handbuch der Kunstwissenschaft), Neubabelsberg, 1926.

A. W. Clapham: Romanesque Architecture in Western Europe, Oxford, 1936.

H. R. Hahnloser: Villard de Honnecourt, Vienna, 1935.

BRITAIN

F. Bond: An Introduction to English Church Architecture, 2 vols., London, 1913.

C. E. Power: English Medieval Architecture, 2nd ed., 3 vols., London, 1923.

E. S. Prior: A History of Gothic Art in England, London, 1900.

E. S. Prior: The Cathedral Builders in England, London, 1905.

T. F. Bumpus: The Cathedrals of England and Wales, London, 1905.

K. Escher: Englische Kathedralen, Zurich, 1929.

A. Hamilton Thompson: The Ground Plan of the English Parish Church, Cambridge, 1911.

A. Hamilton Thompson: The Historical Growth of the English Parish Church, Cambridge, 1913.

J. C. Cox: The English Parish Church, London, 1914.

F. E. Howard: The Medieval Styles of the English Parish Church, London, 1936.

A. Hamilton Thompson: Military Architecture in England during the Middle Ages, London, 1912.

G. Baldwin Brown: The Arts in Early England. Vol. 2: Anglo-Saxon Architecture, 2nd ed., London, 1925.

A. W. Clapham: English Romanesque Architecture, 2 vols., Oxford, 1930–34.

S. Gardner: A Guide to English Gothic Architecture, Cambridge, 1922.

J. Bilson: Les Origines de l'architecture gothique, and Les premières croisées d'ogives en Angleterre, *Revue de l'Art Chrétien*, 1901 and 1902.

C. Enlart: Du Rôle de l'Angleterre dans l'Evolution de l'Art Gothique, Paris, 1908.

FRANCE

H. Focillon: Art d'Occident; le moyen âge roman et gothique, Paris, 1938.

R. de Lasteyrie: L'Architecture réligieuse en France à l'Époque Romane, 2nd ed., Paris, 1929.

J. Baum: Romanesque Architecture in France, 2nd ed., London, 1928.

C. Martin: L'Art roman en France, 3 vols., Paris, *c.* 1910–14.

J. Hubert: L'Art préroman, Paris, 1938.

J. Evans: The Romanesque Architecture of the Order of Cluny, Cambridge, 1938.

E. Gall: Die Gotische Baukunst in Frankreich und Deutschland, vol. 1, Leipzig, 1925.

R. de Lasteyrie: L'Architecture réligieuse en France à l'Époque Gothique, 2 vols., Paris, 1926–27.

C. Martin and C. Enlart: L'Art Gothique en France, 2 vols., Paris, *c.* 1913–25.

P. Abraham: Viollet-le-Duc et le rationalisme médiéval, Paris, 1934.

L. Schürenberg: Die kirchliche Baukunst in Frankreich zwischen 1270 und 1380, Berlin, 1934.

E. Mâle: L'Art réligieux du XIIᵉ siècle en France, Paris, 1922.

E. Mâle: L'Art réligieux du XIIIᵉ siècle en France, Paris, 1902 (English translation, 1913).

ITALY

P. Toesca: Storia dell'Arte Italiana, vol. I, Turin, 1927.

A. Kingsley Porter: Lombard Architecture, 4 vols., Newhaven, 1915–17.

G. T. Rivoira: Lombardic Architecture, 2nd ed., Oxford, 1934.

C. Ricci: Romanesque Architecture in Italy, London, 1925.

C. Martin and C. Enlart: L'Art Roman en Italie, 2 vols., Paris, *c.* 1911–24.

G. C. Argan: L'Architettura Proto-Christiana, Pre-Romanica e Romanica, 'Nemi', Florence, 1936.

M. Salmi: L'Architettura Romanica in Toscana, Milan, 1927.

G. C. Argan : L'Architettura del Duecento e Trecento, 'Nemi', Florence, 1937.

C. Enlart: Les Origines de l'architecture gothique française en Italie, Paris, 1894.

W. Paatz: Werden und Wesen der Trecento-Architektur in Toskana, Burg, 1937.

SPAIN

V. Lampérez y Romea : Historia de la arquitectura cristiana española en la edad media, 2nd ed., Madrid, 1930.

G. G. King: Pre-Romanesque Churches of Spain, Bryn Mawr, 1924.

A. S. Frischauer: Altspanischer Kirchenbau, Berlin and Leipzig, 1930.

M. Gomez-Moreno : El arte románica española, Madrid, 1934.

G. E. Street (revised by G. G. King) : Some Account of Gothic Architecture in Spain, London, 1914.

E. Lambert: L'Art Gothique en Espagne, Paris, 1931.

RENAISSANCE, MANNERISM, AND BAROQUE IN ITALY

J. Burckhardt: Geschichte der Renaissance in Italien, 5th ed., Esslingen, 1912.

W. J. Anderson and A. Stratton : The Architecture of the Renaissance in Italy, London, 1927.

C. von Stegmann and H. von Geymüller : Die Architektur der Renaissance in Toskana, 12 vols., Munich, 1909.

A. Haupt: Renaissance Palaces of Northern Italy and Tuscany, 3 vols., London, c. 1931.

D. Frey: Architettura della Rinascenza, Rome, 1924.

M. Pittaluga : L'architettura italiana del Quattrocento, 'Nemi', Florence, 1937.

L. Becherucci: L'architettura italiana del Cinquecento, 'Nemi', Florence, 1936.

J. Baum : Baukunst und dekorative Plastik der Frührenaissance in Italien, Stuttgart, 1920.

C. Ricci: Baukunst der Hoch- und Spätrenaissance in Italien, Stuttgart, 1923.

G. Giovannoni: Saggi sull' Architettura del Rinascimento, Milan, 1931.

N. Pevsner: The Architecture of Mannerism, *The Mint*, 1946.

N. Pevsner: Gegenreformation und Manierismus, *Repertorium für Kunstwissenschaft, vol.* 46, 1925.

C. Gurlitt: Geschichte des Barockstils in Italien, Esslingen, 1887.

A. E. Brinckmann: Die Baukunst des 17 and 18 Jahrhunderts in den Romanischen Ländern (Handbuch der Kunstwissenschaft), Neubabelsberg, 1919, *seqq.*

C. Ricci: Baroque Architecture and Sculpture in Italy, London, 1912.

D. Frey: Architettura Barocca, Rome and Milan.

A. Muñoz: Roma Barocca, Milan, 1919.

G. Delogu: L'architettura italiana del seicento e settecento, 'Nemi', Florence, 1936.

T. H. Fokker: Roman Baroque Art, 2 vols., Oxford, 1938.

Brunelleschi: H. Folnesics, Vienna, 1915.
    L. H. Heydenreich, *Jahrbuch der preussischen Kunstsammlungen*, vol. 52, 1931.

Michelozzo: L. H. Heydenreich, *Mitteilungen des Kunsthistorischen Instituts in Florenz*, vol. 5, 1932, and *Festschrift für Wilhelm Pinder*, Leipzig, 1938.

Alberti: M. L. Gengaro, Milan, 1939.
    R. Wittkower, *Journal of the Warburg and Courtauld Institutes*, vol. 4, 1941.

Francesco di Giorgio: Papini, 3 vols., Florence, 1946.

Bramante: C. Baroni, Bergamo, 1941.

Raphael: T. Hofmann, 4 vols., Zittau, 1900–14.

Michelangelo: J. A. Symonds, 2 vols., London, 1893.
    H. Thode: Kritische Untersuchungen, 6 vols., Berlin, 1902–13.

Michelangelo's Laurenziana Library: R. Wittkower, *The Art Bulletin*, vol. 16, 1934.

Giulio Romano: E. Gombrich, *Jahrbuch der Kunsthistorischen Sammlungen in Wien*, N.F., vols. 8 and 9, 1935–36.

Serlio: G. C. Argan, *L'Arte*, New Series, vol. 10, 1932.
    W. B. Dinsmoor, *The Art Bulletin*, vol. 24, 1942.

Palladio: A. M. della Pozza, Vicenza, 1943.
F. Burger: Die Villen des Andrea Palladio, Leipzig, *c.* 1909.
Bernini: S. Fraschetti, Milan, 1900.
Borromini: E. Hempel, Vienna, 1924.
H. Sedlmayr, Munich, 1939.

16TH TO 18TH CENTURY IN BRITAIN, FRANCE, GERMANY, AND SPAIN

BRITAIN

T. Garner and A. Stratton: Domestic Architecture of England during the Tudor Period, 2nd ed., 2 vols., London, 1929.
J. A. Gotch: Early Renaissance Architecture in England, London, 1914.
J. A. Gotch: The English House from Charles I to George IV, London, 1918.
S. E. Rasmussen: London, the Unique City, London, 1937.
J. Summerson: Georgian London, London, 1946.

Inigo Jones: J. A. Gotch, London, 1928.
Wren: G. Webb, London, 1937.
L. Weaver, London, 1923.
Wren Society, 20 vols., London, 1924–44.
Bicentenary Memorial Volume, published by the Royal Institute of British Architects, London, 1923.
Wood: M. A. Green, Bath, 1914.
Adam: J. Swarbrick, London, 1915.
A. T. Bolton, 2 vols., London, 1922.

FRANCE

Sir Reginald Blomfield: A History of French Architecture 1494–1774, 4 vols., London, 1911–21.
L. Hautecœur: Histoire de l'Architecture classique en France, parts 1 and 2, in 4 vols., Paris, 1943 and 1948.
F. Kimball: The Creation of the Rococo, Philadelphia, 1943.
F. Kimball: Le Style Louis XV, Paris 1950 (mostly a translation of the previous volume).

A. E. Brinckmann: Die Baukunst des 17 und 18 Jahrhunderts in den Romanischen Ländern (Handbuch der Kunstwissenschaft), Neubabelsberg, 1919 *seqq.*

H. Rose: Spätbarock, Munich, 1922.

E. de Gancey: Châteaux de France, Paris, 1949.

E. de Gancey: Châteaux et Manoirs de France, 11 vols., 1934–38.

J. Vacquier and others: Les Anciens Châteaux de France, 14 vols., *s.d.*

F. Gebelin: Les Châteaux de la Renaissance, Paris, 1927.

W. H. Ward, French Châteaux and Gardens in the sixteenth century, London, 1909.

L. Hautecœur: L'Histoire des Châteaux du Louvre et des Tuileries . . ., Paris and Brussels, 1927.

G. Brière: Le Château de Versailles, 2 vols., Paris, 2c. 1910.

P. de Nolhac: Versailles et la Cour de France, 10 portfolios, Paris, 1925–30.

J. Vacquier and Jarry: Les Vieux Hôtels de Paris, 22 portfolios, Paris, 1910–34.

Pillement: Les Hôtels de Paris, 2 vols., Paris, 1941–45.

A. Blunt: François Mansart, London, 1941.

J. Guiffrey: A. Le Nôtre, Paris, *s.d.*, 1912.

Comte de Fels: A-J. Gabriel, Paris, 1924.

GERMANY

W. Pinder: Deutscher Barock, 2nd ed., Königstein, 1924.

S. Sitwell: German Baroque Art, London, 1927.

M. Hauttmann: Geschichte der kirchlichen Baukunst in Bayern, Schwaben und Franken, 1550–1780, Munich, 1924.

SPAIN

A. Byne and M. Stapley: Spanish Architecture of the Sixteenth Century, New York, 1917.

O. Schubert: Geschichte des Barocks in Spanien, Esslingen, 1908.

19TH AND 20TH CENTURIES

S. Giedion: Spätbarocker und Romantischer Klassizismus, Munich, 1922.

C. Hussey: The Picturesque, London, 1927.

N. Pevsner: The Genesis of the Picturesque, *The Architectural Review*, vol. 96, 1944.

Sir Kenneth Clark: The Gothic Revival, London, 1928, 2nd ed., 1950.

N. Pevsner: Pioneers of Modern Design, from William Morris to Walter Gropius, New York, 1949.

S. Giedion: Space, Time and Architecture, Harvard, 1941.

T. E. Tallmadge: The Story of Architecture in America, London, 1928.

J. M. Richards: An Introduction to Modern Architecture, Pelican Books, 3rd ed., 1945.

Ledoux: G. Levallet-Haug, Paris, 1934.
 M. Raval and Moreux, Paris, 1946.

Soane: J. Summerson, *Journal Royal Institute of British Architects*, vol. 58, 1951.
 A. T. Bolton, London, 1927.

Nash: J. Summerson, London, 1935.

Gilly: A. Oncken, Berlin, 1935.

Schinkel: A. Grisebach, Leipzig, 1924.

William Morris: J. W. Mackail, 2nd ed., London, 1922.
 A. Vallance, London, 1897.

H. H. Richardson: H.-R. Hitchcock, New York, 1936.

Norman Shaw: Sir Reginald Blomfield, London, 1940.
 N. Pevsner, *The Architectural Review*, vol. 89, 1941.

P. Webb: W. R. Lethaby, London, 1935.

F. L. Wright: H.-R. Hitchcock, In the Nature of Materials, New York, 1942.

Some Technical Terms Explained

Only unfamiliar architectural terms are included, and only those which have not already been explained in the places where they first occurred in the text. Bracketed references refer to drawings illustrating technical terms.

Ambulatory: Aisle round an apse or a circular building.

Arcade: Group of arches on columns or pillars.

Architrave: Bottom member of an entablature (C.3).

Attic: Low story above main cornice.

Basilica: Church with aisles and a nave higher than the aisles.

Bay: Vertical unit of a wall or façade; also compartments into which a nave is divided.

Caryatid: Sculptured figure used as a support.

Clerestory: Upper part of church nave with windows above the roofs of the aisles.

Cornice: Projecting top portion of an entablature or any projecting top course of a building (A.3 and C.4).

Cross: Cf. Greek cross.

Cross Rib: (E.1).

Drum: Circular or polygonal structure on which a dome is raised(B.2).

Entablature: The horizontal top part of an order of classical architecture. It is supported by columns and consists of architrave, frieze, and cornice (C.5).

Greek Cross: Cross with all four arms of equal length.

Jamb: Vertical part of the masonry of a door or window (D.1).

Lantern: Small open or glazed structure crowning a dome or a roof (B.1).

Lierne: A decorative rib in a Gothic vault which does not spring from the wall and does not touch the central boss (E.5).

Metope: Panel filling the space between triglyphs (C.1). *See* Triglyph.

Mullion: Vertical division of a window.

Narthex: Porch in front of the nave and aisles of a medieval church.

Ogee Arch: Cf. page 279 (D.).

Pediment: Triangular or segmental upright front end of a roof of moderate pitch (A.1).

Plinth: Projecting base of a building or a column.

Quoins: Corner stones at the angle of a building (A.2).

Ridge Rib: (E.2).

Rustication: Wall treatment with large freestone blocks, either smooth with recessed joints, or with a rough, rock-like surface and recessed joints.

Solar: Chamber on an upper floor.

Spandrel: Space between the curve of an arch; the vertical drawn from its springing and the horizontal drawn from its apex (C.6.)

String-course: Projecting horizontal band along the wall of a building (A.4).

Tierceron: Rib inserted in a Gothic vault between the transverse and diagonal ribs (E.4).

Transom: Horizontal division of a window.

Transverse Arch: (E.3).

Triforium: Wall passage between the arcade of a church nave and the clerestory, or between the gallery and the clerestory. It opens in arcades towards the nave. The arcading can also be blind, with no wall passage behind. Some writers call the gallery a triforium.

Triglyph: Vertical grooved member of the Doric frieze (C.1).

Voussoir: A wedge-shaped block forming part of the arch of a door or window (D.2).

A. – Queen Anne house

1. Pediment   3. Cornice
2. Quoins   4. String-course

B. – Dome

1. Lantern   2. Drum

C. – Classical details

1. *Metope*   3. *Architrave*   5. *Entablature*
2. *Triglyph*   4. *Cornice*   6. *Spandrel*

D. – Ogee arch

1. *Jamb*   2. *Voussoirs*

E. – Gothic vault

1. *Diagonal rib*   2. *Ridge rib*   3. *Transverse Arch*
4. *Tiercerons*   5. *Liernes*

Index

Penguin Books on Planning and Design

*

THE ENGLISHMAN BUILDS
Ralph Tubbs

E32

This book describes by means of a well-illustrated text the history of building in England. The author divides his subject into six sections, each one dealing with a particular period, and discusses the various influences which made the building of that period what it was – the life and beliefs of the people, the tools and materials which were used to build their homes. Nikolaus Pevsner wrote in the *Burlington Magazine* that this book 'is meant to appeal to a very general and uninitiated public and will be of the greatest benefit to them; for it has the outstanding merit of being written with faith and enthusiasm as well as care.'

Three shillings and sixpence each

THE ANATOMY OF THE VILLAGE
Thomas Sharp

E33

This is an attempt to set out in brief and direct form some of the main principles of village planning, a consideration of design in the building of new villages and in extending or rebuilding old ones. The volume, which like the others in this series measures $8\frac{3}{4} \times 7\frac{1}{8}$ in., contains thirty-three photographs (thirteen of which are full-page illustrations) and many line drawings. It was described in *The Listener* as 'a contribution to town planning literature quite out of proportion to its size' which 'objectifies in a narrow compass an idea of incalculable importance.'

Two shillings and sixpence

*

Also available in this series is *Homes by the Million*, by Hugh Casson, a well-illustrated account of the remarkable housing achievement of the U.S.A. from 1940–5. *Building Modern Sweden* by Bertil Hultén will be published shortly.

Pelicans on Art

*

EUROPEAN PAINTING AND SCULPTURE
Eric Newton
A82

A short account of the development of the fine arts, and in particular of painting in Europe from the earliest times to the present day.

PRIMITIVE ART
Leonhard Adam
A67

This reprint, revised and enlarged, of a work specially written for Pelican Books, describes the various forms which the artistic impulse has taken among primitive peoples – from the Stone Age men who roamed the plains of Europe twenty thousand years ago to the modern Negro inventing new ways of carving the human figure among the forests of the Ivory Coast.

RUSSIAN ART
Tamara Talbot Rice
A182

A survey of Russian Architecture, painting, sculpture, and the minor arts from the tenth century to the present day.

THE MEANING OF ART
Herbert Read
A213

Described in the *Star* when it first appeared as 'the best pocket introduction to the understanding of art that has ever been published', this book is illustrated with sixty-six plates and some line drawings. It has been newly revised for the Pelican series.

Two shillings and sixpence each

PELICAN BOOKS
A109

AN OUTLINE OF
EUROPEAN ARCHITECTURE

NIKOLAUS PEVSNER